This extensively researched and
the myth that Christianity ha
culture, politics and society. It w
minded reader.

IVER MARTIN
Principal, Edinburgh Theological Seminary

Having had a hunch for a long time that Scotland was, as they say, punching well above its weight in its influence for the gospel around the world – now I have the proof! In this well researched and well written book, Paul James-Griffiths documents the remarkable story of how God has, in so many ways, used this small nation disproportionately, in terms of its population, to herald the good news of the kingdom to the ends of the earth. This book will both inform and inspire you as well as burden you to pray that what God has done in the past, he might be pleased to do again.

JOHN BRAND
Principal, Edinburgh Bible College

What has Christianity *ever* done for Scotland?

Challenging today from the past

Paul James-Griffiths

CHRISTIAN
FOCUS

Copyright © 2026 Paul James-Griffiths

Paperback ISBN 978-1-5271-1297-1
E-book ISBN 978-1-5271-1403-6

10 9 8 7 6 5 4 3 2 1

Published in 2026
by
Christian Focus Publications Ltd.,
Geanies House, Fearn, Ross-shire,
IV20 1TW, Scotland, U.K.

www.christianfocus.com

Cover Art by Rhian Muir

Cover Design by Daniel Van Straaten

Printed and bound by
Bell & Bain, Glasgow

MIX
Paper | Supporting
responsible forestry
FSC
www.fsc.org FSC® C007785

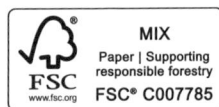

CONTENTS

Dedicated to my wife, Isolde,
who has stood by my side

⟶⟵

To all who seek truth
and righteousness

⟶⟵

Then those who feared the Lord spoke to one another,
And the Lord listened and heard them;
So a book of remembrance was written before Him
For those who fear the Lord
And who meditate on His name
MALACHI 3:16 (NKJV)

Historians are the most powerful and dangerous
members of any society. They must be watched
carefully ... They can spoil everything

NIKITA KHRUSHCHEV
LEADER OF THE SOVIET UNION

ACKNOWLEDGMENTS

My gratitude goes to Alison Carter for her astute counsel, encouragement and watchful proofreading, to Guy Pembroke and Caroline Rouault for their thoughtful feedback, and to many who have inspired and encouraged me in this project.

All quotations from the Bible are taken from the New King James Version, unless otherwise stated.

INTRODUCTION

My inspiration for this book came from a strange encounter with a friend who had watched a comedian on television making jokes about Christianity. The ridicule line had been 'What has Christianity ever done for us?', but after a barrage of jokes, the comedian and presenter began to sober up and realise that Christianity has actually changed the world, largely for the good. It is easy to point the finger of accusation at the church's faults over 2,000 years, but few point out the benefits of our godly ancestors, which we tend to take for granted. At first, as a response to the comedian, I wrote a leaflet entitled *What has Christianity ever done for Scotland?* This morphed into an exhibition, then a series of videos, and now this book, which has taken almost four years to write.

In producing this work, I have been on a personal journey, encountering some people and events I had never heard of that had been buried in the sands of time. On occasions, I have been exhilarated, like a walker who thinks he has reached the top of a mountain, only to find that there is yet more to scale. I have regrouped my senses, battled on, wrestled with the elements of history, and pressed through. At times I have wept at the beauty I have found in such dark and desolate places; sometimes, I have rejoiced with the joy of somebody seeking and finding hidden treasure; I have set my face against turbulent winds, but also run with the wind at my back. In all of this, I have sensed a destiny in unblocking the wells of our Christian heritage in Scotland, that the information might flow to our nation and beyond, in a time of great cultural crisis.

The observant reader might notice that much of this story takes place in Edinburgh and Glasgow; this is not to say that other parts of Scotland do not have their own vibrant and long Christian history to tell, but to do justice to a fuller account would mean producing a longer book, which is beyond the scope of this volume.

PAUL JAMES-GRIFFITHS
Edinburgh
September 2024

CHAPTER 1

THE COMING OF THE CROSS

Edinburgh Festival chaos was upon us again. Over a million visitors were pouring into Scotland's capital city in August, with thousands of performers seeking to draw in their audiences to experience music, theatre, dance, poetry and comedy. Dressed as a monk in a brown cassock, I led a tour group through the masses of humanity, staff in hand, face resolute and steadfast. My destiny was the National Museum of Scotland on Chambers Street. Descending into the quiet basement, we left behind a world of commotion and bustle and entered the world of the early church in Scotland.

There before us stood Celtic crosses, with their intricate weaving and unique symbolism, beckoning to us to unravel their mystical meanings. 'The earliest Celtic crosses that have been discovered in our nation date back to about A.D. 450 and were found in the southern part of Scotland among the Britons,' I told the group. 'Look at the beautiful artistry of these Celtic knots. This symbol was here long before Christianity, but it has a universal meaning of eternity, adopted by Christians. If you start at any point, you always end up where you started – like a circle. See the base of this cross: sometimes these standing crosses were ten or twelve feet tall. The long base represented the tree of life and the *axis mundi*, for Christ, who is God and man, created the world, and broke the curse of sin and death through the cross, bringing forgiveness and eternal life to those who receive Him. Originally the missionary monks would call people to worship with a hand bell, and they would meet under a cross like this one, to have an open-air service.'

'Why is there a circle on the top part of the cross?' asked an inquisitive and sprightly elderly lady. 'Is it true that the Celtic cross is a fusion of Christianity with Paganism? I've heard that the circle represents either the moon or sun god.'

For the next fifteen minutes we explored the mystery of the Celtic cross. We had to go back in time to Emperor Constantine who claimed to have had a vision of a cross and heard the words from heaven: 'In this sign conquer!' Before the Battle of Milvian Bridge in the year 312 he had told his soldiers to paint the Greek abbreviation of Christ, the *chi-rho*, on their shields. He defeated his rival, Maxentius, and then was plunged into war again with Licinius. For many who watched this next battle it was a struggle between Christianity and Paganism. Again, Constantine was victorious, and he became the sole Emperor of the Roman Empire. From the year 327 coins were struck with the *chi-rho* on top of the military *labarum*, with the serpent of Paganism crushed underneath. This celebration was encircled by a victory wreath. On the other side of the coin was the head of Emperor Constantine. By 337 the *chi-rho* with the letters Alpha and Omega appeared on his coins, depicting Christ as God.

If you had been a Briton, Pict or Scot living in Edinburgh, or along the Antonine Wall stretching just west of the city to Dumbarton, you would constantly have seen the symbol of Christ, either on the shields of soldiers, or on the official Roman coins. The wealthy even began inscribing the *chi-rho* on their silverware. The oldest Christian artefacts in Scotland were unearthed from Traprain Law near Haddington in a large stash of silverware, dated to the year 410. Among the silverware were ladles with the *chi-rho* and jugs with scenes from the Bible. It was the cross that began to appear as a victory symbol, originally inside a circular wreath, which eventually became a circle, ring – or nimbus – nothing to do with the sun or moon god at all.

'But when did the Christians first come to Scotland?' asked a burly American guest.

'It was firstly among the Britons,' I answered. 'At the time of Christ, the Welsh-speaking Britons were widespread in tribal groups, from Cornwall and Devon in the south, to Wales, and then north in Scotland – even as far as Aberdeenshire. According to Tertullian, who wrote in about A.D. 200, there were 'haunts of the Britons – inaccessible to the Romans, but subjugated to Christ.'[1] It is likely that the 'haunts of the Britons' meant areas north of the Antonine Wall, which were at the fringes of the Roman Empire. Another Church Father called Origen also had similar information about the Britons, and asked, 'For when, before the arrival of Christ did the land of Britain agree together in the worship of the one God?'[2] Medieval Scottish historians state from earlier records, now lost, that King Donald and his courtiers received Christ in 203.[3] Another ancient tradition says that King Lucius of the Britons was converted to Christ in 179, and he sent bishops to all of the twenty-eight chief cities of the Britons, with Caer-Brython, or today's Dumbarton, being the stronghold in Scotland. So again, we see the Christian faith was anchored in Scotland by the year 200.[4]

---

1. Tertullian, *An Answer to the Jews, The Ante-Nicene Fathers*, editors Roberts A., and Donaldson J., Vol III (Edinburgh: T&T Clark); (Grand Rapids: William B. Eerdmans Publishing Co., 1997), Vol. 7, p. 158.

2. Origen (c. A.D. 240), Commentary on Ezekiel 4:6, *From Origen of Alexandria: Exegetical Works on Ezekiel*, edited by Roger Pearse, trans. Mischa Hooker (Ipswich: Chieftain Publishing, 2014), p. 131. Some scholars have suggested that Britain here means Brittany in France, but the Romans always called Brittany 'Armorica'.

3. John Spottiswoode, *The History of the Church of Scotland: Beginning the year of our Lord 203, and continued to the end of the Reign of King James the VI of Ever Blessed Memory*, third edition, London (original edition, 1639), Book 1, p. 4.

4. The earliest record of King Lucius of the Britons receiving the Christian faith is in the *Liber Pontificalis* (A.D. 530). The entry says: 'He [Eleutherius, bishop of Rome] received a letter from Lucius, King of Britain, asking him to appoint a way by which Lucius might become a Christian.' Bede had access to this information and also recorded the event: Bede (A.D. 725), *Chronica maiora*, 4131, and in his *A History of the English Church and People*, written in 731, Book 1:4 and Book 5:24, p. 42 and p. 332 (Penguin Classics, 1955, 1968). The date given by Bede of A.D. 156 is wrong, because Eleutherius was Bishop of Rome between

As we wandered through the museum basement, I pointed out crosses depicting the symbols of Paganism being driven out by the preaching of the gospel. We encountered Egyptian-style crosses in the circles, showing the influence of the Egyptian desert fathers like Anthony on Scotland's early church; after the Britons, later crosses celebrated the message of Jesus among the Picts, then the Scots, then the Anglo-Saxons, and finally amongst the Vikings.

The cost of the Christian faith to become deeply rooted in Scotland was extremely high. During the severe persecution of Emperor Diocletian (303–313), thousands of Christians were slaughtered all over the Roman Empire, which also stretched to Britain. Eusebius, an eyewitness in Rome, described such a horrendous period, in *The History of the Church*:

> I saw with my own eyes, the places of worship thrown down from top to bottom, to the very foundations, the inspired holy Scriptures committed to the flames in the middle of the public squares .... So many were killed on a single day that the axe, blunted and worn out by the slaughter, was broken in pieces, while the exhausted executioners had to be periodically relieved.[5]

Bede tells us that 'many others of both sexes throughout the land' of Britain were martyred for their faith during this Pagan onslaught.[6] An Irish scribal entry in an A.D. 770 copy of Jerome's *Martyrology* states that 'In Britain was Albinus [Alban] martyr,

---

174 and 189. The traditional date of King Lucius' conversion is 179. Gildas, in the 540s, records the twenty-eight cities of the Britons in his *Ruin of Britain*, but it is Nennius in c.800 who lists them, with Caer Brithon, or Dumbarton, as the most northerly city. *History of the Britons (Historia Brittonum)*, translation by J. A. Giles, in Parentheses Publications (Medieval Latin Series: Cambridge, Ontario, 2000), Vol. 7, p. 5. It is Geoffrey of Monmouth (c.1136) who refers to the twenty-eight bishops sent by King Lucius to the twenty-eight cities of the Britons (*The History of the Kings of Britain*, Book 4:19 and 20). He seems to get this information from a now-lost book of Gildas, who must have had access in his time to early church records.

5. Eusebius, *The History of the Church* (Penguin Classics, 1989), Book 8:2-9, pp. 258-65.

6. Bede, *A History of the English Church and People* (Penguin Classics, 1983), chapter 7, p. 47.

along with others, 889 in number, placed in the list of those whose names are written in the book of life.'[7] Furthermore, Archbishop Spottiswoode, having access to early, now lost, church records, wrote:

> But that which furthered not a little the propagation of the Gospel in those parts was the persecution raised by Diocletian, which at that time was hot in the South parts of Britain. This brought many Christians, both Preachers and Professors, into this Kingdom, who were all kindly received by Cratilinth, and had the Isle of Man given them ... for their maintenance .... In this Isle King Cratilinth erected a stately Church to the honour of the Saviour .... During his Reign Christian religion did prosper exceedingly.[8]

Later that century, and into the next, the Pagan Picts from north of the Forth Estuary and the Scots from Ireland massacred the Britons. When Rome was sacked by the Germanic tribes in 410, the Roman legions departed for Italy, leaving a vulnerable British border. Gildas, writing in the 540s, expressed the despair of the Britons who sent a begging letter to the Roman governor Aetius to help them, with the words: 'The barbarians drive us to the sea; the sea throws us back on the barbarians: thus two modes of death await us, we are either slain or drowned.'[9]

When Rome was finally totally ruined by the Visigoths in 476, the Roman Empire in the West collapsed. By the seventh century the Britons in Scotland had either been killed, driven out as refugees to Brittany in France, Wales, or Cornwall, or had assimilated with the Picts and Scots. However, two courageous

---

7. Hugh Williams points out that in the edition of Jerome's *Martyrology* there is one codex (*Codex Bern.*) dated at about 770, which states this number of martyrs. This codex had been in the possession of someone connected with Ireland (see *Gildas: De Excidio Brittanniae, or the Ruin of Britain*, edited by Hugh Williams, 1901, facsimile reprint by Llanerch Press, 2006), footnote, pp. 25-27.

8. Spottiswoode, Book 1, p. 4.

9. Gildas, *The Ruin of Britain*, Part 1:20, p. 47, edited by Hugh Williams, first published in 1901 for the Hon. Society of Cymmrodorion by David Nutt (Facsimile reprint by Llanerch Press), 2006.

British Christians, Ninian of Whithorn and Patrick of Ystrad Clud (Strathclyde), had a significant impact on the Southern Picts and the Scots in Ireland, in particular. Scottish missionaries from Ireland poured into this nation, as the fruit of Patrick's ministry, and were led by such luminaries as Columba, who established his mission base on Iona, near Mull, in 563. From there, the northern Picts were Christianised.

In turn Aidan was sent from the community at Iona in 635 to pioneer a work at Lindisfarne to reach the Pagan Northumbrians. It would be on Lindisfarne that the beautiful artistic work of the Lindisfarne Gospels would be produced in about the year 700. Lindisfarne would be the inspiration for other monks who would set up education centres in Monkwearmouth and Jarrow, where Bede would become known as the Father of English History, and in York, from where Alcuin would travel to establish a base of higher education under Charlemagne in France.

The later Celtic crosses show the extraordinary Christian story in Scotland, for woven into the artistry are the cultures of the Romans, Britons, Picts, Scots, Anglo-Saxons and Vikings. Every time the church was established in one culture, another culture would seek to destroy the church; this would be followed by the persecuting culture in turn being converted to Christ, only to be persecuted by the next wave, until finally even the rapacious Vikings were tamed by the cross of Jesus.

The church throughout the first nine centuries went through phases of flourishing, persecution, and falling into compromise and worldliness, and yet the foundation for so much of what we came to treasure in Scotland came out of these movements. In the stump of early Christian practice would be the seeds of our law, education, democracy, human rights, social reforms, healthcare, science and Christian values, which would much later become a tree bearing good fruit. In the centuries to come, Scotland would rise up and be transformed, becoming a light to the nations. Now that we have briefly sketched how Christianity became established in this country, we can progress to seeking an answer to the question of this book: *What has Christianity ever done for Scotland?*

CHAPTER 2

TRANSFORMATIONS

On 23rd July 1839, something extraordinary occurred in a Presbyterian church in Kilsyth. William Chalmers Burns, who had been converted to Christ in Edinburgh, was preaching to a packed congregation. The people listened attentively to him as he spoke of his Saviour, but then it was like a spiritual dam burst, with a sudden outpouring of weeping, wailing, groaning, and also shouts of praise from some of the Christians there. Burns wrote in his *Memoir*:

> The appearance of a great part of the people from the pulpit gave me an awfully vivid picture of the state of the ungodly in the day of Christ's coming to judgement. Some were screaming out in agony; others, and among these strong men, fell to the ground as if they had been dead.[1]

From that time on, it was the topic of conversation in the town. Daily services were held in the church and hundreds would gather for morning prayers in the Market Square. Crowds began to come to Kilsyth to find out what on earth was happening. Later, an open-air communion service was held in September with estimated numbers of 12,000 to 15,000 people in attendance. The phenomena occurred in other churches in town. In response to the message of the gospel among the Methodists, 'forty or fifty stout able bodied persons fell to the ground as if dead. On being

---

1. Burns, *Memoir of the Rev. Wm. C. Burns,* pp. 91-93, quoted by Tom Lennie in his *Land of Many Revivals: Scotland's Extraordinary Legacy of Christian Revivals over Four Centuries, 1527–1857* (Christian Focus, 2015), p. 322.

removed to a house, and recovering themselves, they all cried aloud to God for mercy.'[2]

It is not that there was some sort of psychological manipulation going on; there was no use of sensational music or emotional preaching to whip up the crowds. Burns spoke about a 'sweet melting of heart among the audience, and many of the unconverted were weeping bitterly aloud, though I spoke throughout with perfect calmness and solemnity.'[3]

When Dr Thomas Guthrie went to Kilsyth to investigate what was happening and report back to the churches in Edinburgh, he wrote: 'The difficulty at Kilsyth is not, as here, how to get people to church, but the difficulty has almost been to get them away from it, so that the common business of life might not be neglected.'[4]

Revival had hit Kilsyth and, like a stone being dropped into a pond, its waves would be felt in the surrounding areas. When Burns preached in Dundee at the church where he was filling in for its minister, the same effects occurred there as in Kilsyth. The church's godly young pastor, Robert Murray M'Cheyne, was visiting Palestine at the time, but when he returned, he rejoiced to see the revival in Dundee. Within a few years this movement would spread throughout most of Scotland, bringing thousands of unconverted people to Christ.

But what is a revival? It is the supernatural visitation of God to His church in such a tangible way that the Christians become saturated with Him, resulting in double-minded hypocrisy and sin coming to the surface in their lives, so that they become broken and repentant, forsaking sin and living for Christ. This movement of the Holy Spirit can be sensed by those who previously had no interest

2. Drake, *The Wallacestone Reformer,* p. 119, quoted by Tom Lennie in his *Land of Many Revivals* (Fearn: Christian Focus, 2015), p. 323.

3. Michael McMullen, *God's Polished Arrow: W. C. Burns: Revival Preacher* (Christian Focus, 2000), pp. 161-62, quoted by Tom Lennie in his *Land of Many Revivals*, p. 324.

4. David K. Guthrie and Charles J. Guthrie, *Autobiography of Thomas Guthrie and Memoir by his Sons*, quoting from his own manuscript (New York: Robert Carter and Brothers, 1873), Vol. I, p. 396.

in God at all, resulting in multitudes being deeply anxious of their sin, and becoming converted and remaining in the faith. It is not just an emotional high that is exciting for a while, then dies away like a straw fire; it is a genuine, spiritual fire that leaves a permanent and deep transformation in many lives and communities.

Tom Lennie is perhaps the nation's leading historian of revivals in Scotland, and he has painstakingly put together records of these extraordinary movements. Scotland has probably had more revivals in its history than any other nation, and Lennie catalogues them in his three volumes, from 1527 to 1940.[5] It is simply not possible to explain the reason for the tremendous growth and effectiveness experienced by Christians in Scotland, and in its capital, Edinburgh, without understanding this key part of our history. Scientists, psychologists and sociologists might scratch around to try and explain the cause of such a huge Christian influence on shaping Scotland in past movements, but they usually neglect to address the subject of genuine revivals properly.

Such movements must have happened in Scotland since the first coming of Christianity, but reliable eyewitness information is scanty before 1527. We do have Patrick the Briton's letter written in the 450s about what was happening amongst the Scots in Ireland. In his own words he speaks of the miraculous work of God there: 'I am greatly in debt to God,' he wrote. 'He gave me such great grace, that through me, many people should be born again in God and brought to full life. Also, that clerics should be ordained everywhere for this people who have lately come to believe ... the many thousands of my brothers and sisters – the children whom I baptised in the Lord.'[6]

---

5. Tom Lennie's three volumes on revival are: *Glory in the Glen: A History of Evangelical Revivals in Scotland, 1880–1940* (Christian Focus, 2009); *Land of Many Revivals: Scotland's Extraordinary Legacy of Christian Revivals over Four Centuries, 1527–1857* (Christian Focus, 2015); *Scotland Ablaze: The Twenty-Year Fire of Revival That Swept Scotland, 1858–79* (Christian Focus, 2018).

6. Patrick, *Confession* 38 and 14, Royal Irish Academy, 2011.

For 'many thousands' of Pagans to have been converted to Christ and changed to become Christlike is evidence of a miraculous movement that transformed a culture. Later historians record similar significant breakthroughs of this nature through Ninian, Columba, Cuthbert and others working in Scotland, although at later times some of the people would also fall away from the faith.

In this chapter, we will focus on revivals in Scotland between 1839 and the 1880s, which are well-documented. This little window of history will reveal the sort of Christian movements that occurred, leading to the social transformation of Scotland.

The First Wave: 1839

Dr Guthrie describes the conditions in his parish of Greyfriars Kirk when he first arrived there:

> The first winter I was in Edinburgh, 1837–38, was one of extraordinary severity. For six weeks at least there was not a spade put into the ground …. My door used to be besieged every day by crowds of half-naked creatures, men, women, and children, shivering with cold and hunger: and I visited many a house that winter, where there were starving mothers and starving children, and neither bed, bread, nor Bible – till, with climbing stairs, my limbs were like to fail, and, with spectacles of misery, my heart was like to break.[7]

From 1839 we start to hear of a growing transformation across the city. In the Annual Report of Edinburgh City Mission (ECM) that year, it is stated that

> During the past year the people of God have been aroused from lethargy …. Sinners in numbers, not like the gleanings of the vintage, but like the firstfruits of a coming and abundant harvest, have been made to cry, 'What must I do to be saved?' And many have been added to the Lord.[8]

---

7. Guthrie, *Autobiography of Thomas Guthrie and Memoir by his Sons*, Vol. I, p. 192.

8. ECM *Annual Report*: 1838–1839, p. 71.

Before this, the missionaries had reported some encouraging changes amongst the people where they worked in the poor parts of the Old Town, but now something was shifting; the tide was turning and God's blessing was coming to Scotland. The Shelter in the Grassmarket had been established in 1840 as a rehabilitation centre for young women who had been involved in prostitution and crime. ECM missionaries were asked to preach to the women there, with encouraging results. One missionary wrote:

> As I formerly stated, there has been for some time past a considerable awakening among the inmates of this institution with regard to their souls. I held a meeting with them this evening and addressed them from Matthew xiii. 45, 46, 'The kingdom of heaven is like unto a merchant man seeking goodly pearls, who when he had found one pearl of great price went and sold all that he had and bought it.' Not only did an extraordinary deep feeling pervade the meeting, but it might be termed what Scripture calls a Bochim, a place of weeping; many of them wept nearly all the time of the address, and a number of them cried aloud; however I was enabled to get through without my mind being much embarrassed, and I scarcely ever felt more liberty and enlargement of heart. After the exercises were over, a young girl, apparently about fourteen years of age, came to me weeping, and earnestly desired me to go and visit her parents – I said, 'My young friend, what must I say to them?' She replied, 'They are not religious, and I wish you to speak to them about their souls, and about Christ,' but she had much difficulty in telling me this for weeping.[9]

Both William Chalmers Burns and Robert Murray M'Cheyne preached in Edinburgh and Leith between 1839 and 1842, and according to M'Cheyne the spiritual hunger for God was so intense that it appeared 'as if the ever-memorable scenes of Kilsyth, Dundee and Perth were to be repeated in Leith.'[10] It was not just an emotional outpouring amongst the poor and needy, but a life-changing work, which also spilled over into some of the well-to-do churches in Edinburgh, such as in St Luke's near the fashionable George Street, in which Burns was

---

9. ECM *Annual Report*: 1842–1843, p. 10.

10. Tom Lennie, *Land of Many Revivals*, p. 357.

the interim pastor. Here, there were scenes of 'calm weeping' and an 'overflowing church'. If the first revival wave hit Scotland and Edinburgh in 1839 bringing change, a second, and much bigger wave, engulfed the churches in the famous 1859 revival.

The Second Wave: 1859–61

It is difficult to pinpoint where exactly in Scotland the 1859 revival first broke out. Some have suggested it began in Aberdeen in the winter of 1858.[11] However, Lennie suggests that the epicentre was Glasgow. It is clear though that both cities had been influenced by revivals in America and in Ulster. Revivals always begin with passionate prayer, and a network of churches in America and Britain had been doing this for years, but the starting place of the revival seems to have begun with a missionary called Jeremiah Lanphier in the Dutch Reformed Church in New York. At the first lunch time prayer meeting on Wednesday, 23rd September 1857, he was alone until halfway through when six other men joined him. By the third prayer meeting there were thirty to forty men in attendance at the prayer meeting, but by the fourth meeting the church began to fill up with men eager to pray.

The men's prayer meeting exploded when America's worst economic recession hit in October, leaving thousands of men distraught and unemployed. In their desperation they began to call out to God first about the financial crisis, but this then turned to a deep realisation of sin as God's presence met with them. By the beginning of 1858, this prayer meeting had exploded even more. Horace Greeley of the *New York Tribune* travelled by a horse-drawn cab to twelve lunchtime prayer meetings in New York and counted more than six thousand men praying. The revival was covered by the *New York Times* and an article written on 20th March 1858, expressed the utter amazement of many:

> 'The great wave of religious excitement, which is now sweeping over this nation, is one of the most remarkable movements since the reformation,' it said. 'Travelers relate that in cars [horse-drawn

---

11. Tom Lennie, *Scotland Ablaze*, pp. 43-53.

carriages] and steamboats, in banks and markets, everywhere through the interior, this matter is an absorbing topic. Churches are crowded; bank-directors' rooms become oratories; school-houses are turned into chapels; converts are numbered by the scores of thousands. In this City, we have beheld a sight which not the most enthusiastic fanatic for church-observances could ever have hoped to look upon; we have seen in a business-quarter of the City, in the busiest hours, assemblies of merchants, clerks and working-men, to the number of 5,000, gathered day after day for a simple and solemn worship. Similar assemblies we find in other portions of the City; a theatre is turned into a chapel; churches of all sects are open and crowded by day and night. ... It is most impressive to think that over this great land tens and fifties of thousands of men and women are putting themselves at this time in a simple, serious way, the greatest question that can ever come before the human mind, "What shall we do to be saved from sin?"'

Droves of pastors and inquisitive Christians travelled from Britain to America to investigate what was happening and returned with glowing reports of something very special. In a remote little church in Kells, Northern Ireland, a handful of young men had been stirred by what they had heard of the American revival, and they poured out their hearts for such a visitation of God in their nation. By the end of the year in 1858, there were fifty passionate people praying for God's outpouring. Samuel Campbell was converted at this prayer meeting and he went back to his family in Ahoghill to share the gospel with them. They too were converted, which in turn encouraged their minister, Rev. David Adams, who had been praying for revival since 1841, to organise a special Thanksgiving Service for prayer. On 14th March 1859, the unexpected happened: about three thousand people turned up. The church was so packed that the crowds that could not fit inside met outside, and in the mud and pouring rain many fell on their faces, crying out for God's saving mercy. This revival spread to Ballymena and then throughout Ulster, so that in less than two years an estimated one hundred thousand were converted to Christ.[12]

---

12. Edwin J. Orr, *The Second Evangelical Awakening in Britain* (London and Edinburgh: Morgan and Scott, 1949).

In Scotland, an American minister was invited by the Free Church to speak at their General Assembly in 1858. As Rev. Dr Maclean extolled what God was doing in his own country, the Scottish pastors were enthralled and became expectant for a similar visitation of God here. Many eager Irish Christians also poured into Scotland to share their testimony about what was going on in Ulster, stirring up many Scots to go there and witness first-hand what was happening. Of the one hundred and twenty-three clergymen from Britain who travelled to Ulster in 1859 to investigate the Irish revival, 40 per cent were from Scotland, with most of them from the Free Church.[13]

When John Horner came from the Coleraine revival to preach at the Religious Institution Rooms in Glasgow on 24th July 1859, the congregation began to experience what was happening in Ulster and America. According to *The Scottish Guardian*, scores of people were 'in great distress' and 'many were seen weeping'. In less than a week, daily meetings were being held in the Religious Institution Rooms, but as the crowds kept growing, they had to find a bigger venue. The Trades Hall also became too small, so that the hungry masses had to meet in different large buildings in the city, even in the open air. In close conjunction with the Religious Institution Rooms was the Wynd Free Church, which soon became a centre of the revival in Scotland. Despite the cautious nature of most of the Free Church people and ministers who tried to suppress emotionalism as much as possible, God's Spirit was being poured out on people, usually with scenes similar to that of previous revivals. It is a remarkable fact that the Free Church was right at the heart of the movement, witnessing the transformation of many churchgoers and the conversion of thousands.

On 19th August 1860, a crowd of thousands gathered to hear the preaching on Glasgow Green where they witnessed similar scenes to the famous Cambuslang revival of George Whitefield

---

13. Tom Lennie, *Scotland Ablaze*, p. 29. Lennie says that an Irish newspaper reported two hundred and thirty ministers from Scotland coming over to witness the revival in the town of Coleraine between July and August of 1859. Of these 'at least two dozen came from Glasgow and a slightly lesser number from Edinburgh.'

in 1742. Richard Weaver, one of the evangelists there, said that 'The Spirit came in such power that many were struck down under the word and had to be carried into a neighbouring church. There they lay on the floor as if dead.'[14]

This extraordinary spiritual fire broke out almost everywhere in Scotland, leaving in its wake many thousands of transformed lives. Often the scoffers would go to mock and end up encountering God for themselves, leaving them humbled, repentant and broken; often they would be raised up to preach effectively throughout their local districts and beyond; alcoholics and profligates were being changed; the worst of sinners were becoming saints. In Argyll and the Western Isles there was a particularly extraordinary transformation, with many churches doubling, tripling, and even quadrupling within months. In a Rev. Cameron's church in Kilchoman on Islay, his congregation exploded rapidly from sixty to nine hundred regularly attending the daily prayer meeting.[15] In Campbeltown, the Free Church minister reported that the prayer meeting that used to have about a dozen people, and which recently had ceased altogether, now attracted four to five hundred.[16] Such accounts were being reproduced in many parts of Scotland and, for the most part, the converted people remained in the churches.

Edinburgh in the Second Wave of 1859–61

In 1859, the Edinburgh City Mission's Annual Report states that 'A spirit of fervent prayer and of earnest "waiting for the promise of the Spirit", has of late years pervaded, in a remarkable manner, many of the churches in town, and has found the means at once of its expression and its maintenance, in the Union Prayer Meeting, held in Queen St. Hall, and in similar devotional services conducted elsewhere.'[17]

---

14. ibid., p. 75.

15. ibid., p. 320.

16. ibid., p. 321.

17. ECM *Annual Report*: 1859, p. 18.

The same pattern occurred in Edinburgh as in the rest of Scotland, although this revival mostly impacted the working class. In Newhaven, on the outskirts of Edinburgh, a work similar to that described in Glasgow broke out among the tough fishing community in February 1860 at the close of a meeting, in which 'a great weeping and crying began among the people. Many seemed truly to have been brought to Jesus. The whole place was moved. A beloved minister in the village supposed that at that time there were some "five hundred souls wailing after Christ."'[18] The above citation is part of an account of the 1859–61 revival which was put into a tract in the *Monthly Visitor*, and distributed throughout the land to 230,747 people in 1861, thus spreading the movement even more.[19]

In Edinburgh, the missionaries were finding the same deep hunger for God, which startled them, for 'Multitudes who would formerly have resented any direct inquiry respecting their state before God, began eagerly to court opportunities of being conversed with on this topic, and some would follow the missionary to his house, or accompany him in a walk to the country, pressing, in various forms, the momentous inquiry, "What must I do to be saved?"… Coarse and reckless men have become as little children entering the Kingdom; harlots have returned into the bosom of their wondering families, testifying of Jesus; the self-righteous and the secure are asking with burdened hearts, "What shall I do to be saved?"'[20]

Edinburgh City Mission worked closely with Carrubbers Close Mission in the Royal Mile, which became the epicentre for the Edinburgh revival, under the leadership of the Free Church minister, Rev. James Gall. Having been stirred by reports of the revival in Glasgow, the believers there renewed their enthusiasm for prayer. On 14th October 1859, 'the shower came on' and an

---

18. *The Awakening in Scotland*, Monthly Visitor, No. CCCXLIII, January 1861.

19. Edinburgh Society for the Monthly Distribution of Tracts, *Report* in 1861, p. 7.

20. ECM *Annual Reports*: 1860, p. 14, and 1861, p. 15.

'extraordinary ... work of grace' began. Multitudes of people seemed to be drawn to the mission like moths to a light as 'night after night the careless became earnest, the earnest became convicted, and the convicted at length found peace in the blood of Jesus.'[21]

By 1860, multitudes of people had been converted there, and the crowds were so big that 'hundreds had to be turned away', resulting in a temporary move to the Theatre Royal, with extra meetings being put on. Finding again that this was too small, they had to move to the New Assembly Hall, above The Mound and next to the Royal Mile, which became 'densely packed' and where queues of people came, desperately seeking Christ. Working in conjunction with this great harvest of souls were the Free Church evangelist Brownlow North, Rev. James Hood Wilson, and the English evangelists Reginald Radcliffe and Richard Weaver, who saw a large ingathering into the churches, including a hundred and twenty-five prostitutes who were transformed.[22]

Charles Finney and Pilrig School

In his *Memoirs* the celebrated American evangelist, Charles Finney, recorded: 'I remained three months in Edinburgh [from August 1859], preaching mostly in Mr Kirk's church, which was one of the largest places of worship in Edinburgh ... many souls were converted.'[23]

Although it was a fruitful time, Finney found that some of the tendencies in the Evangelical Union denomination, in which he was preaching, caused doors to close to him in other denominations, especially in the Presbyterian churches, thus crippling what he was doing.[24] Sadly, this was reminiscent of what

---

21. *These Fifty Years: The Story of Carrubbers' Close Mission, Edinburgh, 1859–1909*, The Tract and Colportage Society of Scotland, 1909, p. 21.

22. Tom Lennie, *Scotland Ablaze*, p. 164.

23. *Memoirs of Charles G. Finney*, Chapter XXXV: Labors in Scotland and in England, the Gospel Truth www.gospeltruth.net/1868Memoirs/mem35.htm.

24. The Evangelical Union denomination preached 'Morisonianism', a form of Arminianism, which understood that free will was involved in the individual's response to the gospel, and that this gospel was offered to all.

had happened with Wesley over Calvinism during the previous century. With frustration Finney left Scotland, after a trip to Aberdeen, to pursue a seam of openness in England.

One young man, however, had come every night to his meetings in the Brighton Street Chapel. His experience of that week was different from Finney's record of 'many souls' being converted by the end of his three-month trip. William Robertson wrote in his testimony that when he went to hear Finney in November, that 'although large audiences attended, still, however, there seemed to be but little interest.'[25]

On the last day he records that he came to Christ through Dr Kirk after Finney had left. His testimony is fascinating because it relates the quest for God of one individual during the revival. He tells us that, when he lived in Glasgow, he and some of his fellow teachers at East Gorbals Free Church Sabbath School decided to go to the Wynd Church at the end of June in 1859, because they had heard about the revival. William Robertson witnessed the scenes of distress of soul and cries for God's mercy amongst those there, but his 'heart seemed as cold and unfeeling as the stones'. This was in spite of the fact that he was a Bible teacher and known to be a 'Christian' of good character. When others asked him to help them counsel those seeking Christ from his own Bible class, he turned them down. 'I was a hypocrite, at least I was not fit for the position I filled in the Sabbath School,' he wrote, 'I was unconverted .... All around me in the church, both young and old, were in deep distress, and I could look on it all quite unmoved, needing salvation as much as any of them and yet all unconcerned.'[26]

Predestination was the standard position of the Presbyterian churches at the time. The label 'Morisonianism' came from its foremost preacher, Rev. James Morison (1816–1893) of Kilmarnock, who was expelled from the United Secession Church in 1843. The Evangelical Union came out of a merger between his church and the Congregational Union.

25. *William Robertson of the Carrubbers' Close Mission: Reminiscences of a Life of Blessing*, p. 20, edited by his son Rev. R. M. Robertson, with a foreword by Principal Alexander Whyte (Edinburgh and London: Oliphant, Anderson and Ferrier, 1914).

26. ibid., p. 15.

In September, Robertson left Glasgow to take up the headmastership of Pilrig School, which used to be in James Street (now Spey Terrace), off Leith Walk. Shortly afterwards he received letters from teachers and pupils of his former Sabbath school in the Gorbals rejoicing in how the revival had broken out there with many becoming Christians. One of his former pupils asked him to read out his letter to the children at Pilrig School and closed with the words of a popular hymn of that time: 'We're travelling home to Heaven above, Will you go?' He did as was asked, and was stunned that same morning when some of the children asked whether they could start a prayer meeting.

Not long afterwards he was converted and saw his deputy also turn to Christ. They began to pray every morning for the school, and during the Bible class one of the most restless of the children began to break down in tears because of her sins. By the afternoon they had to close the usual lessons because the same phenomena were occurring throughout the school, as virtually the whole school sought Christ. As God's presence hung over the school on Friday 18th November 1859, Robertson, the headmaster, wrote: 'The holy ecstasy with which He filled us cannot be told. We seemed to be translated from the world and things earthly, and on this and subsequent occasions I thought I could not live because of the joy with which the Lord filled me.'[27]

These children became extraordinary evangelists, sharing their faith and seeing many of their parents, families, and neighbours also converted, resulting even in notorious drunkards and violent men being transformed. The *Monthly Visitor* tract expressed what many were thinking in the nation during the 1859 revival. 'In former times,' it said, 'we were wont to hear of an awakening at Kilsyth, or at Dundee, or in Arran, or in some particular and limited district. Now, blessed be God, for the first time, we can speak of the awakening in Scotland.'[28]

---

27. ibid., p. 35.

28. *The Awakening in Scotland*, Monthly Visitor, No. CCCXLIII, January 1861.

If the 1839 wave had brought great times of refreshing to parts of Scotland, the second wave of 1859 eclipsed it in its extent and impact; but a third wave was coming, which some say overshadowed even that.

The Third Wave: 1873–74

When two relatively unknown American men called Dwight L. Moody and Ira D. Sankey arrived to minister in England in 1873, they received an invitation from Rev. John Kelman of Leith to come to Edinburgh with the message of Christ. The previous revival had brought much new life to the city, but there was a need of a fresh movement. When Moody and his singing companion arrived in Edinburgh, they found that the ground was so well prepared that within a week the city was buzzing with their message. Ministers from across the Protestant denominations welcomed them and worked shoulder to shoulder to bring in a huge harvest of converted people. 'Within a short time,' says Lennie, 'the whole city was said to have been moved to its core.'[29]

The unusual working of this revival was that it impacted every class of people, from the poor right up to the well-to-do, professors, national leaders, and especially university students. The *Monthly Visitor* tract distributed to most of Scotland and 'circulated to every Family in the City', covered the 1873–74 revival with gushing words of enthusiasm:

> 'What do you think of it?' was a common saying in Edinburgh, when six months ago this gracious work was beginning. Few who believe in conversion ask that question now .... All classes – the rich and the poor – lawyers, doctors, soldiers, students, merchants, artisans, boys and girls at school, are enlisting for Christ; men of the world, drunkards and blasphemers, infidels, the very chief of sinners, are pressing into the kingdom ....Truly 'Jesus of Nazareth is passing by....' Go where you will, you hear people speaking of salvation, and no one wonders.[30]

---

29. Tom Lennie, *Scotland Ablaze*, p. 513.

30. *Monthly Visitor*, No. 503, May 1874, produced by the Scottish Monthly Visitor Tract Society.

Another report was equally fascinating, as it recalls that 'for all the month of December nothing else was spoken of in Edinburgh. The work, the meetings, and the men were spoken of at breakfast, at dinner, on the streets, and even in the ball-rooms. What does it all mean? What is all this about? At certain hours there seemed no one in Princess [sic] Street who did not carry a hymn-book, the tramway cars were full of hymn-books, and often it happened that nearly everyone in them was interested in the same subject, and pleasant Christian fellowship was exchanged.'[31]

Church Unity

One of the key elements that made this movement such a success was the unity of most of the churches in Edinburgh, Glasgow and across the nation. Presbyterians, Episcopalians, Baptists, Methodists and others prayed together, laboured together and harvested together. As an example of this unity the open-air meetings in Edinburgh, which typically gathered between 10,000 and 20,000 people, were led by ministers from different churches who shared the preaching. Back in 1837, David Nasmith had pleaded for a united gospel movement and preached that 'the object of the mission is not to make people Protestants or Roman Catholics, Baptist, Episcopalians, Methodist or any other sect: its object was in no way sectarian, but to unite all denominations of Christians, and by one strong effort, to pluck sinners as brands from the burning.'[32]

It was this inter-denominational and evangelical approach of the mission societies which broke down the sectarianism in the Scottish Protestant Church. There had already been a partial movement of this during the previous revivals, but now there was fullness. Evangelical leaders were to be found in almost all of the Protestant groupings, and they put their full weight behind Moody's visits. For example, the late Patricia Meldrum wrote her PhD thesis on forgotten evangelicals of the nineteenth

31. Tom Lennie, *Scotland Ablaze*, p. 513, quoting from *Narrative of Awakening* pamphlet in *Times of Blessing*, 1874.

32. Delores Burger, *Practical Religion: David Nasmith and the City Mission Movement, 1799–2000* (*Manchester Guardian*, 3rd May 1837), p. 46.

century in Scotland, and found that the Episcopal Church, which in the past had tended to see mission as the fanatical work of enthusiasts, now had twenty-four chapels in Edinburgh served by ninety-one evangelical clergy, most of whom were English.[33] Besides this, the Evangelical Alliance was founded in London in 1846, nurturing cooperation among gospel-believing Christians across the denominations of Britain. The key person who inspired this alliance was Dr Thomas Chalmers from Edinburgh. Dr John Nicholls, formerly Director of London City Mission, wrote:

> This concern for a 'Universal Home Mission' was also expressed in connection with the new Evangelical Alliance. In 1846 he [Dr Chalmers] published a pamphlet which advocated 'each denomination through all its local congregations co-operating for the evangelisation of their respective neighbourhoods.'[34]

In the same year the World Evangelical Alliance, also held in London, grew out of this, uniting over six hundred million Christians today for world mission.

After Effects

The question must be asked whether these three revivals changed people for the good, long-term, or did most of them return to their old lifestyles after the excitement had died down? Lennie, in his books on revival, gives us a balanced assessment of this. Certainly, there were some emotional excesses of a small minority of people trying to 'work up' an atmosphere, but in the examination process by the ministers afterwards, these sensationalists were usually identified. We also find that the long-term fruit of the revivals also partly depended on the follow-up process. In many churches there was a good nurturing

---

33. Personal notes sent to me by Patricia Meldrum. Her thesis was published in 2007: P. Meldrum, *Conscience and Compromise: Forgotten Evangelicals of Nineteenth Century Scotland*, foreword by Professor David Bebbington, Studies in Evangelical History and Thought (Wipf and Stock, 2007).

34. John Nicholls, *Evangelising Our Cities – The Abiding Challenge of Thomas Chalmers*, p. 28. www.affinity.org.uk. The influential pamphlet which Chalmers wrote was *On the Evangelical Alliance: its design, its difficulties, its proceedings, and its prospects: with practical suggestions*, 1846.

programme to help the new converts; in some churches this was not followed through as efficiently as it could have been.

One of the pioneers on a scholarly appraisal of revival was J. Edwin Orr, whose thesis for a PhD at the University of Oxford was on the second evangelical awakening in Britain. He claimed that out of a population in Scotland in 1859–61 of over three million people, there were about three hundred thousand converts – or about ten percent of the population.[35] Although it is clear that great transformation on a large scale occurred, Lennie points out that Orr missed some important considerations in his calculations, but admits that 'the number of converts from the 1859–61 revival in Scotland remains unknown and completely unverifiable but is universally considered to have run into at least numerous tens of thousands.'[36]

In the Free Church, for example, four hundred and seventy-seven churches recorded over fifteen thousand new members in 1859 alone, and the usual attendance at these churches was recorded at an increase of over 50 per cent for many years after that.[37] Alcoholic addiction decreased between 1859 and 1864 by 55 per cent in Edinburgh[38] and crime was noticeably reduced wherever the revival went. In villages like Ferryden and Cellardyke

---

35. Edwin J. Orr, *The Second Evangelical Awakening in Britain*, p. 5.

36. Tom Lennie, *Scotland Ablaze*, p. 391. In Chapter 1, *Academic Analyses*, Lennie shows that he has sourced information from the main scholarly works on revival in Scotland in the nineteenth century, which are as follows: 1. Edwin J. Orr, *The Second Evangelical Awakening in Britain* (1949); 2. Oscar Bussey, whose PhD thesis at Edinburgh University was in 1947: *The Religious Awakening of 1858-60 in Great Britain and Ireland*; 3. J. Carwardine, *Transatlantic Revivalism: Popular Evangelicalism in Britain and America, 1790-1865*, Westport: Conn., 1978; 4. David Bebbington, *Evangelicalism in Modern Britain: A History From the 1730s to the 1980s*, London, 1989; 5. Janice Holmes, *Religious Revivals in Britain and Ireland 1859-1905*, whose PhD thesis was published in 2000; 6. Clifford Marrs, in his unpublished PhD thesis, *The 1859 Religious Revival in Scotland*, at Glasgow University in 1995; 7. Kenneth Jeffrey, whose PhD, *When the Lord Walked the Land*, was published under the supervision of Professor David Bebbington at Stirling University in 2002.

37. Tom Lennie, *Scotland Ablaze*, p. 400.

38. ibid., p. 401, quoting from James Gall, Superintendent of Carrubbers' Close Mission, p. 6, 1882.

the fruit of the revival made a huge difference to the communities, with almost all of those converted in the movement being faithful Christians twenty-nine years later.[39] George Gardiner of Banff wrote about the long-term positive change that came over the towns in the North East of Scotland, for 'the whole face of society in those villages is so changed that those who have known them before are struck with wonder.'[40] Matthews claims that 'all the mission movements – home and foreign – philanthropic schemes, and measures for the alleviation of human suffering, have been mainly manned and maintained by the converts of the revival of 1859 and the sixties, and those who sympathised with it.'[41]

The Christian movement during Moody's 1873–74 visit grew out of the work in 1859–61, beginning in Edinburgh, and spreading through much of Scotland. Although it was called a revival, it did not have the same deep and purifying effect as before, leading to a higher fall-away rate of the converts, some of whom preferred to worship in 'God's green cathedral' outside, rather than attend church on Sunday; and yet thousands were clearly changed for good, many becoming church ministers and helping with the missionary cause. When Moody returned to Scotland in the 1880s, the evangelical high-water mark was still rising, with a good response to his preaching, and less of a dour dryness about the churches. But his first visit of 1873–74 was always remembered as the most far-reaching.

The nineteenth century was a critical time because it was a period of pioneering mission societies. This century also witnessed three significant Christian revivals and there was a growing unity in the Protestant churches. Out of these movements a godly spirituality spread throughout all classes, and permeated the nation, preparing the church for a most extraordinary expression of social action and mission that would, in turn, have global consequences.

---

39. ibid., p. 402.

40. ibid., pp. 402-03, quoting from Rose, p. 19.

41. ibid., Lennie, *Scotland Ablaze*, p. 406, quoting from Matthews T. T., (Ed.), *Reminiscences of the Revival of Fifty-Nine and the Sixties*, p. xii, Aberdeen, 1910.

CHAPTER 3

EDUCATION

It was an unusually sunny Spring-day when I walked past a primary and secondary school on my way to the University of Edinburgh. During the afternoon, I spoke with some Scottish students there and the discussion turned to education. 'Where do you think our education system came from?' I asked the group. There was a short silence, then one answered, 'Dunno. I guess from the government.' Another chimed in: 'It's always been there.'

Not daunted, I took the same question out on to the streets and asked some Scottish elderly people, thinking that they would know the answer. I was met with a blank stare from some, and embarrassed laughs by others; one man suggested the Labour Party. A petite elderly lady ventured something different. 'The church,' she said quietly and confidently. That simple question revealed something about our nation today: it showed our lack of historical understanding and knowledge, which our forebears would have known straightaway. It was indeed the church that had pioneered and developed education in Scotland.

The crowds pressed in to hear the teacher. Both men and women, as well as children, were eager to listen to what Jesus Christ taught. Before He left for heaven, He told His followers that they should go and make disciples, 'teaching them to observe all things that I have commanded you' (Matt. 28:20). At first, their call was for people to follow after Jesus and obey Him, but in the process of making disciples they soon realised that this meant developing a worldview that would transform society. For example, if we teach the Bible to people, we cannot avoid coming across language, ethics, law, justice, history, geography, sociology, psychology, philosophy, basic natural science, the arts, and more.

As the early church sought to influence the Pagan society around it, Christian scholars realised that they needed to engage with the culture. By about A.D. 150 Justin Martyr had established two catechetical schools in Rome and Ephesus. Following this model, two great colleges of learning arose in Antioch and Alexandria in the 170s. Although theology and literacy were the main subjects taught to the students, they also learnt languages, classical philosophy, rhetoric, history, astronomy, maths and medicine as part of their Christian worldview. Out of these grew cathedral schools between the fourth and tenth centuries, which were maintained by bishops. Sir William Ramsay, the Scottish archaeologist and foremost New Testament scholar of the twentieth century, wrote that the aim of the Christian church was 'universal education, not education confined to the rich, as among the Greeks and Romans ... and it [made] no distinction of sex.'[1]

The output of Christian literature in the first three centuries of the church was enormous. Eusebius, writing in 324, lists many titles, and casually states that 'large numbers of short works composed with commendable zeal by churchmen of that early time are still preserved in many libraries.'[2]

Education Among the Britons and Scots

After the Romans had largely conquered the Britons in A.D. 84, the locals experienced an explosion of Roman culture. Grand buildings arose, along with viaducts, baths, amphitheatres and hippodromes. With this came education amongst the wealthy and élite. Although the Druids had educated their people verbally, Julius Caesar observed that none of their information was written

1. W. M. Ramsay, *The Church in the Roman Empire Before A.D. 170* (Hodder and Stoughton, 1893), p. 345, cited by Alvin J. Schmidt, from *How Christianity Changed the World* (Zondervan, 2001), p. 172.

2. Eusebius, *The History of the Church*, 5:27 (Penguin Classics, translated by G. A. Williamson, 1965, 1989), p. 175.

down by their students, so literacy did not emerge out of Pagan Britain before this time.[3]

The Christians were so keen to get their message out, on the other hand, that the first main library was opened in the time of King Lucius, by bishop Elvanus. This learned man had a significant impact on the Druid leaders, so that many were converted to Christ.[4] Unfortunately, we have such sparse fragments of our history that both Gildas and Nennius bemoan the loss of the early centuries of Christian literacy among the Britons because of the waves of persecution by the Pagan Romans, Picts, Scots and Anglo-Saxons, in which Christian literature and buildings were destroyed.

Christian education and literacy really accelerated in Scotland through Ninian, the British apostle from Galloway, and Patrick, the British apostle from Dumbarton, who established a thriving church among the Scots in Ireland. From this foundation Ireland became known as the 'Land of Scholars and Saints.' It was as if Ireland became a bastion of learning, escaping the upheaval of multiple wars across Europe, as the Roman Empire in the West disintegrated, receiving a final blow to Rome by Odoacer the German in 476. Famous monasteries sprang up in the sixth century, such as the one at Movilla, founded by Finnian who had trained at Ninian's mission centre, and who taught Columba of Iona. Others established great centres of learning at Clonard and at Bangor, which was founded by Comgall. It was from Bangor that Columbanus issued forth to pioneer monasteries in France, Switzerland and Italy. Here in Scotland, Kentigern the Briton set up the education centre as part of an early cathedral at Glasgow.

---

3. Julius Caesar, *The Conquest of Gaul*, 1:1, translated by S. A. Handford (Penguin Classics, 1951, 1976), p. 32. Caesar tells us that the teaching and practice of the Druids in Gaul came from Britain, and that 'the Druids believe that their religion forbids them to commit their teachings to writing, although for most other purposes, such as public and private accounts, the Gauls use the Greek alphabet.' He surmises that the Druids did not want their teaching to be in public property through written records.

4. David J. Knight, *King Lucius of Britain*, p. 93, citing from Stow's *Survey of London* (1598), who cited from Jocelyn's twelfth century now-lost *Book of British Bishops*, a compilation taken from earlier sources.

The Scotsman who Founded Education in Paris

What an eccentric scene was beheld by the people of Paris in 792: two Scotsmen called out daily to passers-by with their rough accents: 'Whosoever covets wisdom, let him come to us and get it, for we have it for sale.' News of these two strange monks came to the ears of King Charles the Great, or Charlemagne, and being a lover of learning, he invited them to his court. 'We not only have wisdom,' they said to the king, 'but are ready to give it to those who seek it in the name of the Lord.' Intrigued, he cross-examined them and found them indeed to have great knowledge. He appointed Clement to establish his school in Paris, and John, or Albinus, to pioneer his other school at Pavia in Italy. From this foundation a great movement of education grew in France.

The above account is taken from Fordun's *Chronicle of the Scottish Nation*, volume one, written in 1363, but he himself cites from Vincent of Beauvais, a thirteenth century historian, who quotes from the tenth century *Chronicles of Arles*. The earliest historian to record this extraordinary event was Notkerus Balbulus, a French monk of St Gall, who wrote the *Life of Charlemagne* in 883/4. He tells us that 'two Scots came from Ireland to the coast of Gaul along with certain traders of Britain. These Scotchmen were unrivalled for their skill in sacred and secular learning.' Fordun says they were 'from Scotland' and were 'two Scottish monks'.

Now herein lies the confusion! Were they Scots from Ireland or from Scotland? This problem appears frequently in Scottish history for Alba (later called Scotland) was made up of Britons, Picts and Scots. When the Scots came from Ireland, they settled on the western coast of this nation in an area known as Dalriada – which was part of Ireland's expansion. John, who came with Clement, was known as Albinus after his native country, Alba. As the Britons, Picts and Scots fought for dominance, the Scots rose to the top of the pile, and so the nation was called Scotland. Despite this, for centuries the Scots living in our nation were called Irish – just to confuse everyone. If we are confused about it, I'm not surprised the French were too!

The wonderful point about this history is that it shows the Scottish Christians in Ireland and Scotland raising the standard of education to such prominence, that a king like Charlemagne would grasp this opportunity with all of his might. Eric of Auxerre could write to Charlemagne's grandson, Charles the Bald: 'What shall I say of Ireland, which is migrating with almost her whole train of philosophers to our coasts?'[5] From the seeds of this Scottish foundation the famous University of Paris would be born in 1150.

Another great luminary of education at the time of Charlemagne was Alcuin of York. Einhard, one of the king's courtiers, exuberantly confessed that he was 'the greatest scholar of the day'.[6] His impact on both Charlemagne and King Alfred the Great of Wessex were enormous, as they strived to establish education in their nations. Alcuin himself had been educated by Archbishop Egbert at his school in York where there was a famous library, but Egbert's influence was from Bede. The great Northumbrian scholars of York, Jarrow and Wearmouth all trace back to the community at Lindisfarne, which had been pioneered by Aidan in the seventh century. This Irish Scot had come over from Iona for this purpose. It was this movement, which began with the Britons, then transferred to the Irish and Anglo-Saxons, which became the foundation of our education in Scotland.

The first university to emerge in Britain was at Oxford, the world's second oldest continually active university. From an eighth century beginning with Frideswide's abbey, a college sprang into life by 1096, so that by 1167 it was developing as a university,

---

5. George Metcalfe, *The Life and Writings of St. Columban 542?–615*, Preface, first published in Philadelphia in 1914, a facsimile reprint (Felinfach: J.M.F. Books, 1993).

6. Einhard, *The Life of Charlemagne*, translated by Samuel Epes Turner (New York: Harper and Brothers, 1880), p. 25. The reference here says: 'Another deacon, Albin of Britain, surnamed Alcuin, a man of Saxon extraction, who was the greatest scholar of the day, was his teacher in other branches of learning. The King spent much time and labour with him studying rhetoric, dialectics, and especially astronomy; he learned to reckon, and used to investigate the motions of the heavenly bodies most curiously, with an intelligent scrutiny.'

based on the model of the University of Paris. Out of Oxford came the University of Cambridge in 1209. Both universities were inspired by the monastic movement, and developed by the Dominicans, Franciscans, Carmelites and Augustinians. Today, their mottos show their Christian origin, with Oxford's being 'The Lord is my light' and Cambridge's being 'From here light and sacred draughts'.

At that time most of the Scottish students had to either travel to these two universities, or to Paris, but in the fifteenth century national universities began to emerge. First came the University of St Andrews in 1413 through Benedict XIII's papal bull and the Augustinians, followed by the University of Glasgow in 1451, with its biblical quotation from Jesus: 'The Way, The Truth, The Life.' Next came the University of Aberdeen in 1495, through the untiring work of bishop William Elphinstone. The motto for this university is 'The fear of the Lord is the beginning of Wisdom'.

The fourth to become established was the University of Edinburgh in 1583. The origin of this famous seat of learning grew out of Magdalen Chapel in the Cowgate. Mary de Guise, the mother of Mary, Queen of Scots, encouraged by bishop Robert Reid, who also left a legacy for the foundation of a college in Edinburgh, accepted the appointment of Alexander Sym as a lecturer. The Edinburgh town council made a contract with him in 1556 and gave him 'ane powpet', or lectern, for him to 'reid in the Magdalene Chapel'.[7] He was joined shortly by his colleague, Edward Henryson, and the two professors lectured to students there. Soon after, due to the lack of space, they had to move elsewhere.

When the Reformation erupted in 1560, the reformers were enthusiastic to improve and transform education, so the University of Edinburgh officially came into being in 1583, being founded by the Town Council under the care of the Presbyterian Church.

---

7. John Durkan, *The Royal Lectureships under Mary of Lorraine*, from *The Scottish Historical* Review, Vol. 62, No. 173, Part 1 (Apr., 1983), pp. 73-78, published by Edinburgh University Press, stable URL: http://www.jstor.org/stable/25529507 Accessed: 1906–2017 13:02 UTC.

The reformers James Wilson, who was John Knox's successor at St Giles, and William Littil, the Lord Provost, were the key movers for this. William's reformer brother, Clement, founded the university library. Even today, when students receive their degrees in the McEwan Hall, they are doffed on the head with a black cap, traditionally believed to have been made from the trousers of John Knox! The actual university college began on the site of Kirk O' Field, which was previously known as St Mary in the Field, a collegiate church founded by the Augustinians.

Professor Renwick points out that by 1800 there were only two universities in England: Oxford and Cambridge, but four in Scotland, and that the English universities had a combined intake of 1,000 students, whereas the University of Edinburgh alone had 993 students. By 1830, the English universities had less than 3,000 students, but the Scottish universities catered for 4,400, despite the fact that the population of England was eight times that of Scotland.[8]

Grammar schools were also established by the church and began to emerge in the sixth century through the early monastic orders. At first these schools were pioneered for the purpose of training up future priests and monks. Typically, the pupils would be taught Latin, the language of the church and legal business, music, astronomy, maths and law. From these some of the early private boarding schools developed, such as at Winchester (1382), Oswestry (1407), and Eton (1440). After the Reformation these schools proliferated. In Scotland, the Choir School of Glasgow Cathedral (1124) and the Grammar School of the Church in Edinburgh (1128) were transformed into schools run by local councils. The latter school mentioned is known today as the Royal High School, which is one of the oldest schools still functioning today. It was founded by Alwin, abbot of Holyrood Abbey, with his Augustinian monks, under the Christian patronage of King David I.

---

8. A. M. Renwick, *The Story of the Scottish Reformation* (Inter-varsity Fellowship, 1960), p. 118.

A School in Every Parish

With the reformers came the vision for 'a school in every parish', which was achieved throughout much of Scotland by 1660. This was a revolutionary vision because before that, education had been limited in the country, being in the hands of monastic orders, such as the Augustinians, Dominicans and Franciscans, who tended to teach those mostly from the middle and aristocratic classes. The reformers' vision for a universal national education was so astounding, that I will quote from the extract of their manifesto called *The First Book of Discipline*, produced in Edinburgh in 1560:

> Of necessity therefore we judge it, that every several church have a schoolmaster appointed .... And further, we think it expedient that in every notable town, and especially in the town of the superintendent, [there] be erected a college, in which the arts, at least logic and rhetoric, together with the tongues, be read by sufficient masters, for whom honest stipends must be appointed; as also provision for those that are poor, and are not able by themselves, nor by their friends, to be sustained at letters, especially such as come from landward .... Last, the great schools, called universities, shall be replenished with those that are apt to learning; for this must be carefully provided, that no father, of what estate or condition that ever he be, use his children at his own fantasy, especially in their youth; but all must be compelled to bring up their children in learning and virtue.[9]

In this manifesto for universal education, we can clearly see the vision for every child in Scotland to have a basic education through the church network, including provision for the poor, so that even the children of poor parents could have an opportunity

---

9. *The First Book of Discipline (1560): The Fifth Head: Concerning the Provision for the Ministers, and for the Distribution of the Rents and Possessions Justly Appertaining to the Kirk: For the Schools and The Necessity of Schools*, based upon the published edition in the *Works of John Knox*, edited by David Laing (Edinburgh: James Thin, 1895), Vol. 2, pp. 183-260, and produced in an edited version to comply with contemporary English, by Presbyterian Heritage Publications, 1993.

to be educated. This huge and costly vision would take centuries to work through, and would take a lot of encouragement and development. In 1616, the Scottish Parliament passed the School Establishment Act, so that every parish would have a school and a teacher, paid for by the parishioners, and under the supervision of church leaders. The later Education Acts of 1633, 1646 and 1696 strengthened this policy.

By the eighteenth century, most of Scotland was receiving a basic education and it was among the most literate nations in Europe. However, the Highlands were a different matter. *The Society in Scotland for Propagating Christian Knowledge* (SSPCK) was founded in Edinburgh in 1701, but given its royal charter eight years later. Apart from having a passion for producing and distributing Christian literature, the founding members also realised that mission work in the form of pioneering schools needed to be done in the Highlands, among the predominantly Roman Catholic and Gaelic-speaking people, often in remote regions. Four years later, SSPCK had established twelve schools in the Highlands, and by 1781 these had mushroomed to one hundred and eighty.[10]

Sabbath or Sunday Schools

In 1780, a Christian newspaper publisher called Robert Raikes, together with Rev. Thomas Stock, pioneered what became known as the Sunday School Movement. Most of the education being done in England was amongst the children of the wealthy. Typically, parents would hire a private tutor to teach the children and would send their sons through a private school system known as Public Schools. The working-class children were expected simply to follow in their parents' footsteps and pursue the same careers, without being given the opportunity to learn to read and write.

Raikes and Stock saw the desperate need of liberating the masses from a treadmill existence through a Christian-based

---

10. Henry Hunter, *A Brief History of the Society in Scotland for Propagating Christian Knowledge* (London: SSPCK, 1795), p. 16.

education. At first, they met with opposition from politicians and liberal churchmen, who saw this as a threat to the established order; often parents themselves also opposed the idea, thinking that if their children were educated they might desert the family business to pursue another career, leaving the parents stranded and deprived of an extra income. Despite this opposition, the Sunday School Movement took off, so that by 1850 over two million children in Britain were receiving a basic education.[11] Dr J. Wesley Bready could write:

> By 1786 no less than 200,000 English children were regularly attending Sunday schools. In 1791 the movement was planted in America. In 1831, when Lord Shaftesbury unveiled a statue to Raikes, it was claimed that already in Great Britain alone 1,250,000 children were attending Sunday schools. When the Sunday School centenary was celebrated in 1880, the movement had taken root in every continent, and its voluntary teachers far exceeded a million.[12]

To be sure, the idea of Sunday schools was not a novel one, for John Wesley's disciple, Hannah Ball, had taught a flourishing Sunday school in High Wycombe eleven years before. Here in Scotland, schools had been sprouting up everywhere through the Presbyterian Church since the Reformation, and the existence of Sabbath or Sunday schools was not a new thing. Dr John Brown stated that 'Mr Raikes was the founder of the English schools, and that he had no acquaintance with the prior existence of these schools in Scotland ... we had Sabbath Schools of a superior order long before the days of that eminent philanthropist.'[13] Brown

---

11. Thomas Walter Laquer, *Religion and Respectability: Sunday Schools and Working Class Culture* (New Haven: CT Yale University Press, 1976), p. 44.

12. J. Wesley Bready, *England: Before and After Wesley: The Evangelical Revival and Social Reform* (Hodder and Stoughton, 1938), p. 354, whose references are taken from *Raikes* in the *Dictionary of National Biographies*, and also from *Sunday Schools* in the *Encyclopaedia of Religion and Ethics*, and also from the *Encyclopaedia of Education*.

13. John Brown, *The Origin of Sabbath Schools in England and the Existence of these Schools in Scotland Fifty Years Before those of Mr Raikes*, from the *Scottish Christian Herald: Origin of Sabbath Schools*, Vol I, p. 182.

then cites examples of Sabbath schools in Norham in 1757 and in Simprin in 1707.

It was, however, Raikes' business acumen to develop a big vision, and to spread the idea through his newspaper publishing, which enabled the Sunday School Movement to take off in Scotland as well, where it acted in conjunction with the already existing parish schools, giving fresh impetus to the national education movement. It was in another newspaper of 1787, the *Scots Magazine*, that we first read about Raikes' Sunday School vision in this nation, although there must have already been discussions about it, and we learn that Christians in Aberdeen and Glasgow had already started them.

By the 1790s, Sunday schools were dotted throughout most of lowland Scotland. This work inspired the Haldane brothers, James and Robert, who were evangelists, so that in 1797 they established the first free schools, supported by a network of patrons. These schools spread rapidly through the Haldanes' *Society for the Propagation of the Gospel at Home* (SPGH), but because they were Baptists, they were opposed by the Church of Scotland. Unfortunately, this was exacerbated by the run up to the Napoleonic Wars that lasted from 1803 to 1815, during which time there was suspicion in Britain of any potentially subversive networks which could undermine the national war effort against the French. William Pitt, the Prime Minister, called Sunday schools 'dangerous',[14] fearing that they might be spawning grounds for revolution, and the Archbishop of Canterbury, John Moore, called them 'nurseries of fanaticism'.[15] In 1799, the General Assembly of the Church of Scotland issued a Pastoral Admonition against SPGH and the Sunday schools in general, saying that the teachers were 'persons notoriously disaffected to

---

14. BBC Magazine online, 2nd July 2008, http://news.bbc.co.uk/1/hi/magazine/7484282.stm as at 15th December 2015, referred to from *The Little Book of Non-Violent Extremists*, 2016, The Christian Institute, p. 26.

15. W. M. Ramsay, *Church History 101: An introduction for Presbyterians* (Geneva Press, 2005), p. 103, quoted from *The Little Book of Non-Violent Extremists*, p. 26.

the Civil Constitution of the country'.[16] Although the evangelical party in the Church of Scotland fully supported Sunday schools in the 1830s, it was not until 1849 that the national Presbyterian denomination gave its full official sanction.

By 1819, there were 452 Sunday schools in Scotland, most of which were run by Independent or interdenominational church groups, although the Sabbath School Union for Scotland claimed that there were also 567 schools affiliated with them, with 39,000 pupils.[17] By 1842, Glasgow alone was educating 25,000 pupils with its Sunday school growth outstripping the population growth by four times; this was largely due to the evangelical movement. By 1891, 46 per cent of children between the ages of five and fourteen were in Sunday schools there; this amounts to 108,205 pupils, being taught by an army of over 10,000 teachers. Illiteracy in that city had also fallen through this work between 1850 and 1870, from 18.3 per cent to 5.8 per cent.[18]

In the Sunday school records we can see a pattern emerging across Scotland: there was huge growth from the 1830s to the 1890s, and then the numbers begin to tail off. At its height in 1890, the Church of Scotland had 217,207 pupils; the Free Church had 166,166; and the United Presbyterian Church had 103,010 – or a total of 486,383 children in Sunday/Sabbath schools, and this did not include the Independent and other churches, missions and societies.[19] This is a staggering record, causing Callum

---

16. Callum Brown, *The Sunday School Movement in Scotland 1780–1914*, p. 10.

17. *Sabbath School Union for Scotland: Third Annual Report*, 1819. The Sabbath School Union for Scotland claimed 567 affiliated schools altogether, with 39,000 pupils: Callum Brown, *The Sunday School Movement in Scotland 1780–1914*, p. 13. Callum Brown says of the 452 Sunday schools, 181 were interdenominational; 133 were run by Independent churches; ninety-three were 'countenanced' by Church of Scotland clergy; seventeen were established by 'titled gentry'; nine by Methodists; nine by Burghers (a Presbyterian grouping); three by Anti-Burghers (another Presbyterian grouping); three by tradesmen; two by factory owners; and two by day schools.

18. Callum Brown, pp. 14-15.

19. ibid., Appendix, pp. 25-26.

Brown to state that the 'Sunday school teachers had been the most numerous, and arguably the most influential, educators and educationists in the country.'[20]

The Monitoring Method

At the age of fourteen, a passionate English Christian secretly travelled to Bristol in order to secure a crossing to Jamaica to 'teach the poor blacks the Word of God'. Unfortunately for him funding was not available, and so he sought to find another avenue for God's service. Six years later, this evangelical Quaker, Joseph Lancaster, began a small school in 1798, in which he began to experiment with teaching methods. In 1801 he took a large room in London in Borough Road and launched his free school. An amusing notice was hung over his school, which read: 'All who will may send their children and have them educated freely, and those who do not wish to have education for nothing may pay for it if they please.'[21]

Lancaster developed a method by which many children could be taught in one place at low cost, by using a monitorial system. This meant that older children, who had been taught by the teachers, could be used to help teach the younger ones in small groups. This method also meant that future teachers were being trained up. The Lancastrian Method took off and his popularity opened the way for a personal interview by King George III in 1805, who, being amazed about Lancaster's success, became his patron, saying, 'It is my wish that every poor child in my dominions should be taught to read the Bible.'[22]

Unfortunately, Lancaster fell into debt and had to be rescued by some fellow Quaker Christians, who reorganised his finances and called the movement the *Royal Lancastrian Institution*. Lancaster struggled with having a committee, being an autocrat, so the directors and supporters had to eject him, following which

---

20. ibid., p. 17.

21. J. Wesley Bready, *England: Before and After Wesley*, p. 355.

22. ibid.

they renamed the institution the *British and Foreign School Society*. This had a name change yet again to the *National Society for the Education of the Poor in accordance with the Principles of the Church of England* – or the *National Society*. It was the Scottish Christian, Dr Andrew Bell, who took this over and developed it so well, that by his death in 1831, when he was buried in Westminster Abbey, almost 13,000 National schools had been formed.[23]

As with the Sunday schools, the Scots again claimed that their own Dr Bell had pioneered the monitorial method before Joseph Lancaster, having done so in Madras in India, when he was the Superintendent for the Madras Male Orphanage Asylum. Dr Bell had even published his *Experiment in Education* in 1797, a year before Lancaster has opened his first school, outlining the monitoring system he had pioneered there. He was born in St Andrews in 1753, where he also studied at the university. For a short time, he practiced as a Church of England priest in Edinburgh, but when he gave his full strength to promoting his 'Madras System' of monitorial education, he made sure that these schools were established in Scotland too, thus bringing another important ingredient in the advance towards our national education.

Industrial and Ragged Schools

Since 1707, when the Union Treaty was signed, Scotland had come under the authority of the Parliament in London, which meant that both English and Scottish Christians began to work more closely together to see transformation in all areas of society. Lord Shaftesbury, an evangelical Christian reformer, who was dearly loved as 'The Poor Man's Earl', realised that in order to provide a proper education for many children, they had to be delivered from the workforce. Multitudes of children under the age of thirteen toiled twelve hours a day or more, six days a week, and often in horrendous conditions. By battling as a dogged politician,

---

23. ibid., p. 357, whose references are found in the *Encyclopaedia Britannica* and *Dictionary of National Biographies* (under Bell), and also in Meiklejohn's *An Old Educational Reformer*.

Shaftesbury finally had his 1833 Factory Act passed, which now meant that children under the age of nine were protected from factory work, and no child under thirteen was allowed to work longer than nine hours a day, or forty-eight hours a week. This freed the younger ones to receive a basic education, and those under thirteen could now have classes at the factories and other places of work.

The Ragged School Union was an offshoot of the Sunday School Movement and 'its purpose was to catch, befriend, and educate, "human eels in the mud".'[24] In 1798 Thomas Cranfield of Southwark, London, saw the terrible plight of the children from the slums who were too ragged to attend Sunday schools. Many of them lived on the streets and were beggars, pickpockets and prostitutes. For some this was a safer existence than being at home to face the drunken brawling and abuse of their parents. Cranfield set up several schools for these urchins, waifs and strays, under the supervision of Rev. Rowland Hill. John Pounds of Portsmouth attempted the same vital work, but neither of these men saw a breakthrough which would see continuity. This would change with the visionary work of another Scottish man called Rev. Dr Thomas Guthrie.

When Guthrie was appointed in 1837 as assistant minister at Greyfriars' Kirk in Edinburgh, much of his work was focused among the poor of the district, for whom he poured out his life. It is hard for us to imagine what it was like in the Edinburgh slums of that time. What better person than Guthrie to tell us in his own expressive and emotive style:

> I wandered in those houses for whole days without ever seeing a Bible, or indeed any book at all. I often stood in rooms bare of any furniture; where father, mother, and half a dozen children had neither bed nor bedding, unless a heap of straw and dirty rags huddled in a corner could be called so. I have heard the wail of children crying for bread, and their mother had none to give them. I have seen a babe pulling breasts as dry as if the starved-

---

24. ibid., p. 358.

looking mother had been dead. I have known a father turn his step-daughter to the street at night – bidding the sobbing girl who bloomed into womanhood, earn her bread there as others were doing. I have bent over the foul pallet of a dying lad to hear him whisper how his father and mother – who were sitting half drunk by the fireside had pulled blankets off his body to sell them for drink. I have seen children blanched like plants growing in a cellar – for weeks they never breathed a mouthful of fresh air for want of rags to cover their nakedness; and I used often to observe in these dingy dwellings, where the air is poison, and the food is scanty, and the cold is bitter, and short is the gleam of sunshine, and they live in continual terror of a drunken father or mother, and where when they cry they are not kissed but beaten, that the children have an air of sadness, and look as if they never smiled. I don't recollect of ever seeing a mother in these wretched dwellings dandling her infant, or of hearing the little creature crow or laugh as he leapt with joy. There, infants have no toys; and mothers' smiles are rare as sunshine. Nobody can know the misery I suffered amid those scenes of human wretchedness, woe, want, and sin.[25]

For Guthrie, healing the plight of the poor seemed like scaling a towering mountain with sheer rock faces, and many would have turned back at the knowledge of the real condition he knew so well, a condition that was hidden from most of the people in the city. And yet he steeled himself for the task of transformation through God's help. He could have fled to the security of the suburbs, but he held firm to his deep conviction that 'if a man won't live among the scum of the Cowgate, I would at once say to him "you can't be its minister."'[26]

The first thing that Guthrie realised was that many of the poor did not come to church because they could not afford the pew tokens. This was due to an old custom that money for the church's upkeep was raised in this way. Guthrie's friend, Dr Chalmers,

25. Thomas Guthrie, *Out of Harness* (New York: Alexander Strahan, 1867), p. 3.

26. David K. Guthrie and Charles J. Guthrie, *Autobiography of Thomas Guthrie D.D. and Memoir* (New York: Robert Carter and Brothers, 1873), Vol. 1, p. 370.

had been successfully working on the Church Extension Project to increase the number of church buildings within the growing parishes, and had raised £300,000 from the Christian population – about £35 million in today's money, so that between 1835 and 1841, two hundred and twenty-two new churches had been built and erected.[27] Realising that he could not overcome the church token custom in Greyfriars' Kirk, Guthrie gained permission to use Magdalen Chapel – the chapel famed for the reformers and Covenanters – and set up a church service for the poor who could not afford to buy tokens. Although the stench of the body odour in that place would drive the well-to-do away, for Guthrie it was a fragrance of heaven, as the poor responded with tears to the good news of Christ. But he soon realised that this small chapel could not contain the crowds that started coming. Something had to be done.

In 1840, St John's on Victoria St was erected with money sacrificially raised by many, and the crowds poured in. The gallery was let to people of the city who could easily afford it, but the main floor was open free of charge to six hundred and fifty, thus allowing many of the poor that Guthrie had befriended to join the church. When the Disruption broke out in 1843 over the patronage system, most of the evangelicals left the Church of Scotland to form the Free Church, which meant that Guthrie lost this building. By 1845, Free St John's (today's St Columba's Free Church) had been built opposite his old church, so he resumed his work there.

In 1841, Sheriff William Watson had set up the first Ragged School in Scotland in Aberdeen, and Guthrie, inspired by his relative's work, found that such a ministry needed to be set up in Edinburgh. The Ragged School Union had already been established in London in April 1844, with Lord Shaftesbury as its first president, but Guthrie was to play a prominent part in spreading this movement for the children in rags. When he and his congregation moved into Free St John's, they decided to use the

---

27. Guthrie and Guthrie, *Autobiography*, ibid., p. 380.

basement for the first Ragged School in Edinburgh, but the elders and deacons changed their mind when they realised the reality of what this would mean. Not being thrown into despondency, Guthrie picked himself up, and raised the funds for the first Ragged School in the city, built in 1847, which today stands next to the Camera Obscura on the way up to the castle. It is estimated that 300,000 poor children went through the Ragged Schools in London between 1844 and 1881,[28] but Guthrie was the key mover in Scotland, with thousands of children been plucked out, like 'human eels' from 'the mud' of society's degraded underbelly.

Guthrie's Committee of Management consisted of members from the Episcopalian Church, Church of Scotland, Free Church, United Presbyterians, Baptists and Independents, so it was a non-denominational evangelical ministry. They did however hit trouble – this time from the Roman Catholics. Guthrie said that he had never seen a Roman Catholic priest working in the slums in twenty years where 'the girls were left to grow up as prostitutes, and the boys to become thieves,' but as soon as the children of Roman Catholic parents started to receive help to improve their lives and to learn to read the Bible, opposition broke out, as Guthrie put it: 'Father Keenan of Dundee ... boldly stated that he would prefer to see children perish in the streets rather than get food and education and God's Word in the Dundee Ragged Schools.'[29] This caused a rumpus, and the city of Edinburgh was 'stirred to its depths' as a four-hour debate raged in the Music Hall. But when the vote was taken to continue the Ragged Schools as they were, a sea of hands was seen, with only five people standing against the motion.

The fruit of the Ragged Schools spoke for itself, as Guthrie pointed out in 1859:

I. The results of our Schools are to be found in many happy homes, the abodes of those that, once wretched, ragged outcasts, are

---

28. J. Walvin, *A Child's World: A Social History of English Childhood 1800–1914* (Pelican, 1982).

29. Guthrie, *Out of Harness*, p. 5.

now honest men and virtuous mothers, useful citizens and heads of families .... We – and in these results I include the influence of other, though smaller schools, have cleared the streets of Edinburgh of juvenile beggars, a feat that the Magistrates and Police, with cells and prison at their back, were far from ever being able to achieve, that when our School was set on foot, their name was Legion. They swarmed through all the town – it was creeping with them.

II. We are fast emptying the prisons ...

III. The Original Ragged School [founded in 1847] alone has rescued from great misery and certain ruin not less than five hundred children. They are now blessings to society .... And if we make the much more probable supposition, that but for our school – its useful, kind, and holy training – two-thirds of those five hundred children would have developed into full-blown criminals, we have saved the country not less than £72,000 [about £9.8 million in today's money]![30]

National Education

As the different streams of schools expanded in Britain, there was a growing realisation that we needed to have a national education system to pull everything together. Before this could be done though, an in-depth assessment of the standards of schools needed to be carried out, for some schools excelled; others were good, but needed improvements; and in some cases, the standards were poor. The Newcastle Commission in England (1858–61) in its *Report on the State of Popular Education in England* discovered that about 2.5 million children in England were receiving a daily education, which meant that about one seventh of the entire population was attending day schools. England and Wales embraced a national education system shortly after in the Education Act of 1870.

---

30. ibid., p. 6. In just twelve years, Guthrie reckoned the taxpayer had been saved almost ten million pounds through one school alone in Edinburgh. It would be an interesting task for someone to calculate the total amount of money reckoned to have been saved through *all* of the Scottish Ragged Schools between 1847 and 1859.

Scotland was not far behind, when we accepted the same thing in the Education Act of 1872.

In 1866 George Campbell, the eighth Duke of Argyll, had been commissioned to investigate the condition of education in Scotland and, as with the English schools, there was a mixed bunch of standards from excellent to poor. Campbell was a regular supporter of Christian enterprises, also being an external director for Edinburgh City Mission (ECM). In the Annual Meeting at the Music Hall, he gave an address to the supporters and missionaries of ECM gathered there and said, 'I approve of this society exceedingly, in one respect, especially, that it employs lay missionaries ... I rejoice ... in the unsectarian character of this society.'[31]

He wholeheartedly backed the numerous churches and Christian volunteers, and was determined, as one of the key movers for a national education system, to pull everything together and raise the standards to the highest possible level in Scotland. With this came the 1,000 regional school boards to develop and oversee the standards. Christian leaders like the Haldane brothers in Edinburgh had pioneered free education in Scotland, but now it was the time to establish compulsory education for all children from five to thirteen, and eventually a free National Education System in 1890 that would teach children from Primary to Secondary, with the money not coming from private donations, but through the taxpayers, and run by the State.

Teacher Training Colleges

In the long march to a National Education System in Scotland, there were some key Christian figures that played a significant part, such as William Watson, Thomas Guthrie, Andrew Bell and John Wood, but David Stow was instrumental in developing teacher training in Britain. In 1828 he set up his first Sunday school in Glasgow, out of which came the *Glasgow Educational*

---

31. Address of the Lord Provost, the Duke of Argyll, at the ECM Annual Meeting, Music Hall, Dec 23rd, 1850, Annual Report: 1850: pp. 7-8.

Society. Many educationalists came to observe his methods, in what was called the Normal School, meaning the norms, or standards of teaching used, and then established the model throughout Britain and the colonies. One of the most important of these observers was Sir James Phillips Kay-Shuttleworth, who had studied medicine at the University of Edinburgh. He went to England and pioneered the Battersea Normal College in 1840 as a teacher training college with Edward Tufnell – this becoming a model for other colleges to follow. Most of the colleges that came out of this movement dropped the word 'Normal', and simply called themselves teacher training colleges, which were eventually attached to universities.

The politician, Sir Thomas Chambers, after the national school boards had been established, asked, 'Who are they that have brought about this marvellous improvement in the amount of Education given, and in the Educational machinery involved? Who but the members of all the Evangelical Churches throughout the country? Who have filled the Sunday Schools, and the Ragged Schools, and the British and Foreign Schools, and to a great extent, the National schools, with teachers? Who but the men who have acted from religious motives, and whose conduct has been influenced by the teaching of the Gospel?'[32]

---

32. J. Wesley Bready, *England: Before and After Wesley*, p. 361, quoting from C. J. Montague, *Sixty Years in Waifdom*, p. 310. Note: when Chambers uses the word 'men' in the nineteenth century, he meant men and women. Thousands of the teachers who were involved in education were women.

CHAPTER 4

HEALTHCARE

At the end of 2019 the Coronavirus broke out in Wuhan, China. By Christmas 2021, over 148,000 people were dead in Britain and over five million worldwide. Today's global death rate stands at almost 6.9 million, with the UK losing over 226,000 people. Fear paralysed nations as the virus spread, leading to a global financial crisis because of lockdown, and huge social unrest. During this time two vital words were often discussed: antiseptics and vaccines. Antiseptics help us in the battle against spreading the virus, and vaccines enable us to be more protected: both are connected with Scotland. The first person was Lord Joseph Lister, the pioneer of antiseptics, the father of sanitising; the second was Edward Jenner, the pioneer of vaccination.

Oxford University's Jenner Institute, named after Edward Jenner, worked long and hard, among others, and produced a vaccine, with millions of doses being manufactured by the pharmaceutical company called AstraZeneca. Amidst all the fear, multitudes found relief and hope because of the vaccines being rolled out. Few, though, would realise the connection of an English Christian with Scotland.

Edward Jenner, the son of Rev. Stephen Jenner, grew up in Berkeley in Gloucestershire. In 1763, he was appointed as an apprentice with a surgeon at Chipping Sodbury, where he gained invaluable experience in surgery. Seven years later he furthered his career by becoming an apprentice in surgery and anatomy with the nation's leading Scottish surgeon, John Hunter, at George's Hospital in London. By 1773, Jenner was practising as a family doctor and surgeon in his home town of Berkeley. It was later, in 1792, that Jenner applied for the degree of MD from the University of St Andrews, because Scotland was a world leader in medicine during that period.

Although Jenner has been rightly credited as being the pioneer of vaccination against smallpox, he had already been influenced by John Hunter in London, for this Scotsman had not only been using an earlier form of inoculation, but they had also discussed the possibility of cowpox being a cure for smallpox. The writers of an article from the *Journal of the Royal Society of Medicine* (Vol. 83, April 1990), state that 'The overriding question is as to why Jenner waited until 1798 to complete his experiments and publish his results – five years after Hunter's death?'

By 1979 the World Health Organisation declared that they had finally eradicated smallpox, which had killed millions of people. It was from Jenner's work that the science of immunology grew. As a Christian, he remarked to a friend as he was dying in 1823: 'I am not surprised that men are not grateful to me; but I wonder that they are not grateful to God for the good which He has made me the instrument of conveying to my fellow creatures.'[1]

Joseph Lister (1827–1912): The Father of Antiseptics and Sanitising

The surgeon had just finished successfully operating on a patient. It was the last one for the day and he was eager to get back home to his family. As he walked back, he mulled over his work. He had done his best job, but he knew that over 50 per cent of patients successfully operated on died of infection afterwards; in parts of Europe, it was as high as 80 per cent. Scientists believed that infections arose spontaneously within the body, so there was nothing that could be done about this: we just had to live with it. This was all to change in 1860.

One day the French Roman Catholic, Louis Pasteur, triumphantly proclaimed that his experiments had proved that life came from

---

1. John Baron (1838), *The Life of Edward Jenner M.D. LL.D. F.R.S.* Vol. 2 (London: Henry Colburn), p. 310. hdl:2027/nc01.ark:/13960/t2t523s95, Hathi Trust.

life rather than from spontaneous generation. Before this, scientists had observed that an unsealed glass of water, when left alone, will eventually produce bacteria. Their conclusion was that water spontaneously evolved into simple life forms. When Pasteur boiled water and sealed off all of the air in special glass tubes, no bacteria formed. In one fell swoop he had vanquished a popular theory that had held back science for centuries, and demonstrated the new germ theory, that contamination comes from outside bacteria.

Joseph Lister came up to Edinburgh from England in 1853 to learn from Professor James Syme, a Christian who was regarded as the country's best teacher of surgery. Lister came from a devout Quaker family, but when he met Syme's daughter Agnes, he fell in love with her and they were married. Lister remained in Edinburgh, as Syme's assistant, attending an Episcopal Church with the family. In 1860, during the year of Pasteur's discovery, he became the Professor of Surgery in Glasgow. It was there that a friend lent him some papers by Pasteur. As he read about Pasteur's work, his heart and mind were racing with excitement. This new germ theory could be extended to medical science and save lives. He needed a chemical which was harmless to people, but which would disinfect the body, cleansing it of potentially lethal bacteria. He found out that carbolic acid was being used safely by workers to disinfect sewers.

By 1865, Lister was using carbolic acid in his surgery: he washed his hands in it, before and after operations; he cleansed his surgical instruments with it, as well as bandages, and even sprayed the air with it. Lister published the results of his antisepsis method in the medical journal *Lancet* between March and July in 1867, reporting that his surgical wards were clear of sepsis. Between 1864 and 1866, before he had introduced antisepsis, 46 per cent of his own patients died after surgical operations (which was better than average); after introducing his new treatment there was a dramatic change, with only 15 per cent of his patients dying between 1867 and 1870.

Two years later he took up the post as Professor of Clinical Surgery in Edinburgh, replacing his father-in-law. From there he wrote to Pasteur in 1874, thanking him for his 'brilliant researches', which he said had 'proved to me the truth of the germ theory ... and furnished me with the principle upon which alone the antiseptic system can be carried out.'[2] By 1875, Lister was highly acclaimed in Europe, with post-operation fatalities rapidly falling as surgeons applied his principles, and in some cases, as in Munich, fatalities dropped dramatically from 80 per cent to a much lower percentage.

But Lister was not a one-trick pony: he went on to invent surgical instruments, introduce sterilised wiring to aid healing bones, rubber drainage tubes, and sterilised catgut, which would harmlessly disintegrate in the body after a time. Lister was made the first Lord in British medical history and was a committed Christian, who wrote, 'I am a believer in the fundamental doctrines of Christianity.'[3] We have become used to antiseptics, especially during the Coronavirus pandemic, but without Lister's work in medical science, so many more people would have died.

Healthcare for Everyone

Back in the first century, Jesus told his disciples to heal the sick through miraculous prayer, but he also encouraged medical care and nursing. In the Parable of the Good Samaritan, care is shown by the Samaritan, who bound up the wounds of the victim and applied wine and oil for antiseptic and healing. Christ also expressed his love of those suffering with illness with the words, 'I was sick and you looked after me' (Matt. 25:36). The apostle Paul not only practised healing prayer but took along Luke, his medical doctor, on his mission trips.

By the year 325, the great persecutions against the church in the Roman Empire had abated and Christians could come out

---

2. J. H. Tiner, *Louis Pasteur – Founder of Modern Medicine* (Milford [Michigan]: Mott Media, 1990), p. 111, cited by Ann Lamont in *21 Scientists who believed in the Bible* (Creation Science Foundation Ltd., Brisbane, Australia, 1995), p. 193.

3. Ann Lamont, *21 Great Scientists who Believed in the Bible*, p. 196.

from being an underground, despised movement to dominating the spiritual landscape. At the Council of Nicaea the bishops agreed that 'the hospital ... be established in every city' in the Roman Empire.[4] The first fully established hospital complex was pioneered by Basil, the bishop of Cappadocia, in 369, which, apart from a large hospital, also included 'a large number of buildings, with houses for physicians and nurses, workshops, and industrial schools.'[5] When we get to the sixth century, hospitals can be found all over Europe, usually being looked after by monastic orders. By the 1450s there were 37,000 monastic communities that looked after the sick.[6]

In Scotland the early monks cared for the sick and dying during the early centuries, and were keen to experiment with and develop medicinal herbs as 'leaves ... for the healing of the nations' (Rev. 22:2). The first large hospital in this nation was founded by the Augustinian monks in 1164, as the House of the Holy Trinity at Soutra Aisle at Fala, not far from Edinburgh. Today only partial ruins can be found, but the hospital once measured about seven hundred square metres. The complex also included an almshouse for the poor and a hostel for weary travellers. It was situated in a bleak place, which in winter is exposed to the biting Scottish wind, but the spot was well-chosen because it was near the main route from Northumbria to Edinburgh, known as Dere Street, a Roman road which today forms part of the A68.

Sadly, there were allegations of scandal and corruption within the House of the Holy Trinity, so in the 1460s it was abandoned and the work was transferred to Edinburgh to a site just below Calton Hill, where it became known as Trinity College Hospital. This hospital, with its adjoining Trinity College Kirk, was founded

---

4. Canon Law LXX, Council of Nicaea, A.D. 325, *The Seven Ecumenical Councils, the Nicene and Post-Nicene Fathers*, Vol XIV, second series (Wm B. Eerdmans Publishing Co, 1899), p. 50.

5. H. Garrison Fielding, *An Introduction to the History of Medicine* (Philadelphia: W. B. Saunders, 1914), p. 118, cited by Alvin J. Schmidt from *How Christianity Changed the World* (Zondervan, 2004), p. 156.

6. Alvin J. Schmidt, *How Christianity Changed the World*, p. 157.

in 1460 by Mary of Gueldres, the wife of King James II. When the Town Council built the railway in 1848, they decided to demolish both buildings in the name of progress, promising that this beautiful and old Gothic church would be rebuilt as before with its own stones elsewhere – a promise which was not kept, although a different church of Gothic character, called Trinity Apse, was opened in 1877.

King James IV was a great patron of medicine, and in 1505 the Royal College of Surgeons was founded in Edinburgh as the Incorporation of the Surgeon Barbers of Edinburgh, which is one of the oldest medical fellowships in the world.

Corruption of the Roman Catholic Church and monasteries in Scotland meant that the Reformation was necessary. With the settlement of the Protestant Church of Scotland, a renewed and purified vision was established in the *First Book of Discipline* in 1560. The Presbyterian manifesto for the health and welfare of the Scottish people is stated thus:

> But for the widow and fatherless, the aged, impotent, or lame, who neither can nor may travail for their sustenance, we say that God commands his people to be careful. And therefore, for such, as also for persons of honesty fallen in[to] decay and penury, ought such provision be made that [of] our abundance should their indigence be relieved. How this most conveniently and most easily may be done in every city, and other parts of this realm, God shall show you wisdom and the means, so that your minds are godly thereto inclined.[7]

It was this Christian vision of caring for the sick and the poor that was developed to eventually become our National Health and Welfare Services today.

The reformers were keen to see better medical practice happening in Scotland and we find a prayer, attributed to John

---

7. *The First Book of Discipline*, 1560: *The Fifth Head: Concerning the Provision for the Ministers, and for the Distribution of the Rents and Possessions Justly Appertaining to the* Kirk, https://www.fpchurch.org.uk/about-us/important-documents/the-first-book-of-discipline-1560/

Knox, in the Surgeons' Hall. This prayer for surgeons to use was contained within the Minutes of the Barber Surgeons in 1581, with the words:

> O eternal God, our loving and merciful Father – Jesus Christ – seeing we are convened to treat of those things which concern our calling, we beseech thee, O Lord, to be merciful to us, and give us grace to proceed therein without malice, grudge, or partiality: so that the things we do may tend to the Glory of God, and weal of our vocation, and the comfort of every member of it, through Jesus Christ our only Lord and Saviour. Amen.

Gilbert Primrose, a devout Christian in the Reformation, became the Royal Surgeon for King James VI and in 1583 he raised surgery to the prime position in the Edinburgh Guilds. Peter Lowe, another dedicated Christian, went to Glasgow and founded the Faculty of Physicians and Surgeons there in 1599.

Edinburgh: Medical Training Capital of the World

It is the 1720s and over two hundred Scotsmen have travelled to study under Europe's greatest teacher of medicine. The elderly and frail professor at St Augustine's Medical School in Leiden, Holland, holds the class spellbound as he explains aspects of medical practice in simple ways. Suddenly he looks up, his eyes impassioned, as if in rapture, to encourage his students to treat their patients as Christ would have us do, not as mere living machines, but as precious individuals for whom Christ died, for 'the excellency of the Christian religion was the frequent subject of his conversation.'[8]

Of the two hundred Scots students who learnt from Professor Herman Boerhaave, five went on to set up the world-famous Edinburgh Medical School in 1726, based on his model. In the museum at Edinburgh's Surgeons' Hall, we read that 'The torch of learning ... which had been lit in Greece and passed to

---

8. Herman Boerhaave, from *The Works of Samuel Johnson*, Vol. 14 (Troy, New York: Pafraets Company, 1903), pp. 154-84.

Salerno then to Montpelier and Padua then to Leiden and early in the eighteenth century [was] ... handed on to Edinburgh, which then became the centre of medical learning.'[9]

In the eighteenth and nineteenth centuries, Edinburgh was the leading medical college in the world, with many students being dedicated Christians. Among them was John Fothergill, who copied Boerhaave's Christian ethics and bedside manner with his patients. Fothergill combined this with the careful scientific approach of Boerhaave and the English Christian, Thomas Sydenham, so that he opposed the popular but destructive medical practice of bloodletting[10] which was eventually banned. James Ramsay, one of the leading slavery abolitionists of his day, became a notable surgeon; John Coakley Lettsom founded the London Medical School, also standing with his Christian friend Edward Jenner, persuading many British doctors to accept his vaccination methods; Sir Charles Bell pioneered the anatomy of the nerve system; Sir John Richardson was a famous naval surgeon and arctic explorer; and Thomas Hodgkin discovered Hodgkin's Disease.

Besides these, Benjamin Rush studied at Edinburgh Medical College, and as a dedicated Christian he returned to America to be a leading medical man of his day there, becoming the father of American psychiatry. Nathan Smith, another Christian, also studied at the Edinburgh Medical College and returned to America to establish five medical colleges that would be foundational for the nation's healthcare. Dan Graves wrote that 'As an educator of doctors and the creator of educational institutions, he stands unrivalled in the annals of American medicine.'[11]

---

9. From the text of the medical historian, Douglas Guthrie, in the Museum at Surgeon's Hall, Edinburgh.

10. The pseudo-science of bloodletting involved doctors cutting a patient's body (usually the arm) to allow blood to flow out in order to prevent or heal illness and disease, and balance 'the humours'. This Pagan practice lasted over 2,000 years before it was rejected.

11. Dan Graves, *Doctors Who Followed Christ*, p. 80.

Sir James Young Simpson: Father of Anaesthetics (1811–1870)

The next patient came in for an operation, fearful and agitated. He was tied down and given alcohol to drink to help deaden the pain. Despite this, as the surgeon cut through his body there was searing pain, agonising cries, and a traumatic experience. James Young Simpson, the observing medical student, was horrified. He left, his heart racing, determined to find a more effective form of pain relief.

It was not Simpson who introduced chloroform: this accolade goes to three men at the same time in 1831: Samuel Guthrie of America, Soubeiran of France, and Liebig of Germany, but Simpson is credited as being the pioneer of using chloroform for medical purposes. When Sir James Young Simpson was elected to the Chair of Obstetric Medicine at the University of Edinburgh in 1840, he went on to carry out a series of risky experiments on himself and his friends with various suggested potential anaesthetics.

It was a strange and epoch-making day on 4th November 1847, at 52 Queens St, Edinburgh. For days Simpson and his assistants, James Matthews Duncan and George Keith, had sought to discover the best form of anaesthetic. Professor James Miller, a devout Christian surgeon and Simpson's next-door neighbour, had come in to check up on the three, 'just to inquire if everyone was still alive,'[12] for this was a hazardous series of experiments. Finally, following the earlier suggestion of David Waldie of Liverpool, Simpson took a bottle of chloroform out of a waste-paper basket, which had been made up by Professor William Gregory, and the three brave adventurers sniffed the solution. Soon they were unconscious, without any bad side-effects. History was being made.

The first patient on whom Professor James Miller operated, with Simpson assisting with the use of chloroform, was a

---

12. Douglas Guthrie, *Centenary of Chloroform Anaesthesia*, British Medical Journal, p. 701, 1st November 1947.

Gaelic-speaking lad from the Highlands. Encouraged by their success, Simpson, as Professor of Midwifery, was keen to try it on a woman giving birth. Again, they were delighted at the outcome: a girl named Anaesthesia was born to the daughter of Dr Carstairs. Simpson light-heartedly nicknamed her his 'patron St Anaesthesia'. Growing support from the medical establishment enabled Simpson to promote this form of pain relief, but the general public was suspicious. It was only when Queen Victoria gave birth to Leopold with the use of chloroform that the suspicion of most dissolved. In 1866, Simpson was made baronet in Scotland for his pioneering medical work.

One day an interviewer asked him, 'What do you consider was the greatest discovery you ever made?' He expected the professor to speak about the medical use of anaesthetics, but instead Simpson looked intently at him, replying, 'That I have a Saviour.'[13] Simpson went on to write his own personal account of how he became a Christian. 'I saw another sight – it matters not when – myself a sinner standing on the brink of ruin, deserving nought but hell,' he wrote. 'For one sin? No; for many sins committed against the unchanging laws of God. But again, I looked and saw JESUS, my substitute, scourged in my stead and dying on the cross for me. I looked and cried and was forgiven. And it seems to be my duty to tell you of that Saviour, to see if you will not also look and live .... How simple it all becomes when the Holy Spirit opens the eyes!'[14]

During his last days he suffered with great pain in his home in Queens Street. His nephew, Robert Simpson, visited him often and recorded a diary, which his own descendant, another Robert, transcribed and gave to me. He left a moving account of his uncle's last battle. 'I shall never forget our conversation,' he wrote. 'How he was cheered and comforted amid pain and weariness by his Saviour's grace I cannot rightly describe. It was heaven begun on earth. He who had seen suffering in so many forms and had done so much to alleviate the pain of others was now in the furnace of

---

13. E. B. Simpson, *Sir James Young Simpson* (Edinburgh: Oliphant, Anderson and Ferrier, 1896), p. 127.

14. *A Scientist's Testimony: Sir James Simpson, Bart., M.D.*, Sovereign Grace Union.

affliction. But there he was sustained by the presence of the Son of Man. He who had so often stood by the bed of death and softened so many dying pillows was now face to face with the last enemy. Yet there was no murmuring under suffering, no terror in prospect of death. He had learnt to count these afflictions as but for a moment; he had been taught the secret of victory over death.'[15]

The National Health Service (NHS)

During lockdown we admired the courage of our NHS as the staff in hospitals battled to save lives from Covid-19. We lined the streets and clapped them every Thursday evening for a few months, showing our appreciation. The NHS has been doing the best it can, although it has faults, but few pause to think about how it came into being. As with the National Education Board system, the NHS was the culmination of the hard work of many before who had developed healthcare in Britain, with a great influence coming from dedicated Christians, as we have already seen in this chapter. Although the atheist, Aneurin Bevan, led the Labour Party in setting up the NHS in 1948, the movement for this had been well underway for centuries.

An example of the way in which Christianity was hugely significant in developing healthcare can be seen by what happened with the Royal Infirmary of Edinburgh, one of Scotland's leading hospitals. One of the students from Scotland who studied under the Christian, Hermann Boerhaave, in the Medical School at the University of Leiden, was John Munro. Inspired by Boerhaave's model, he became the catalyst and mover for a charity hospital in Edinburgh when he produced a plan in 1720. The project for the hospital was supported by the Royal College of Physicians, who had already been giving free health care for the poor, the Incorporation of Surgeons and Apothecaries, and the University of Edinburgh, represented by his son Alexander Munro, who was the Professor of Anatomy there. After discussions, the leading

---

15. Robert Russell Simpson, *A Diary of the Last Days of Sir James Young Simpson*, p. 5, Sunday, 10th April 1870, transcribed by R. R. Simpson (Pansmanse Publications, December 2008).

group of men wrote that 'As men and Christians we have the strongest inducements and even obligations to this sort of charity as it is warmly recommended and enjoined in the gospel.'[16] As such, they were also following the vision laid out in the reformers' *First Book of Discipline* of 1560.

With funding from the stockholders of the Fishery Company and donations from private individuals, alongside the support of numerous Presbyterian and Episcopal churches, the Hospital for the Sick Poor was established at the head of Robertson's Close on 6th November 1729, which was run by six surgeon-chemists. Seven years later, in 1736, King George II granted it a Royal Charter, and it was named the Royal Infirmary of Edinburgh.

By the late 1730s it was soon realised that this hospital was far too small, and plans were made to build a bigger and better one. Alexander Munro and the Lord Provost, George Drummond, led the movement to raise funding for this new hospital. Drummond seemed to combine a Christian faith with Freemasonry. After going through a crisis of faith because of personal issues, he was warmed by the preaching of the evangelical minister, Rev. Alexander Webster of the Tolbooth Kirk, who encouraged him in the process of building the new infirmary, and so the funding drive began; Drummond remarked 'The Lord gives remarkable success to all our applications.'[17] Of those who gave funding there were many wealthy individuals, but again, powerful support came from the churches, including the special fundraising of the evangelist George Whitefield. In 1741, the new Royal Infirmary was opened with two hundred and twenty-eight beds.

At the instruction of the Lord Provost, Thomas Boyd, a new site was again found for this hospital in 1879, and it opened at Lauriston Place, near the university. Only recently was a new Royal

16. Guenter B. Risse, *Mending Bodies: Saving Souls: A History of Hospitals* (Oxford and New York: Oxford University Press, 1999), p. 240. Guenter Risse was the Professor and Chairman of the History of Health Services Department.

17. *George Drummond's Diary*, EUL DC, 1.83, Vol. 2, f.167, cited by James Buchan in *The Capital of the Mind: How Edinburgh Changed the World* (John Murray Publishers, 2003), p. 182.

Infirmary built in Little France on the outskirts of Edinburgh in 2003. The Royal Hospital for Sick Children (popularly known as the Sick Kids' Hospital) at Sciennes in Edinburgh, moved to a new building at the Royal Infirmary in 2019, making it one of the top medical facilities for children in the world. This hospital for children was founded in 1859 through the tireless work of the Christian dental surgeon, John Smith, and by a board, which was chaired by the Rev. Dr James Hodson, Rector of The Edinburgh Academy. The hospital opened the following year. Its first surgical ward was begun by the Christian, Sir Joseph Bell, famous, along with another Edinburgh Christian, Sir Henry Littlejohn, for pioneering forensics and being the inspiration behind Sir Arthur Conan Doyle's Sherlock Holmes' character.

In 1948 most of the hospitals, like the schools, came under the government's authority, and so the Royal Infirmary, Glasgow Infirmary, Sick Kids, and many other healthcare streams all over Scotland, poured into the river of the NHS.

Pioneer of Scotland's Modern Nursing: Angélique Lucille Pringle

In 1872, Joseph Lister was becoming frustrated as he worked as the Professor of Clinical Surgery in the Royal Infirmary Edinburgh. This Christian had introduced antiseptics and hygiene in healthcare, and by now his methods were being welcomed in many hospitals, saving the lives of countless people. However, right under his nose, he saw another kind of infection in the Royal Infirmary – that of the immorality and bad practice of the nurses. At his instigation, the hospital board appointed Deputy Surgeon General Charles Hamilton Fasson to liaise with Florence Nightingale, who had become famous during her nursing exploits among the wounded soldiers in the Crimean War, and who became known as the 'Lady with the Lamp'.

This dedicated Christian lady became the pioneer of modern nursing, teaching her students to be professionals with Christian values at St Thomas' Hospital in London. When Fasson contacted her about the possibility of sending 'Nightingale Nurses' to improve the nursing standards at the Royal Infirmary, she wrote in 1872: 'Edinburgh Royal Infirmary. We are going to undertake the nursing of this beastly "den of thieves". (Nothing that I have ever known except the Vienna General Hospital approaches it in badness ...).'[18] Thus, a team of seventeen Nightingale Nurses came up to Edinburgh, led by the English Quaker Christian, Elizabeth Barclay, to pioneer professional nursing in our capital, and set up the first Scottish school for training nurses. Although Barclay was the first superintendent of the nurses, the stress of trying to deal with 'the drinking, profligate (old) night nurses' and the uncooperative doctors, drove her nearly to a breakdown, and she resigned in the first year, in December 1873, leaving a vulnerable staff.

Florence Nightingale sent a powerful Christian rallying call to her team at the Royal Infirmary on 6th December, 1873. 'My dear friends, our good nurses ...,' she wrote, 'What is *His* will for us nurses? I will not tell *you* how He likes His wards kept, for *that* you know right well, as well as I do. Nos. 1, 2, 3-20 medical wards, and Nos. 1, 2, 3-20 surgical wards, are *His* wards, are they not? And all those patients in them are *His* patients, and we are His, *His* nurses .... In nursing, each of us may be about her "Father's business", each in her degree, *as Christ was.*'[19]

Florence chose Angélique Pringle (1846–1920) to replace Elizabeth Barclay as the superintendent of the nurses. Angélique had trained under Florence Nightingale at St Thomas' in London in 1868, and was soon noticed for her exceptional qualities, becoming her favourite 'disciple'. The other nurses endearingly called Angélique 'Pearl', for she was a pearl of great price in nursing. This young woman of twenty-seven took the bull by the horns and turned Royal Infirmary Edinburgh nursing into a professional arm of Scotland's healthcare, for which it became famous worldwide. She was a Scottish woman from Hawick, with

---

18. *Florence Nightingale: Extending Nursing: Collected Works of Florence Nightingale,* edited by Lynn McDonald (Wilfrid Laurier University Press, 2009), p. 312.

19. ibid., p. 332. Source: *'Letter to the dear Nurses of Edinburgh Infirmary,'* University of Edinburgh, LHB1/111 letter 1, draft ADD MSS 47765 ff, 119-131.

a strong Christian faith, which can be seen in the motivational letters between her and Florence, as she led the work in Edinburgh between 1873 and 1887.

After her ground-breaking work in Edinburgh, Angélique was promoted, as Florence's protégée, to being the Superintendent of the Nightingale Training School for Nurses at St Thomas' in London. However, she resigned under pressure in 1890, because she had converted to Roman Catholicism in an era that was still suspicious of this expression of church.

Her book, A Study of Nursing (1905), became an important influence in practical nursing, in which she also wrote that one of the important tasks of the nurse with dying patients is to 'prepare them to enter the Dark Valley' and direct them to Christ, the light of the world. She also encouraged the nurses to attend regular prayer meetings at the hospital. A plaque has been dedicated to her inside the chapel at the Edinburgh Royal Infirmary.

Auld Reekie and Sanitation

'Gardyloo!' came a shrill voice from one of the upper windows in a dark alleyway in Edinburgh's Old Town. With little time given to step aside, the pedestrian sought to avoid the effluence hurled from above, and with an angry shout, he sought to clean his trousers of faeces and other nasties that had splattered on him. Welcome to old Edinburgh! Much of the stench in the city, which gave it the unenviable name of Auld Reekie, came from the thick smoke from the abundant chimneys; but this other stench was stomach-wrenching and disease-ridden, a breeding-ground for plagues.

Back in 1761 Rev. John Wesley the revivalist could cry, 'How long shall the capital city of Scotland, yea, and the chief street of it, stink worse than a common sewer? Will no lover of this country, or of decency and common sense, find a remedy for it?'[20] Wesley's cry would be answered in 1865 through a fellow

---

20. W. Forbes Gray, John Wesley in Edinburgh, from The Book of the Old Edinburgh Club, eighth volume (Edinburgh, 1916), p. 164.

Christian, Sir Henry Littlejohn, an elder at St Giles Kirk. Three years earlier he had been appointed as the first municipal medical officer in Scotland. With precise research he mapped out the city, painstakingly collecting accurate statistics about the sanitary conditions, and presenting the evidence and solutions for a new sanitary system to the leaders of the nation with a shrewd confidence.

Readily assisting him were the missionaries, especially from Edinburgh City Mission (ECM), who were the social workers of the period. Bailie Pollard, being one of the directors of ECM, became the natural bridge between the missionaries and the town council later in 1896, with the development of the revolutionary and new underground city sanitation system, as he was appointed Chairman of the Public Health Committee of the Town Council.[21] Henry Littlejohn's *Report of the Sanitary Condition of the City of Edinburgh* was shocking and revealing, but it led to a transformation of sanitary conditions in Edinburgh and Scotland, becoming a model to many other cities in the world to copy, thereby saving the lives of millions.

Dentistry

If any of you have ever experienced severe toothache, you will be glad of modern dentists. John Smith was not only the pioneer of The Royal Hospital for Sick Children in 1860, but in that same year he also founded the Edinburgh Dental Dispensary with three other dentist colleagues: Francis Brodie Imlach, Peter Orphoot and Robert Nasmyth. John Smith was a Presbyterian elder at St Andrew's Parish Church and Francis Imlach was an elder at St Stephen's Church in Stockbridge. By 1880, their work had developed into the Edinburgh Dental Hospital and School, with the twin vision of providing dental treatment for the poor and training up dentists in a professional way. Before this, back-street dentistry had been commonplace in Scotland,

---

21. Paul James-Griffiths, *The History of Edinburgh City Mission: David Nasmith, A Dynamic Founder of Missions (1799–1839)*, p. 13, which can be found online at https://www.christianheritageedinburgh.org.uk/category/ecm/

with both competent and charlatan practitioners operating in an unregulated fashion.

The four friends worked together to revolutionise dental standards in Scotland, with Imlach being the first person in history to use Simpson's chloroform anaesthetic in a dental procedure, and Nasmyth went on to pioneer gold fillings for teeth. The four friends pressed for government reform in the dental practice, so that only properly qualified dentists could practice. In 1878 the Dental Act was passed, thereby ensuring that only professionals could be on the official register. The Edinburgh Dental School was taken over as part of the University of Edinburgh Faculty of Medicine in 1948. Today's Edinburgh Dental Institute continues in the same standard of excellence as its founders.

Edinburgh Medical Missionary Society

If you had lived in the Cowgate part of Edinburgh in the 1800s, you would have been shocked at the squalor and poverty there. The once fashionable and large houses had been sold when the New Town was built. The wealthy moved there, and the Cowgate houses were converted into apartments in which poor crowded families huddled together in despair. The Edinburgh City Mission, recognizing this terrible situation, appointed a medical doctor to assist the missionaries, who besides doing their usual gospel work acted as social and healthcare workers. The mission has a handwritten nineteenth century leather-bound medical volume, which acted as a manual to help the missionaries with their parishioners in the hovels that they visited.

One evening in 1841, in the drawing room of 19 York Place in Edinburgh, a fascinating discussion was in progress. Dr John Abercrombie, Scotland's leading medical consultant and a dedicated Christian, had invited some medical and pastor friends to join him at his home to hear about the work of Dr Peter Parker. Dr Parker explained how he and his colleague, Dr Thomas Colledge from Aberdeen, had pioneered the Medical Missionary Society in China in 1838. The listeners were so enthusiastic they proposed that a formal meeting should be launched for leading medical people, pastors and others to assess what to do. The public gathering was thronged with the curious at Waterloo Hotel on 26th July, in 1841, with Dr Thomas Graham, the President of the Royal College of Physicians, and Dr Richard Huie, the President of the Royal College of Surgeons, giving their backing. As a result, another public gathering took place on 30th November in the Royal Hotel on Princes Street, resulting in the formation of the Edinburgh Medical Missionary Society (named so in 1843).

The august body of medical experts, along with the Lord Provost, Sir James Forrest, had whole-heartedly agreed to this medical missionary enterprise, which included the spread of the gospel, combined with Christian medical missionaries who would, by their work, demonstrate 'proofs of the nature and practical operation of the spirit of love, which ... [is] the fruit of our holy religion.'[22] It was understood by all that Edinburgh was favoured 'in being the seat of a Medical School of the first excellence' with many Christian medical students, so that a call should go out to raise finance to support medical missionaries abroad, and also train them up and send them out to pioneer healthcare and hospitals there. On the first board were Dr John Abercrombie as its president, Rev. Dr Thomas Chalmers, the leading churchman of that time, and others such as Professor James Syme and Dr Joseph Bell.

As the work of The Edinburgh Medical Missionary Society (EMMS) took off, it settled in the Cowgate. A base was built adjacent to Magdalen Chapel, famous for reformers and Covenanters, and named the Livingstone Memorial Missionary Training Institute, after the intrepid missionary doctor in Africa, Dr David Livingstone, who was a member of EMMS. Over the years a pattern emerged: Christian medical students would graduate from the university, train with senior doctors in

---

22. John Wilkinson, *The Coogate Doctors: A History of The Edinburgh Medical Missionary Society, 1841–1991*, citing from the Minutes of the inaugural meeting, The Edinburgh Medical Missionary Society, 1991, p. 3.

the Cowgate dispensary, giving free healthcare to the poor, and be also trained in theology at the Magdalen Chapel. After this, those who were called to do so, would be sent out to establish healthcare worldwide in conjunction with churches and mission societies. In this way, not only were the poor of Edinburgh being cared for, but the model was also being replicated by the Americans and Europeans. In time, a network of healthcare centres and hospitals would spring up all over the world as a result, and free health clinics for the poor would mushroom all over Scotland.

An Experience in a Scottish Hospital

As I looked around the High Dependency Ward at the Western General Hospital in Edinburgh, feelings of gratitude welled up inside me for the dedicated staff, who day and night gave themselves to saving lives. I had been rushed into A&E with severe sepsis, following a prostate biopsy the day before. Unfortunately, I was among the one-percenters who had developed a particularly resistant form of E-Coli infection. After the battle for my life gave way to victory, I had time to reflect on my experience. All around me in the ward was evidence of the legacy of Christian pioneers in Scotland who had changed the world, and whose work had saved the lives of millions.

A team of anaesthetists came into the ward to discuss pain control with one of the patients. As they did, I recalled Sir James Young Simpson, the Christian father of anaesthetics in hospitals. The doctors had been fighting with me to overcome the virulent infection. Having discovered that four standard antibiotics had not worked because of bacterial resistance, they proceeded to use Tazocin, a treasured weapon. It was another Scotsman, this time a Presbyterian who became an Anglican churchgoer, who had discovered penicillin which became the foundation of antibiotics. It has often been said that Sir Alexander Fleming (1881–1955) discovered penicillin through a series of chance events in 1928, but he stated clearly, 'Discoveries of this magnitude are rare .... God took care to hide that country till he judged his people ready; then, he chose me for his whisper and I found it and it's yours.'[23]

One of the nurses came back to me. She had been well trained at nursing college and was looking forward to becoming a full-blown practitioner the next week. As we discussed her nursing career, I remembered how an English Christian called Florence Nightingale had pioneered professional nursing, and on the request of the Christian, Lord Joseph Lister in Edinburgh, had sent the Quaker Christian, Elizabeth Barclay, up to the city to pioneer this standard in Scotland.

That night I discussed with another nurse about the stress for the NHS staff during the Covid pandemic. During that terrible period, the name Jenner Institute and the vaccination called AstraZeneca became well-known. The institute at Oxford University had been named after Edward Jenner, the Christian pioneer of vaccination who had vanquished smallpox. Both vaccination and the sanitizing of Lister had been vital during the pandemic, but Lister's pioneering of antiseptics has saved the lives of millions more.

As a patient in the High Dependency Ward, you soon become accustomed to the various machines bleeping away. Surrounded by impressive-looking equipment, I was led to ponder about the dynamic foundational work in physics by the dedicated Christian, James Clerk Maxwell. His famous Maxwell's Equations inspired our technological revolution; indeed, Albert Einstein had this hero on a poster above his office desk, and he once stated, 'I stand not on the shoulders of Newton, but on the shoulders of James Clerk Maxwell.'[24] Out of Maxwell's work came a crowd of inventions: among them X-ray machines; computers, televisions and radios.

---

23. L. J. Ludovici, *Fleming: Discoverer of Penicillin* (London: Andrew Dakers Ltd., 1952), p. 196.

24. Joyce McPherson, *The Light of Knowledge: The Story of James Clerk Maxwell*, back cover (Amazon Publishing, 2022). Further information on Maxwell can be found in Lewis Campbell's and William Garnett's book, *The Life of James Clerk Maxwell*, which came out three years after Maxwell died. This book was almost lost, but James Rautio republished it, with further details.

As I looked around the ward I studied the saline drip, another invention by an Edinburgh Christian doctor. Thomas Latta grew up in the Kirkgate Church in Leith where his father was an elder and Thomas went on to develop this vital hospital appliance in 1832. It was the saline drip that would be the means of healing millions suffering with cholera.

Pioneer of the Saline Drip: Thomas Latta (1796–1833)

When cholera broke out across all continents in the nineteenth century, millions were left dead in the wake of a horrible pandemic. At that time nobody knew that contaminated water could lead to such horrible plagues with the victims dying in just a few hours from continual diarrhea and vomiting. Again, God raised up a Christian from Scotland to find a cure.

Thomas Latta grew up in the seaside village of Newhaven, near Edinburgh, and the family were members of the Presbyterian Associate Congregation of Leith. Graduating in medicine at the University of Edinburgh in 1819, Latta practised as a doctor in both Leith and Edinburgh. In 1831, the cholera plague had spread to Britain, killing many thousands, and the medical scientists did not know how to combat it. Latta observed that the victims lost copious amounts of fluids before they died and he realised that water, with a small amount of salt, had to be injected into the body to prevent dehydration and replace a key depleted mineral. The idea was not entirely new, as Dr William Brooke O'Shaughnessy, an Irishman who had graduated at the University of Edinburgh and who had worked with William Alison in a practice in the same city, had already experimented with an intravenous solution in dogs. However, Latta, convinced that the principle would work for humans, applied a saline solution into the bloodstream of a woman in the Edinburgh Cholera Hospital on Drummond Street, where the Old Surgeon's Hall used to be. The result in 1832 was stunning:

> 'She had apparently reached the last moments of her earthly existence, and now nothing could injure her,' he wrote. 'Indeed, so entirely was she reduced that I feared I should be unable to get

my apparatus ready ere she expired. Having inserted a tube into the basilic vein, cautiously – anxiously, I watched the effect; ounce after ounce was injected, but no visible change was produced. Still persevering I thought she began to breathe less laboriously; soon her sharpened features and sunken eye and fallen jaw, pale and cold, bearing the manifest impress of death's signet, began to glow with returning animation; the pulse which had ceased returned to the wrist, at first small and quick, by degrees it became more and more distinct, fuller, slower and firmer, and in the short space of half an hour when six pints had been injected she expressed in a firm voice that she was free from all uneasiness ... her features bore the aspect of comfort and health. This being my first case, I fancied my patient secure and from my great need of a little repose left her in charge of the hospital surgeon.'[25]

Unfortunately, with the saline drip treatment finished too early, the woman died within a few hours, but the breakthrough for cholera had begun. Latta published his results in the journal *Lancet* on 23rd June 1832, much to the excitement of the medical world. The saline drip method would be developed and effectively used throughout the world by 1902, bringing a cure to millions suffering with cholera, with about 99 per cent of patients being saved. It has been so effective that it is regularly used in hospital wards for those who need it. It would take the combined work of the medical doctor John Snow, and the Rev. Henry Whitehead in London a few decades later, to prove that the cause of cholera was contaminated water, rather than the speculated miasma, or polluted air, leading to council improvements to prevent outbreaks of this terrible plague.

Pioneer of the Hypodermic Syringe: Alexander Wood (1817–1884)

During my time of recent recovery from severe sepsis, the nurses regularly worked with hypodermic syringes: in some cases, blood samples were needed; in other cases, cannulas were inserted

---

25. *The Medico-chirurgical Review and Journal of Medical Science*, 21:241-42, 1st July 1832.

into my veins for the intravenous antibiotics, saline drip and a catheter. As I lay in bed, I thought I would look on the internet to discover who invented the hypodermic syringe, something that was used on millions during the Covid vaccines. Again, I discovered a Christian from Edinburgh.

Dr Alexander Wood grew up as the son of a dedicated Christian medical doctor in Fife. After receiving his MD at the University of Edinburgh in 1839, he used his keen sense of observation and experiment to advance medical science. In 1853 he became the first person to use the proper hypodermic syringe, which he invented using a glass tube and a plunger with the hollow needle, which had been invented by Francis Rynd. He treated neuralgia by injecting morphine in the area of pain in his patient, giving welcome relief. It was because of his noted medical ability that he was made President of the Royal College of Physicians in Edinburgh, just five years later.

Although his invention has now been taken for granted, it has been the means of saving and helping the lives of countless people. However, his dedicated Christian faith has largely been forgotten. He was a firm believer in combining Christ and the Bible with science and medicine, just as a person looking through binoculars can see things more clearly. It was this sharp and investigative mind that also inspired him to examine the scientific evidence for homoeopathy, after which he debunked it with his book *Homoeopathy Unmasked* (1844). This caused a stir because homoeopathy had become a popular practice, but his love of truth drove him to expose it as false science.

Between 1846 and 1852, he was the Chairman of the Association for the Improvement of the Condition of the Poor, which existed to provide food and employment for the poor. Besides this, he was also a key leader in Edinburgh for supporting the establishment of Sabbath schools, as well as teaching in one himself. Those who knew him admired his Christian faith as a member of the Free Church of Scotland. 'The part of his home life,' his wife said, 'which I think so peculiarly characteristic of him, was that even in the midst of his many arduous duties he found time for years to make – I may say – a profound study of his Bible. He used to rise early in the mornings and study hard before going out to his public duties; and eleven bound volumes of his MS. notes bear testimony to his industry .... The truth, once delivered to the saints, was the foundation of all his hope.'[26] His favourite written prayer was: 'Lord, give us a heart to turn all knowledge to Thy glory, and not to our own. Keep us from being deluded with the lights of vain philosophy. Keep us from the pride of human reason. Let us not think our own thoughts, nor dream our own imaginations, but in all things, acting under the good guidance of the Holy Spirit, may we live in all simplicity, humility, and singleness of heart unto the Lord Jesus Christ, now and for evermore. Amen.'[27]

For fifteen years he suffered with illness, but instead of becoming bitter, his faith grew deeper. His pastor, the hymn-writer Dr Horatius Bonar, shared that, 'During the last weeks of his life, weeks of weariness, weakness, and pain, he could speak but little, but what he did say, brokenly and by snatches, showed that his thoughts were of things above. "Behold the Bridegroom cometh," he said at one time; and then at another, "Peace which passeth all understanding."'[28]

Pioneer of Obstetric Ultrasound: Sir Ian Donald (1910–1987)

As I lay in the hospital ward I thought about my daughter-in-law; our son had recently told us she was pregnant. One of the great medical instruments to have been invented in Scotland is the obstetric ultrasound scanner. With this we can see the baby grow in the mother's womb, and any abnormalities can also be detected. The leading pioneer behind this breakthrough was Sir Ian Donald. Together with his colleague, John MacVicar, and engineer Tom Brown, they developed the first diagnostic

---

26. Thomas Brown, (his brother-in-law), *Alexander Wood: A Sketch of his Life and Work* (Edinburgh: MacNiven and Wallace, 1886), pp. 191-92.

27. ibid., p. 90.

28. ibid., pp. 202-03.

applications of ultrasound at the Glasgow Royal Maternity Hospital. In 1958 they published an article in the journal, *Lancet*, revealing to the medical world the first images of a baby in the womb. By the 1960s Ian Donald and James Willocks had improved the machinery and the first public Fetal Ultrasound Scanner was launched, which they called the Diasonograph. As a result, most areas of medicine would be impacted.

Ian Donald was born in Cornwall, of Scottish parents, and attended Warriston School in Moffat and Fettes College in Edinburgh. For a time, the family lived in South Africa, where he graduated at the University of Cape Town in 1927 with a degree in the arts and music. However, it was when he came to live in England that he pursued a career in medicine at the University of London where he practiced at St Thomas' Hospital Medical School. When World War II broke out, he worked as a medical officer with the Royal Airforce, and received the MBE for his bravery in rescuing some of the aircrew from a crashed bomber which was on fire.

After experience in obstetrics at both St Thomas' Hospital and Hammersmith Hospital, he was promoted to the position of Regius Professor of Obstetrics and Gynaecology at the University of Glasgow (1954–1976). It was here that he became famous for the invention of the obstetric ultrasound scanner. In later years he became the consultant with Nuclear Enterprises in Edinburgh.

The *Journal of the Royal Society of Medicine* (March 2005) highlights 'the strongly held Christian faith of this man and how it ruled his culture and attitudes to contraception and abortion and the battles this led him into.' For Professor Donald, the ultrasound scanner gave scientific proof of the baby in the womb in the face of the pro-abortion movement of the 1960s. He became a strongly outspoken champion for the unborn child, often being at the centre of heated opposition. 'And when you destroy a baby by abortion that is what you are destroying,' he said. 'I think you have got to face the fact honestly .... There can be no argument about it and if I have done nothing else in my life, I have killed that dirty lie that the foetus is just a nondescript meaningless jelly, disposable at will, something to be got rid of.'[29] It was a heart-breaking moment for him when the Abortion Act was passed in 1967.

As a staunch Christian in the Scottish Episcopalian Church, he continued to raise his voice on ethical issues of abortion, methods of contraception and euthanasia. It was also through his work that the Queen Mother's Maternity Hospital was built next to the Royal Hospital for Children in Glasgow. The record of his scientific medical work and faith, which inspired his ethical concerns, have been preserved by James Willocks and Wallace Barr in their book, *Ian Donald: A Memoir*. Both men had worked with Ian Donald for about twenty years and knew him well. James Willocks, whom the *Herald* newspaper states, 'had a strong Christian faith,' along with his wife Elma, was keen to make sure Ian Donald's faith was not sidelined in history.

Besides these Scottish Christian pioneers of medicine, I discovered that the first successful kidney transplant in the UK was by Sir Michael Woodruff, who also went on to establish one of the world's leading transplant units in Edinburgh, and who wrote his autobiography *Nothing Venture Nothing Gain*, with his last chapter, *The Faith of a Scientist*, demonstrating the dual purpose of Christianity and medical science. But there were others too: Sir Patrick Forrest, an elder at St Giles in Edinburgh, introduced Breast Cancer Screening, saving the lives of many women; and Sir David Brewster, the Edinburgh Free Church lay preacher, whose Brewster's Law paved the way for laser technology in medicine. I realised that Scotland has punched far above its weight in advancing medical science, with most of the major luminaries being Christians.

During some chats with the staff at the hospital, I mentioned some of these pioneers from Scotland. The typical reaction was

---

29. Ian Donald (undated but after 1978) *Predicting ovulation*, unpublished lecture, tape-recording in BMUS Archive. Cited by Malcolm Nicolson, from his article, *Ian Donald, Diagnostician and Moralist*, online publication, Royal College of Physicians of Edinburgh, 2000: https://www.rcpe.ac.uk/heritage/ian-donald-diagnostician-and-moralist.

the standard 'was like us' quote, a nurturing of Scottish pride, but the connection with the Christian faith has been lost over time. Even our hospitals themselves grew out of the work of the church from the medieval period onwards. Today, I thank God for all the healthcare workers who do a great job, but I also thank God for the Christians He raised up to advance medical science and healthcare itself. May He continue to do so.

CHAPTER 5

LAW AND JUSTICE

'Law chief urges Scots courts: consult the Bible in judgments' ran the heading of an article in *The Herald* newspaper. Immediately the critics' feeding frenzy began, like sharks drawn to the scent of blood. The cause of this furore in 2009 was Lord Mackay of Clashfern, a former Lord Chancellor of Great Britain and Lord Advocate of Scotland. Unashamedly standing up for his Christian faith, Lord Mackay had backed the Scottish Bible Society's bicentennial project of getting a Bible into the hands of every court in Scotland. 'I have found it immensely important in my life and I trust it will be the same with many who have access to it through this initiative now,' said Lord Mackay in an accompanying leaflet. 'The Bible is a unique resource as the foundational source book for Scotland's legal system. The SBS is pleased to have the opportunity to donate a Bible to courts, so that it is readily available for reference in any case which may arise.'

Terry Sanderson, President of the National Secular Society and a homosexual activist, was incensed: 'What Lord Mackay is proposing could put the Sharia laws of the Middle East to shame,' he warned. 'He and the SBS make absolutely no concessions to the progress of legal thought over the past two millennia. Killing witches and homosexuals and stoning adulterers are all clearly stated legal requirements in the Christian holy book. Are they seriously suggesting that Scottish sheriffs and judges should follow the Bible to the letter?'[1]

---

1. *Former Lord Chancellor says 'Use Bible to judge crooks': A Former Lord Chancellor has sparked controversy after calling on judges to consult the Bible*

The University of Edinburgh School of Law entered the fray with 'the greatest hesitancy', on the one hand backing Lord Mackay historically and vindicating his statement about Scotland, that 'institutional writers [were] informed by Roman and biblical law for civil law and by biblical law for criminal law', but cautioning its readers on the other hand, in a multi-cultural world and sceptical era, to treat the Bible 'with circumspection, critical thought and awareness that much of its content is informed by the ideas and values of times completely different from our own.'[2]

The Early Medieval Geneva Convention

Adomnan surveyed the scene of a bloody carnage. Dead bodies from the tribal war near Drogheda in County Louth, Ireland, were strewn so thickly that he could have walked across the field without stepping on the ground. It was not just the carnage that filled him with grief, but the loss of innocent lives: the women who had been raped and butchered with their children, and the unarmed clergy. Distraught and tearful he left the scene, vowing to see justice done for the innocents of war.

So in the year 697 ninety-one leaders converged on Birr in Ireland. Among them were fifty kings from among the Irish, Scots and Picts, and many bishops and abbots. They had come to support a legal document called *Cáin Adomnáin*, or *Law of Adomnán*, which was also known as the *Lex Innocentium*, or *Law of Innocents*. This document has been hailed as the 'Geneva Convention' of the early Middle Ages, and had been instigated by Adomnan, the ninth abbot of Iona since Columba, to protect non-combatants in war. It would play a key part in the process of justice and human rights within the context of war, setting a precedent that others would follow and develop.

---

before passing sentence on criminals (*The Express*, Dean Herbert, Monday, 16th August 2010).

2. *The Bible in Scots Law*, *Scots Law News*, 22nd August 2010. hmacqueen, uncategorized, University of Edinburgh, Edinburgh Law School, https://www.sln.law.ed.ac.uk/2010/08/22/the-bible-in-scots-law/.

All cultures have had laws and a justice system, but even before Christianity began to influence the ancient world, the Jewish law 'became famous and like a fragrant breeze penetrated to every corner of the world. From the Jews the movement spread, and soon the characters of most heathen races began to grow gentler, thanks to the lawgivers and thinkers in every land. Savage and cruel brutality changed to mildness ...'[3] Eusebius meant the ancient world of the Roman Empire when he wrote this in the fourth century A.D. He may have exaggerated the Jewish influence being in 'every corner of the [known] world', but certainly the law of God was spreading in cultures, like yeast in the dough.

The Bible describes God as being passionate for law and justice. One Scripture says about God that 'Righteousness and justice are the foundation of Your throne; mercy and truth go before Your face' (Ps. 89:14); another Scripture expresses God's command: 'Do not pervert justice; do not show partiality to the poor or favouritism to the great, but judge your neighbour fairly' (Lev. 19:15). God says through the prophet Isaiah: 'For law will proceed from Me, and I will make My justice rest as a light for the peoples ...' (Isa. 51:4-5).

Christian Law in Western Europe

During the first three centuries of persecution in the Roman Empire the church multiplied under enormous pressure, seeking to model a new society. But it was only when freedom came, and the church could influence emperors, governors and senates, that laws could be passed at the highest level, bringing about a fairer and more compassionate culture. For example, the bishops in the Roman Empire influenced Constantine and successive emperors, who claimed to have a Christian faith, with their senates, to pass laws. Constantine's government banned crucifixion as a method of execution; temple prostitution was abolished; he provided for the poor, orphans, widows and churches, and had laws passed to make sure wills were processed properly and laws enacted

---

3. Eusebius, *The History of the Church* (Penguin Classics, 1989), 1:2:20, p. 8.

to respect childless couples. Emperor Honorius outlawed the horrendous gladiatorial combats by which thousands were slaughtered to entertain the masses.

With the collapse of the Roman Empire in 476, Western Europe fell into ruin with rival kings fighting for territory and dominance. In desperate need of stability, the people turned to the bishops for leadership. It was from this period onwards that the church started to have a direct and influential role in developing a legal system. By the sixth century, the Frankish King Chilperic complained that 'there is no one with any power left except the bishops. No one respects me as king; all respect has passed to the bishops in their cities.'⁴ Typically, the bishops saw this as a golden opportunity to shape European culture to a more Christian way of thinking. Scholars would pore over the existing cultural laws, sanitise them by removing the Pagan elements, and combine them with a more biblical understanding, purified Roman law, and the Christian-based code of Emperor Theodosius. To give us an understanding of the rising authority of the bishops, we only need to look at the case of Emperor Theodosius himself. Theodosius, after massacring people in Greece, who were mostly innocent, humbled himself before Bishop Ambrose at Milan in 390 and performed penance for his sin. This act of the most powerful man of that era demonstrated to all that even kings were under the law of God and could not do whatever they wanted. It would be an inspiration for the famous 1215 Magna Carta, one of the vital documents in English history.

With the prominence of the church, a unified legal system was developed, which was established on the foundation of the equal subjection of individuals under God. In 529, Emperor Justinian of the Eastern Empire commissioned a team of lawyers to revise the Roman legal system, which needed to be updated and have conflicting laws harmonised. This Justinian Code was rediscovered in the West by the end of the eleventh

---

4. A citation from the chronicler Gregory of Tours, taken from Larry Siedentop's *Inventing the Individual: The Origins of Western Liberalism* (Penguin, 2014), p. 137.

century. By 1153, Bernard of Clairvaux felt obliged to warn his former disciple in the Cistercian Order, who was now a pope, complaining that 'thy palace is made to resound daily with noisy discussions relating to law, but it is not the law of the Lord, but the law of Justinian.'[5]

Bernard was overreacting though, for what was being hammered out under Pope Eugenius III was the framework of canon law and our Western system of jurisprudence, interpreted through a Christian understanding. Gratian, the famous Italian church philosopher, wrote in his *Decretum*, which became the cornerstone of our Western legal system, based on canon (church) law: 'Natural law is what is contained in the Law and the Gospel by which each is to do to another what he wants done to himself and forbidden to do to another what he does not want done to himself.'[6] This, then, became the fountainhead of the twin pillars of law and justice in our modern Western civilization.

Scots Law

This land was once inhabited by many tribes with different laws until the ninth century, when it became known as Scotland. As these tribes became Christianised over the centuries, they may have held a basic unifying Christian understanding, but their own laws could be contradictory: there was Pictish law; Brehon law (Gaelic); British law; Anglo-Saxon law; Roman law and later, Dane and Norman law, to add to the mixture. From 664, the Picts, Scots, Britons and Anglo-Saxons came under the authority of the church at Rome at the Synod of Whitby, so a mixed legal system began to be gradually superseded by a combination of a Christianised Roman legal system and church canon law, which dominated by the fifteenth century. It is from this that most of our modern Scottish law has arisen. Scotland began to follow the feudal system of Europe in the

---

5. Larry Siedentop, *Inventing the Individual*, p. 213, citing from Tierney, Brian, *The Crisis of Church and State, 1050–1300* (Toronto, 1988), p. 92.

6. ibid., p. 216.

Middle Ages with the establishing of Burgh Courts, Barony and Regality Courts, Sheriff Courts and Ecclesiastical Courts. With the Reformation of 1560, Roman law began to lose its influence through the *Regiam Majestatem*, and a fuller biblical framework developed.

In Scotland, the principles of law were pulled together by what are known as the Institutional Writers. The most influential of them were Stair, Hume, Erskine, Mackenzie and Bell. Among them they had essentially codified Scottish legal practice by the eighteenth century in books collectively known as the Institutes of Scots Law. It is worthwhile looking at some of these men to see what inspired their legal minds.

'James Dalrymple, later 1st Viscount Stair,' says Dr G. M. Hutton, 'one of Scotland's most eminent scholars and statesmen, has been universally acknowledged as the genius who first established Scots law as a complete and coherent rational system, and the most complete master of jurisprudence that Scotland has ever produced!'[7] That is an extraordinary accolade for Stair. What is not appreciated, however, is that this man was a dedicated Christian Covenanter. His *Institutions of the Law of Scotland*, first published in 1681, and then revised in 1693, 'set out the whole of Scots private law in a rational and systematic fashion for the first time based on natural law.'[8] Another scholar could write of him: 'He was a committed Presbyterian, an allegiance which affected both his personal life and his formulation of the law. For Stair was intent not only on creating a rational system of law, but one which was godly in character and would, in turn, yield godly Scottish citizens.'[9]

---

7. G. M. Hutton, *Stair's Public Career* in D. M. Walker (ed.), *Stair Tercentenary Studies* (Stair Society, Volume 33) 1 at 1, cited by Stephen Allison in *Stair, Natural Law and Scotland*, L&W Journal 1112-2: L&W Journal 1009 14/12/2012 09:19, p. 189.

8. ibid., p. 190.

9. D. Reid, *Thomas Aquinas and Viscount Stair: the Influence of Scholastic Moral Theology on Stair's Account of Restitution and Recompense* (2008), 29 Journal of Legal History 189 at 189, cited by Stephen Allison, ibid, p. 191.

David Hume, Professor of Scottish Law at the University of Edinburgh, and the nephew of David Hume the philosopher, wrote a book entitled *Commentaries on the Law of Scotland Respecting Trial for Crimes* (1797), which is still influential in today's Scottish courts. Like Stair, Hume's work and influence is embedded in Christian thinking. After his wife Jane died in 1816, he erected a memorial to her at his uncle's tomb and inscribed the following caption above the door: 'Behold I come quickly. Thanks be to GOD which giveth us the victory, through our LORD JESUS CHRIST.' The influence of Stair, Hume and other key Christian lawyers is significant, for it was they who established the laws for evidence and procedure, jurisprudence, the body of criminal law, and private law.

The Christian influence on our Scottish legal and justice system is so considerable that the LLB degree from Scottish universities dates back to the beginning of these departments, which were based on both biblical (canon) law and civilian law, which was inspired by the Bible. The motto of our Scottish courts is 'In my defence God defend me,' and the law lords still wear the symbol of the Christian cross on their gowns.

Lord Mackay, with whom I began in this chapter, listed several of the ways in 2009, in which the Bible has played a key role in shaping our legal system:

1. The overarching concepts of justice tempered by mercy and proportionality, some of our procedural and evidential principles and some areas of our substantive common law are directly derived from the Bible.

2. The works of Hume (criminal law) and Stair (civil) are thoroughly informed by biblical principles and precept.

3. In more modern times, at her coronation, the Queen accepted the Bible as the Royal Law and is bound by solemn oath to have regard to its guidance. All authority of the Crown Prosecution Service is constitutionally derived from this undertaking, continuing in the pattern set by previous monarchs over hundreds of years.

'Extract from the Coronation Oath:

'Will you to your power cause Law and Justice, in Mercy, to be executed in all your judgements?'

Queen: 'I will.'

'Our gracious Queen: to keep your Majesty ever mindful of the law and Gospel of God as the Rule for the whole life and government of Christian princes, we present you with this book, the most valuable thing that this world affords.

'Here is wisdom.

'This is the Royal Law.

'These are the lively oracles of God.

'Be strong and of a good courage:

'Keep the commandments of the Lord thy God, and walk in His ways.'

Woven into the fabric of the coronation are many threads of biblical and Christian historical ideas, and it is noteworthy that the Dean of Westminster Abbey hands the Bible to the Moderator of the Church of Scotland to give to the monarch, because of the Presbyterian stand for God's Word as the truth, and because the Authorised Version of 1611 was produced under the care of King James VI, who was born in Edinburgh. In both the Royal Family and the House of Lords and House of Commons we find Christian art and symbolism everywhere, showing the huge influence on our constitution.

In 1841, Parliament asked the Fine Arts Commission to decorate the new Westminster Palace after the disastrous fire of 1834. The commission was chaired by Prince Albert, a dedicated Christian, and he made sure that among the stunning paintings representing the key events of Great Britain over the centuries, there were many displaying Christian themes. We see William Dyce's mural above the monarch's throne in the House of Lords, showing the baptism of King Aethelberht of Kent, the first English king to convert to Christ. It was he who introduced the first Anglo-Saxon legal code on this island. Then there is J. R. Herbert's painting of Moses with the Ten Commandments on Sinai in the 'Moses Room', signifying the importance of God's law in developing our legal system. In the Central Lobby can be found the four patron saints of the United Kingdom, with St. Andrew of Scotland, flanked by St. Kentigern and St. Margaret. In St. Stephen's Hall the mural of Wycliffe with his Lollard preachers can be seen; Wycliffe is pointing to his English translation of the Bible, for the Bible became the foundational source of inspiration for our culture.

Lord Mackay goes on to list the biblical influences on our Scottish legal system, with references given from the Bible. The fruit of this can be seen in the following areas in which our courts operate to seek to bring righteousness: access to justice; accidental death; admonition to judges/sheriffs; adultery; aggravated sentence for leaders; animal welfare; appeal courts; bribery; citation of witnesses (duty to give honest evidence); contempt of court; corroboration of evidence for solemn procedure; defamation; defence of the disadvantaged; disability rights; diversion from prosecution (at instances of accused); culpable and reckless conduct; accidental death; equality before the law; evidence on oath; fabrication of evidence; fraud; general principles of legal aid, equality and purity of process; health and safety; incest; independence of judiciary; legal aid (for the poor); lesser fines for the poor; malice; miscarriage of justice; murder/culpable homicide; murder; perjury; preparation before a trial; purity of law; racial equality; reparation; rule of law; strict liability for statutory crime; submission to authority; theft and deception; weights and measures.

You may have noticed Terry Sanderson's remark in opposition to biblical influence in our laws at the beginning of this chapter, for he says: 'What Lord Mackay is proposing could put the Sharia laws of the Middle East to shame. He and the SBS make absolutely no concessions to the progress of legal thought over the past two millennia. Killing witches and homosexuals and stoning adulterers are all clearly stated legal requirements in the Christian holy book. Are they seriously suggesting that Scottish sheriffs and judges should follow the Bible to the letter?'

What Sanderson is doing is a common ploy of the enemies of Christianity: they focus on a few difficult issues over the centuries and ignore all of the benefits that have been inherited by us, so that people like Sanderson can have the freedom of speech and justice in our culture today. Yes, it is true that the Old Testament said that homosexuals, witches and adulterers should be stoned to death at the time of Moses until the coming of Christ, but when Christ came, notice what happened. He said to the Jews who were about to stone an adulteress, 'He who is without sin, cast the first stone' (John 8:7); to those who might curse Christians, which would include witches, He said, 'Love your enemies ... bless those who curse you ...' (Luke 6:28). He regarded adultery and witchcraft as sin, but as God in human form He was introducing a more merciful way of justice. Whether or not the church through the ages has followed this may be disputed, but, as always, we need to return to Christ, the Head of the Church, for His ways. Likewise, the Old Testament death sentence was eventually overturned in Scotland because it was realised that as humans we do not have a justice system which is good enough to bear this verdict, and Christ's example of mercy was followed instead.

Professor Montgomery, as a law specialist, tackles the difficult subject of witch- burning in his *Law Above the Law*. He points out that the death sentence for witchcraft mentioned in the Old Testament concerned a practice that some people used to harm and murder others, either through curses or poisoning. The death sentence for such a custom was enacted through a vigorous process of cross-examination of witnesses. Neither the burning of witches, nor the extracting of information by torture, appear in the Old Testament, but both ordeals are due to a revival of Roman law in the twelfth century in the Bologna school, which combined both canon law and Roman law. The church lawyers should have purged the legal system of the Pagan practice of burning heretics and using torture, but they failed to do so. This great error resulted in the horrendous sufferings of supposed heretics, whether witches, Christians, or others.

Tertullian, in his *Letter to Scapula* (c.217), was the first known person in Western civilization to promote religious freedom in the context of human rights. As a leading Church Father, he wrote: 'We worship the one God .... There are others whom you regard as gods; we know them to be demons. Nevertheless, it is a basic human right that everyone should be free to worship according to his own convictions .... Religion must be practiced freely, not by coercion.'[10] Augustine, in 426, expressed his horror at Roman law which entitled the magistrates to torture their victims to extract information: it is a well-known fact that people will often say anything you want them to say, as long as you take away the pain.[11]

Both Pope Gregory 'the Great' (sixth century) and Pope Nicholas I (ninth century) opposed this Roman law. In Gratian's *Decretum*, which became a key document in developing our Western legal system, this kind of torture is repudiated.[12] The French jurist, Augustin Nicholas, expressed his disgust at torture in 1682, with the words: 'I shall never accept as legitimate ground for conviction what has been admitted under torture, for it is an invention of the devil and has never been condoned by Scripture.'[13]

It has been estimated that about 2,500 of the 3,837 people accused of practicing witchcraft were killed in Scotland between 1563 and 1736,[14] when such cruel treatment was abolished; most were not witches at all and they fell foul of personal vengeance by their enemies, particularly through accusations of plotting against the King's life, as with the 1590 North Berwick persecution at the

10. Tertullian, *Scapula*, Vol. III, The Ante-Nicene Fathers (Edinburgh: T&T Clark); (Grand Rapids: William B. Eerdmans Publishing Company, reprinted 1997), 2, p. 105.

11. Augustine, *City of God*, 19:6 (Penguin Classics, 1984), pp. 859-61.

12. Gratian, *Decretum*, Caus. XV, qu.6, can.1.

13. James Warwick Montgomery, *The Law Above the Law*, Chapter 2, *Witch Trial: Theory and Practice* (NRP Books, 1975), p. 67.

14. *Survey of Scottish Witchcraft*, History Department, University of Edinburgh, The National, Hamish MacPherson, 16th February 2021.

time of James VI. With such a fear that witches were plotting his death, he was inspired to write his *Daemonologie* in 1597, which inflamed some of the populace into an irrational frenzy. It is true that the General Assembly of the Church of Scotland also agreed with the Scottish government's Roman law during the 1649–1650 and 1661 witch-hunts. They had sought to extend the Witchcraft Act of 1563 to eradicate witchcraft, leading to a witch-hunt with the deaths of three hundred people. Such harsh judgment is inconceivable when viewed through Christ's teaching.

In March 2022, Nicola Sturgeon, on behalf of the Scottish Parliament, rightly issued an apology acknowledging this 'egregious historic injustice', following pressure from The Witches of Scotland campaign. The Church of Scotland followed the example of the Scottish Parliament a few months later in May, apologising for 'feeding the witchcraft fury' and for allowing some former church elders to capture and cross-examine accused witches, before handing their victims over to the secular courts.

The Rule of Law in Scotland

Tom Bingham was the Lord Chief Justice of England and Wales and the Senior Law Lord of the United Kingdom. Regarded by *The Guardian* as 'the most eminent of our judges', he published a short work called *The Rule of Law* (2010). In the second chapter of his book, he identifies the key milestones in the development of the rule of law in Western civilization, such as Magna Carta (1215); Petition of Right (1628); Habeas Corpus Act (1679); Bill of Rights (1689, with the Act of Settlement in 1701); the American Constitution (1787, coming out of the Declaration of Independence in 1776, with the 1791 American Bill of Rights); and the French Declaration of the Rights of Man and the Citizen (1789).

Bingham freely admits, 'In my choice of milestones I am highly selective and shamelessly Anglocentric.'[15] It is a much-needed book in our time of confusion, in which the anchor of the rule of law needs to be kept fast, but like most scholars he

---

15. Tom Bingham, *The Rule of Law* (Penguin Books, 2010), preface viii.

has left out the Scottish part, which was vital in the development of the English Bill of Rights and the Scottish Claim of Rights (1689), all of which grew out of the Scottish National Covenant (1638) and Solemn League and Covenant (1643), both drawn up by the Scottish theologian, Rev. Alexander Henderson. We will uncover this significant part of our history, but in a later chapter on human rights.

The Christian Institute: Whistle-Blower

In August 2019 it was as if people woke up from a deep sleep, or trance-like state. The *Daily Mail* trumpeted such headings as 'SNP urged to abandon its "unworkable" snooper plan', and 'It's time to put SNP's zombie plan out of misery for good.' The controversy was all about the so-called Named Person Scheme in Scotland. The Scottish National Party had drafted a document proposing that every child in the nation would have a State-appointed guardian, from nursery until eighteen years old, to which the child would report, without parental consent. The idea sounded good at first, for it was promoted as establishing a safety network in Scotland for vulnerable children who could otherwise be abused. When the Members of Scottish Parliament (MSPs) voted for this to be made law, the support was overwhelming, with one hundred and three for and none against it. Even children's charities queued up to support it. If it had not been for the lawyers of the Christian Institute bothering to examine the small print in the document, Scotland might well have adopted a nanny policy with increasing State control, which some have likened to Communist regimes.

The Christian Institute, sensing the direction in which the Named Person Scheme was potentially taking Scotland, blew the whistle on it, and even took the Scottish Parliament to the Supreme Court where it was investigated carefully and declared to be in breach of human rights. Suddenly, the scheme was in the national news and in the glare of the spotlights. The Scottish government was rebuked and told to produce a robust code of practice that would also safeguard the law in accordance with the Human Rights Act of 1998. Despite attempts to do this, they floundered, and the scheme ended up being shipwrecked on the hard rocks of the law.

The Article in question was number 8 (1): 'Everyone has the right to respect for his private and family life, his home and his correspondence.' Clause 2 continues: 'There shall be no interference by a public authority with the exercise of this right except such as in accordance with the law and is necessary in a democratic society in the interests of national security, public safety or the economic well-being of the country, for the prevention of disorder or crime, for the protection of health or morals, or for the protection of the rights and freedoms of others.' Thus, the Named Person Scheme was weighed in the scales of law and justice and found wanting, rightly being dismissed.

A similar case also emerged with the so-called Hate Crime Bill in Scotland. Again, it was the Christian Institute that blew the whistle on this attempt of the Scottish Parliament to sneak in another law to punish those accused of offensive hate speech. As with the Named Person Scheme, it was as if people were sleep-walking into a potentially dangerous system of control. As the Christian Institute grappled with this Bill, concerned that free speech would be butchered, celebrities stirred from their somnolence. Comedians began to agitate. Mr Bean (Rowan Atkinson) said 'the bill could frustrate rational debate and discussion which has a fundamental role in society.'[16] John Cleese of Monty Python fame could state that 'it's disastrous to the creative process .... if you're having to edit everything you say before you say it then nothing is going to happen creatively.'[17] Top lawyers, leaders of our police force, and others joined the protest. Once the potential traps in this Bill had been made known publicly, a poll was taken among Scots and 87 per cent believed that 'free speech is an important right'.[18]

---

16. *Hate Crime and Public Order (Scotland) Bill*, The Christian Institute, Scotland, October 2020.

17. ibid.

18. ibid.

The debate centred on the loose wording of the document and the harsh punishment of up to a seven-year prison sentence for those charged with 'hate speech'. Almost everyone agrees that abusive behaviour must be punished, but the word 'abusive' could be aimed at somebody who holds a different opinion in today's hyper-sensitive culture. In September 2020, Humza Yousaf, the then SNP Cabinet Minister for Health and Social Care, tried to tweak the wording of the document to say that a person could be punished if that person 'intended' to stir up hatred, rather than 'likely' to stir up hatred. The Faculty of Advocates stated that the Scottish government had not addressed the concerns many had about freedom of expression. Another poll was taken amongst Scots, with 69 per cent agreeing that 'For a criminal offence to be committed, there must be a proven intention to stir up hatred.'[19]

Again, the loose wording of the Hate Crime Bill has come under the scrutiny of lawyers who weigh up law and justice through the Human Rights Act 1998. In this document, Article 10 (1) says: 'Everyone has the right to freedom of expression.' This Article adds the following: 'This right shall include freedom to hold opinions and to receive and impart information and ideas without interference by public authority and regardless of frontiers.'

If, as the SNP claims, that they are on the right side of history, they need to listen to the voice of the people in a democratic culture. Yes, we need to develop a caring and just society for all, but under the rule of law. But how did democracy arise in Scotland? This is the subject of our next chapter.

---

19. ibid.

CHAPTER 6

DEMOCRACY

In 2014, the eyes of the world turned towards Scotland. Millions wondered whether this nation would break away from the United Kingdom and become independent. In the highest recorded referendum turn-out in the United Kingdom since 1910, with 84.6 per cent of people voting, a decision was made: we would, at least for the time being, remain, and not leave.[1] There were no bombings, and massacres of people, and no rigged elections; we had no concentration camps for dissidents, bribery, serious corruption, or people being forced to vote against their will through threats of torture and death. It may have been an emotional time for some, but what the world saw was essentially a peaceful exercise of democracy.

This has not always been the case in Scotland. Like any nation we have had our atrocities and bloodshed, as we have walked the long, arduous road to democracy. All the way back in the 540s, Gildas of Strathclyde could lament the desperate situation among the Britons, whose tribes spread all the way up to today's Edinburgh. He could speak of the 'truly diabolical monstrosities of my native country', and cite from the Pagan author Porphyry who wrote that 'Britain is a province fertile in tyrants'.[2]

---

1. The final result was 55.3 per cent in favour of Scotland remaining in the UK, and 44.7 per cent against.

2. Gildas, *De Excidio Brittanniae, or The Ruin of Britain*, pp. 18-19, edited for the Hon. Society of Cymmrodorion, Hugh Williams (1901), a facsimile reprint by Llanerch Press, 2006.

It has been assumed by most people that our democracy emerged, firstly from the Greeks in Athens in the fifth century B.C., and then with the Roman Republic, after which these ideas triumphantly spread through the Enlightenment of the eighteenth century. However, this is a superficial understanding. It is true that both eras influenced the democratic movement in our Western culture, as evidenced in America with its Senate, Republican Party, Democratic Party, and Capitol. But such a portrayal of the rise of democracy in the modern Western world is biased and unfair. In Athens, democracy arose in the sixth century B.C., flourished in the next century, and collapsed in 322 B.C. at the hands of the Macedonians. At its height, only ten to twenty per cent of the population could vote, with women and slaves barred from this right. It was not a secular democracy, for the Pagan religion dominated much of the culture, thus making it more of a Pagan semi-democracy. Similar sentiments could be expressed for the Roman Republic, which flourished between 509 and 27 B.C., but was never a genuine democracy with full participation of the population, women and slaves. In reality it was another Pagan semi-democracy, in the hands of the aristocracy.

Typically, people will point to the American War of Independence and the French Revolution in the eighteenth century, as being the key movements that brought about our modern democracy. The cry of the French revolutionaries was 'Liberty, Equality, Fraternity,' expressing democratic values, but the origin of this cry had come from Christianity. John Robison, Professor of Natural Philosophy at the University of Edinburgh, revealed in 1797 that the French Revolution had emerged out of a secret society called the Illuminati. This society had wormed its way into the lodges of Freemasonry, much to the concern of Robison, himself a committed Freemason. He cites from many letters of the leaders, who had code names. 'Spartacus' their leader (Adam Weishaupt), wrote to 'Cato' (Franz Zwack), his right-hand man:

> Jesus of Nazareth, the Grand Master of our Order ... speaks of a
> kingdom of the upright and faithful; his Father's kingdom, whose

children we also are. Let us only take Liberty and Equality as the great aims of his doctrines.[3]

Although Freemasonry is clearly contradictory to biblical doctrines in other ways, the fact is that the principles of equality, fraternity and liberty were taken straight from the Christian ethic, just as Rousseau's *Social Contract* was inspired by the Presbyterian National Covenant (1638) and Solemn League and Covenant (1643).[4] It is true that Rousseau was no friend of Christianity, even writing against it, but he knew that the purest form of equality came from the New Testament.[5]

Likewise, the inspiration for the American constitution came largely from Christian ideology, a fact evidenced by the large

---

3. John Robison, *Proofs of a Conspiracy Against All The Religions And Governments Of Europe, Carried On In The Secret Meetings Of Freemasons, Illuminati, And Reading Rooms*, 1798, p. 57, reprinted by Amazon in Great Britain. The original manuscript was published in Edinburgh in 1797, with the second edition being printed in London in the same year by T. Cadell and W. Davies. The third edition (1798), from which I have cited, was reprinted in Philadelphia, USA, by T. Dobson and W. Cobbet. The monk Alexander Horn acted as an undercover agent and provided much of Robison's material. In the same year that Robison's book came out, Abbé Augustin Barruel independently published another book, called *Memoirs Illustrating the History of Jacobinism*, showing the same evidence of the Illuminati conspiracy.

4. Although Rousseau does not mention these Presbyterian covenants in *The Social Contract*, his early friendship with David Hume from Edinburgh meant that he was fully aware of them. Rousseau wrote: 'But the social order is a sacred right which serves as a basis for all other rights. And as it is not a natural right, it must be founded on covenants. The problem is to determine what those covenants are .... All power comes from God, I agree ... all legitimate authority among men must be based on covenants.' Rousseau, Jean-Jacques, *The Social Contract*, translated by Maurice Cranston (Penguin Classics, 1968), Chapters 1–4, pp. 50-53.

5. In 1762, the year in which Rousseau published *The Social Contract*, he also published the *Profession de foi du vicaire Savoyard*. This was his diatribe against revealed religion, for which he was exiled from France, and fled to England where he met up with his old friend, David Hume, only to become his enemy. However, in *The Social Contract*, he regards the New Testament early church, which was based on the gospel of Christ, to be the best example of equality, but critiques it because he thinks it is heavenly, and not practically obtainable in normal society (Book IV, Chapter 8, p. 182).

number of Presbyterians who were influential in its formation. President Theodore Roosevelt, in his book, *The Winning of the West*, acknowledged this. 'It is doubtful if we have realised in the leadership of our country,' he wrote, 'the part played by that stern and virile people, the Scots-Irish, whose predecessors taught the creed of Knox and Calvin. They became the vanguard of our civilization ... these were the men who first declared for American independence ... they were kinsfolk of the Covenanters, they deemed it a religious duty to interpret their own Bible ... for generations their whole ecclesiastical and scholastic systems have been found fundamentally democratic.'[6]

In the American Declaration of Independence, we find the following memorable statement, penned by Thomas Jefferson: 'We hold these truths to be self-evident, that all men are created equal, that they are endowed by their Creator with certain unalienable Rights, that among these are Life, Liberty and the pursuit of Happiness.' It is a cry for equality and freedom based on the Christian democratic ideal, but where do the phrases, 'self-evident', 'unalienable Rights', and 'the pursuit of Happiness' come from? For this, we have to look back to Scotland and to the city of Glasgow and to two Christian professors of Moral Philosophy at the university there.

The phrase 'self-evident' truth comes straight from Rev. Thomas Reid who pioneered the Scottish School of Common Sense as a reaction to the sceptical rationalism of David Hume. Reid's book, *An Inquiry into the Human Mind, on the Principles of Common Sense* (1764), was a sensation in America. Its teaching was enthusiastically spread by evangelical Christians in the universities, by such men as Rev. Dr John Witherspoon, a key influence behind the Declaration, and Benjamin Rush. It was a great source of inspiration too for Thomas Jefferson. Professor Arthur Herman, who wrote *The Scottish Enlightenment: The Scots' Invention of the Modern World*, calls Reid's Common Sense

---

6. Cited by William S. Anderson, former historical archivist of the Free Church, in his *A Guide to the Free Church of Scotland College and Offices* (Edinburgh: Knox Press, 1994), pp. 23-25.

argument 'a science of human freedom', and says it 'Democratised the intellect, by insisting that the ordinary man could be as certain of his judgements as the philosopher was.'[7] In his defence of the five senses of humans, which are common to all of us, and better guides than the mists of philosophy and conjecture, Reid repeatedly calls them 'self-evident' truths.

For the phrases 'unalienable Rights' and 'the pursuit of Happiness' we have to look to Rev. Francis Hutcheson. It is in his *Inquiry into the Original of Our Ideas of Beauty and Virtue* (1725) that we find his phrase 'unalienable rights' in conjunction with the right to resist tyranny, a concept which became embedded in Harvard and other colleges of that time, and was taught by the Scot Rev. Dr John Witherspoon at Princeton as part of his Moral Philosophy course. The phrase, 'the pursuit of Happiness', is the central message of Hutcheson's message of Christian virtue, which inspired the Swiss philosopher Jean-Jaques Burlamaqui and Thomas Jefferson. Hutcheson wrote in his *Inquiry* (1725): 'That Action is best, which procures the greatest Happiness for the greatest numbers' (Treatise II, section III).

It might come as a shock to many today to realise that our modern democracy came largely from Christian movements of the past, accustomed as we are to denigrating Christianity and attributing to it the oppression and intolerance of religious bigotry, but the facts will speak for themselves. It remains for me now to outline how our essential democratic process developed in Scotland and England and disentangle truth from error.

Christ and Equality

In the fifteenth century B.C., Moses said to the people of Israel: 'Choose wise, understanding, and knowledgeable men from among your tribes, and I will make them heads over you,' to which the people answered, 'The thing which you have told us to do is good' (Deut. 1:13-14). It is true that Moses acted as a prophet

---

7. Arthur Herman, *The Scottish Enlightenment: The Scots' Invention of the Modern World* (Harper Perennial, 2001), p. 251.

for the people, receiving God's commands for the Israelites, but here we see a glimpse of a theocratic democracy, in which the people participated in the election of their leaders. 'Oh, that all the Lord's people were prophets,' Moses cried out from his heart, 'and that the Lord would put His Spirit upon them' (Num. 11:29). God's desire that his people would be 'a kingdom of priests and a holy nation' (Exod. 19:6) was revealed in the time of Christ and the New Testament church, when the Holy Spirit was poured out in great measure.

In Christ we see God expressed in human form. Instead of only giving us commands from heaven, He became one of us to identify with us. Instead of lording it over people, He stooped down at the Last Supper and washed His disciples' feet as a servant would do, showing us the model of servant-leadership. When James and John requested to be on either side of His throne in the future heavenly kingdom, He told them that 'the Gentiles lord it over' people, yet among Christian leaders 'it shall not be among you; but whoever desires to become great among you shall be your servant. And whoever of you desires to be first shall be the slave of all. For even the Son of Man did not come to be served, but to serve, and to give His life a ransom for many' (Mark 10:42-45).

In the community that Jesus pioneered, both men and women could select their leaders before God as 'brethren' (Acts 1:14-26). Both men and women alike, as brethren, could receive the Holy Spirit (Acts 2:16-18), and could elect their deacons to serve the church (Acts 6:1-6) and choose leaders to represent them (Acts 15:22). Paul could express this equality under the authority of Christ with the memorable and revolutionary words: 'There is neither Jew nor Gentile, neither slave nor free, nor is there male and female, for you are all one in Christ Jesus' (Gal. 3:28, NIV).

Such an equality, however, was not a uniform equality, but it was expressed in diversity, for just as there is one Holy Spirit, there were diverse gifts from Him in the church, expressed through men and women (1 Cor. 12). Their community was radical, for wealthy Christians sold land and property to provide for those in need (Acts 2:44-45), and class favouritism was rebuked (James 2:1-4).

Paul's cry was 'that there may be equality' (2 Cor. 8:13-15). Thus, many centuries before France was resonating with the call for equality, fraternity and liberty, the Christians were already living this. It would be a mistake, however, to compare Christian democracy with the secular democracy of Scotland today. The biblical boundaries are different, with Christ as King and Head of the Church, and yet the essence of our democratic culture comes from this Christian fountainhead in which we are called to love God with everything and love our neighbour as ourself, for as Jesus said: 'On these two commandments hang all the Law and the Prophets' (Matt. 22:40).

The Early Church

By the end of the first century, the triad leadership structure of bishop, elder and deacon had become established.[8] Such a model worked really well, as long as the bishops remained humble servants of Christ and did not seek to lord it over the people. We read in about the year 250 that a bishop 'is chosen in time of peace by the suffrage [voting] of an entire people'.[9] Certainly, the pyramid system of power and control that emerged later was unknown in the early centuries of the church. If this is the case, how on earth did we end up with such a controlling and tyrannical system in the church by the medieval period?

For the first three centuries of the church the Christians intermittently suffered horrendous persecution at the hands of

---

8. This structure of the church by A.D. 96 can be seen in the letter of Clement, Bishop of Rome, to the Corinthian church in sections 42–44, *Early Christian Writings* (Penguin Classics, 1968), pp. 45-46. Clement remarks that 'our Apostles knew, through our Lord Jesus Christ, that there would be dissensions over the title of bishop,' but they went ahead to appoint a leading elder over each new church, along with elders and deacons, thus setting a model for the churches that followed. Similarly, Ignatius, Bishop of Antioch (martyred in A.D. 107), where Jesus' disciples were first called 'Christians', addresses the bishop, elders and deacons in the church at Philadelphia (*Epistle to the Philadelphians* 1, Penguin Classics, p. 111).

9. Cyprian (Bishop of Carthage, died 258), *Epistles*, 54:6, The Ante-Nicene Fathers, Vol. V (Edinburgh: T&T Clark); reprinted 1992 (Grand Rapids: William B. Eerdmans Publishing Company), p. 341.

the Pagan Roman Empire, and yet they multiplied. Constantine, who professed to be a Christian after his vision at the Battle of Milvian Bridge, later became the most powerful man on earth as sole Emperor of the Roman Empire. With the Edict of Milan in 313, Christians and Pagans were allowed freedom 'so that every man may have permission to choose and practise whatever religion he pleases.'[10] However, when Constantine clashed with Licinius in 324, it was seen as a battle, not just about the rulership of the empire, but between Paganism and Christianity. With Constantine's victory established we now witness a shift from a beleaguered and despised Christian culture to a dominant and powerful worldview. Roman emperors were used to exercising absolute power, so Constantine 'either closed or destroyed the temples of the pagans, and exposed the images which were in them to popular contempt.'[11]

You can imagine the rejoicing and celebrations of the Christians as they bathed in the glow of their freedom. With pride they could proclaim the emperor as a Christian, and Eusebius, the court historian, gushed out his praise for all the good laws that Constantine passed: abolition of the barbaric gladiatorial entertainment, banning of temple prostitutes, support for the poor and needy, restoration of Christian properties, and the programme for grand church buildings. Eusebius noted that 'cathedrals were again rising from their foundations high into the air', and 'a stream of personal letters from the emperor reached the bishops, accompanied by honours and gifts of money .... The basilica itself he built solidly of still richer materials in abundance, never for a moment counting the cost ... he furnished it with thrones high up, to accord with the dignity of the prelates [or bishops] ...'[12]

---

10. Eusebius, *The History of the Church*, 10:5, translated by G. A. Williamson (Penguin Books, revised and edited by Andrew Louth, 1989), p. 323.

11. Socrates Scholasticus, *Ecclesiastical History*, 1:3, Nicene and Post-Nicene Fathers, Second Series, Vol. 2, edited by Philip Schaff and Henry Wace (Hendrickson Publishers, 1999), p. 2.

12. Eusebius, 10:3-4, pp. 305, 315.

By rewarding the bishops with 'thrones high up' he was unwittingly opening up the door to invite a new kind of bishop who would eventually rule over the people like a prince, rather than shepherd them with servant-leadership.

When the emperor summoned the famous Council of Nicaea in 325, the church had really come out of the shadows into the limelight – and into temptation. And yet another, more sinister, edict was also enacted by Constantine at the Nicaean Council: that of the execution of heretics. Arius had gained many converts to his belief that Christ was not God, the second person of the Trinity, but the created Son of God. Christians were horrified at this false teaching, as it cut to the very core of the foundation of their faith. Unsurprisingly, they wanted to see the church protected from this heresy. Constantine stepped in on their behalf with his edict, writing in a letter to the bishops and people that 'if anyone shall be detected in concealing a book compiled by Arius, and shall not instantly bring it forward and burn it, the penalty for this offence shall be death; for immediately after conviction the criminal shall suffer capital punishment.'[13] Thus, Roman law would justify the execution of heretics from this time forth, resulting in a heritage of carnage and bloodshed, particularly from the medieval period onwards, that would match that of the Pagan Roman emperors.

With a string of 'Christian' emperors emerging after Constantine, it is not surprising that many saw the church as a gateway to power and influence. Disaster struck in 476 when the Germans came sweeping into Italy and did the unthinkable – they completely sacked Rome. The Western Roman Empire began to disintegrate, but the Bishop of Rome had the ability to pull different peoples together through the church. When Gregory I came to the pontifical seat (590–604), the imperial power had collapsed, and he found himself pushed into the role of papal supremacy for both church and state – a job which he did well. John Calvin, the Swiss reformer, saw Gregory I as the last of the

---

13. Socrates, *Ecclesiastical History* 1.9.30, and Gelasius, *Church History* 2.36.1.

'good popes'. We now enter a different phase of the church in which popes and their councils could wield great power. Increasingly, bishops came to proudly lord it over the people, rather than serve them as the apostles had done in humility. With this pride there also came a lack of regard for biblical authority.

Columbanus, an Irish scholastic monk, wrote a letter to Pope Boniface IV in 613 in which he refers to himself as 'an uncultured rustic, the humblest and most insignificant of men', but addresses the Pope like the Roman Emperor: 'The most beautiful Head of the Churches of all Europe, the most sweet Pope, the Supreme Pontiff, the Pastor of pastors, the venerable Sentinel ...' The letter is a call to the Pope to stop the immoral rot in the church, but there is also a key issue which he raises for the reason of this backsliding: 'Let us return to the book,' he says, 'which we left on one side.' The reformers saw that the key issue at stake in the church was the authority of men over God's word, the Bible. It was for this reason that their slogan later became *Sola Scriptura* – Scripture alone.

From the corrupt spring and gradual neglect of biblical authority arose many immoral beliefs, such as simony, the practice of buying a bishop's ministry for money, something which Gildas of Strathclyde bemoaned in the 540s. It is understandable that Christians would want to honour the memory of their martyrs and godly examples, but from about 375 the saints of the past were being venerated, with prayers to the Virgin Mary being accepted by some bishops in 431.

The spring became a stream as other unbiblical beliefs poured into the mainstream church between 593 and 995, such as purgatory, kissing the pope's feet as if he were the Roman Emperor, the temporal power of popes, adoration of the cross, images and relics, and canonisation of dead saints with prayers to them. In 1079, priests had to be celibate by law, and in the eleventh century the church accepted the rosary, inquisition of heretics, and sale of indulgences.

Pope Innocent III made transubstantiation church dogma in 1215, which required people to believe that the priest had the power, by saying *hoc est corpus meum* ('this is my body'), for the bread and wine of the Mass to turn magically into the literal body and blood of Christ. With this came the adoration of the wafer (1220), in which the consecrated bread could be worshipped. In 1229 the common people were forbidden to read the Bible at the Council of Valencia, thus causing a great famine of biblical understanding and ensuring a tight control by the church hierarchy. Thus, the phrase 'Rome knows best' became a catchword.

The power and wealth held by the popes, cardinals and bishops became colossal, so much so that they could have control over kings – indeed kings would bow the knee to the pope and hand over their crowns in submission to him. The institutional church became so sought after that the sons of kings and lords vied with each other for positions of power in it. 'Christianity' had become a thin covering for a monster of depravity. The year 1409 was known as the Year of the Three Popes, in which Pope Gregory XII of Rome fought it out with Pope Benedict XIII of Avignon and Pope Alexander V. No wonder the world watched in disbelief, for this was a replay of the warring emperors in the Roman Empire!

It is not surprising that the corruption at the top of the church pyramid filtered down to the priests in the local churches throughout Europe. The great scholar Erasmus of Rotterdam, himself a dedicated Roman Catholic, who remained faithful to the pope, could write in 1526: 'The world had become bewitched by ceremonial, evil monks reigned unchecked, theology had been reduced to subtle sophistries, while bishops and priests acted like tyrants in the name of the Roman pontiff.'[14]

In Scotland we saw the same sort of corruption in the church as in the rest of Europe. Aristocratic families tended to put their children in places of power in the church as abbots and bishops. King James IV of Scotland, whilst he was building his Holyrood Palace in Edinburgh, in 1504 nominated his illegitimate son

---

14. D. Bentley-Taylor, *My Dear Erasmus: The Forgotten Reformer* (Christian Focus, 2002), p. 185, quoting from the *Collected Works of Erasmus*, 1526 (University of Toronto Press, 1969), pp. 45-46, 116-148.

Alexander, aged eleven, to the position of Archbishop of St Andrews.[15] Christianity was often far from the minds of those appointed. Pope Clement VII agreed to let King James V put the three wealthiest abbeys in the hands of his three illegitimate sons.[16] When Sir David Lyndsay published *A Satire of the Three Estates* (1540), which was levelled against the corrupt clergy, lords and burgesses, his descriptions were unfortunately accurate and damning for the church, and all of the abuses he wrote about can be confirmed by church records. The cathedrals might have looked artistically beautiful, but inside they were full of rottenness.

The Monastic Movement

It was a deep consternation over the worldliness that was creeping into the church which drove men and women to seek a purer faith in the deserts and wilderness, away from the new model of the bishop princes and power and wealth politics in the church. Beginning in Egypt, the monastic movement flourished from the fourth century, as thousands sought simplicity, equality, fraternity and liberty through Christ. 'Therefore brothers, let us be equal, from the least to the greatest, whether rich or poor, perfect in harmony and humility,' was the call of one leading monk.[17]

If the church leadership model was starting to reflect that of an aristocratic secular hierarchy, the monastic movement was a determined attempt to preserve the early church practice of Christian democracy. Around these monastic groups, such as the one at the mountain of Nitria in Egypt, in which over five thousand men lived and thrived, self-supporting communities

---

15. Alexander Stewart, the illegitimate son of King James IV of Scotland, was made an archdeacon of the church at the age of nine. In 1504 he was nominated as Archbishop of St Andrews by his father when he was eleven, but he died at the Battle of Flodden in 1513 (aged twenty), so he never actually performed his role as archbishop.

16. Gordon Donaldson, *Scotland: Church and Nation through Sixteen Centuries* (Bloomsbury St, London: SCM Press Ltd, 1960), p. 48.

17. L. Siedentop, *Inventing the Individual: The Origins of Western Liberalism* (Penguin Books, 2014), pp. 84-85.

with trade, healthcare and hospitality emerged, based on such principles. The abbot, being elected by the monks, was seen as a spiritual leader whose Christ-like example would inspire them all – a far cry from the later medieval abbots who were imposed on the monks through the aristocracy.

The monastic spring bubbling up in Egypt streamed forth in France through Martin of Tours, and to Ninian and Patrick, the Britons of Scotland, and from their influence to the Irish-Scottish monastic movement that produced such a galaxy of stars, such as Columba, Comgall, and others. In the Irish-Scottish model of monasteries the local abbot was the leader, rather than the bishop. This may have been very frustrating for a bishop who wanted total control, but it enabled the monasteries to operate in a more democratic way.

Columbanus, who was mentored by Comgall in Bangor, Northern Ireland, had a dramatic impact, especially in France, but also in Germany, Switzerland and Italy. When he arrived in France in 589, monasticism was at a low ebb, but through his work it underwent a renaissance. Benedict had previously pioneered a similar monastic work in Italy and had put together his Rule for his monks to follow. When the Benedictine and Columbanian Rules joined hands across the Alps, and were embraced by Charlemagne in the eighth century, a standard and model was set for Western monasteries to follow. The ideas of a written constitution, law and democratic practice amongst equals under Christ became partially embedded in Europe and rose up through the guilds and civic boroughs of the medieval period.

The Reformation

A volcano started to stir in France in the twelfth century. Peter Waldo of Lyon, incensed at the corrupt hierarchy of the national church, began publicly calling people back to Christ and the Bible. It was one thing to have monastic orders operating as they did in their retreats, but to have firebrands stirring up the general population was another issue. As his movement grew and became influential, so did the persecution by the religious authorities.

Waldo had the Bible translated into the language of the people because he believed that, as God's Word was read, it would bring light and understanding. As the beliefs and practices of the corrupt medieval church were compared with Scripture, the Waldensians, as the movement was later called, began to cast out unbiblical traditions. Part of this reformation saw a restoration of the New Testament teaching that all Christians are priests, and a democratic structure was reintroduced, also allowing both men and women to preach from the Bible. It was not just the Waldensian movement which angered the Roman Catholic tyranny, but other similar groups, such as the Berengarians and Albigenses, were also influencing the people. Centuries later these various streams would converge together in the river of Protestantism.

From Oxford in England, John Wycliffe's fourteenth-century preachers of reformation came up to Scotland, stirring and shaking multitudes, so that they were banned and hunted out as heretics. It was Wycliffe who penned in 1384 the notable words of Christian democracy: 'The Bible is for the Government of the People, by the People, and for the People,' as found in the prologue of his Bible translation from the Latin Vulgate into English. With Luther's stand in Germany in 1521 the volcano erupted, bringing the Reformation period to Europe.

Here in Scotland, Luther had some significant influence in inspiring the Protestant outpouring, especially through the preacher, Patrick Hamilton, who was burnt at the stake at St Andrews, but it would be the reformers in Switzerland, such as Calvin, Zwingli, Bullinger, and others, who would really shape the national church here through John Knox and other Scottish leaders. For the reformers, their united battle cry was *Sola Scriptura* – Scripture Alone. When John Knox returned from Geneva to Scotland to lead the Reformation, the nation experienced a transition from Roman Catholicism to Protestantism in 1560.

For decades, the Scots had been examining the Bible to test everything in the church by it, and the Reformation here was more radical than in England. With the overthrow of a controlling and tyrannical papal system with its lord bishops and cardinals, Knox and the leaders called for a New Testament pattern of leadership, which would flower into the Presbyterian Church by 1578. It was this restored democratic system of a church led by elders, elected by the people, which would be hugely significant in shaping not only Scotland, but the United Kingdom, America, Europe and many other parts of the world.

In 1560, John Knox and other leaders produced *The First Book of Discipline*. Amongst the text are some extraordinary values that helped transform Scotland and the world from Edinburgh. Here we find their desire for a democratic form of church government. 'The election of elders and deacons ought to be used every year,' it says, 'by common and free election ... every man may give his vote freely, every several church may take such order as best seems to them.'[18]

Taking a Stand for a Presbyterian Government

Whilst Scotland and England existed as two separate kingdoms, the Presbyterian Church could function peacefully and well. This all changed when, in 1603, King James VI of Scotland also became King James I of England, in the Union of Crowns. In England, James followed the practice of the monarchs from the time of Henry VIII, which meant he became the Head of the Church of England as his 'divine right'. Desirous of a uniformity between England and Scotland in church polity, he began to put pressure on the Presbyterian Church to conform to that of the Church of England, with its lord bishops. As the years progressed, the Presbyterians were cowed into submission, losing their freedom and democratic rights. However, it would not be until the reign of Charles I that this system of control would flower into absolutism. If Scotland had escaped the tyranny of the papal system through the Reformation, it had now become imprisoned in the tyranny of the 'divine right' of monarchs.

---

18. *The First Book of Discipline*, 1560: *The Eighth Head: Touching the Election of Elders and Deacons, etc.*

When Charles I forced the Scots to accept the Anglicised Book of Common Prayer in 1637, without consulting either the Scottish Church or Parliament, the nation was on a knife edge. The reading of this book in the High Kirk of St Giles in Edinburgh led to a riot, as the crowded audience understood the wording to be a pretext to force the nation back to Rome. Out of this protest came a significant document called the National Covenant (1638), which led to what some scholars call the Second Reformation in Scotland. The National Covenant was essentially a legal and binding agreement by many thousands of Scots from all social classes, who contracted before God that they would stand for their faith. It was also a petition to the king and authorities for freedom of conscience.

In 1641 the Civil War erupted in England between Charles I's royalist army and the parliamentarians. The English parliamentarians needed Scottish help to win the war. When the Puritan John Pym, the leading parliamentarian in Westminster, asked Rev. Alexander Henderson, the minister of St Giles in Edinburgh, to put together a second document, the Solemn League and Covenant emerged. Along with Magna Carta (1215), Petition of Right (1628), and the Habeas Corpus Act (1679), the National Covenant (1638) and Solemn League and Covenant (1643) were documents of vital importance in developing our democratic constitution in Britain.

The actual text of the Solemn League and Covenant is shorter than that of the National Covenant, and it was signed by people in Scotland, England and Ireland. The document itself represented the opinion of many noblemen, barons, knights, gentlemen, burgesses, citizens and commoners. The agreed uniting factor was that those who signed it would be of 'one reformed Religion' for the sake of 'the true publick Liberty'. After 'mature deliberation' it was resolved that the document would reflect 'the example of the best Reformed Churches' that agreed with a Presbyterian 'form of Church-government', which was democratic and acknowledged Christ as the Head of the Church. Along with this came the section that deplored the hierarchy of the Church of England and called subscribers to endeavour to remove 'Popery, [and] Prelacy (that is, Church-government by Arch-bishops, Bishops ... and all other Ecclesiasticall Officers depending on that Hierarchy)', with its pyramid control structure.

This document was more political than the National Covenant. In section 3 it expressed the subscribers' desire to 'preserve the Rights and Priviledges of the Parliaments, and the Liberties of the Kingdoms.' There was no defiant broadside against the monarchs, for the people were also called to 'defend the Kings [sic] Majesty's Person and Authority', providing those monarchs kept within their boundaries. The leaders were well aware of the 'Malignants' who were scheming and plotting as 'evil instruments', seeking to divide the king from his people, contrary to the League and Covenant. Such people, they agreed, should be judged and punished.

The document finishes with a humble confession of their sins before God, recognizing that the people had not laboured for purity of the faith, and had not always walked in a worthy manner. There is a call for a 'real Reformation' amongst them and a conscious effort to realise that this document should not be signed lightly, because it was a covenant made before a holy God, 'the Searcher of all hearts.' Lastly, there is an 'encouragement to other Christian Churches groaning under, or in danger of the yoke of Antichristian Tyranny ... to joyn in the same, or like Association & Covenant.'[19]

The Solemn League and Covenant stands as a document of great importance, because it combines both the Reformed Christian faith, together with the civil liberties of the English and Scottish Parliaments and people. It also shows how much the Presbyterian model of church democratic governance had impacted the English churches and Parliament in Westminster, at this crucial stage of our long march towards a fairer and more democratic constitution.

---

19. H. Watt, *Recalling the Scottish Covenants* (Thomas Nelson and Sons Ltd, 1946). The entire Solemn League and Covenant document is reproduced in the appendix (pp. 106-109).

Lex Rex: Samuel Rutherford's Revolutionary Book

When the soldiers came for Rev. Samuel Rutherford to arrest him for treason, which would have led to his execution, they found him weak and dying of natural causes, so he was left. It was 1661 and King Charles II was determined to remove all opposition to his desire for absolute rule, and Rutherford was seen as a key agitator and enemy of the State. Rutherford, a Presbyterian pastor, Covenanter, and the Professor of Divinity at the University of St Andrews, had been one of the four main Commissioners representing the Church of Scotland at the Westminster Assembly.

Now, as he lay dying, he reflected on his revolutionary book, *Lex Rex, or The Law and The Prince*, which he had published in London in 1644. In those heady days of Presbyterianism, which had not only transformed Scotland, but had hugely impacted London too, he was recognized as a hero, a Christian celebrity, because of his preaching and his book. Copies of his book had flown off the printing press and had been devoured by intellectuals everywhere, even in the colonies of America. Now, he was a criminal, and copies of his book were being publicly burnt by the hangman at Mercat Cross in Edinburgh's Royal Mile, at St Andrews and in London.

Lex Rex is a tyrant's nightmare. In this extraordinary book, Rutherford outlined his main points: 1. The legal enforcement of a monarch to be stripped of his absolutism and to become a constitutional monarch under law; 2. The government to consist of the House of Lords and the House of Commons, but with the voice of the common people to be properly represented; 3. The democratic constitution of the Presbyterian Church governance should become standard practice, because he believed it was the most biblical, and that Christ is the Head of His Church; 4. The right of the people to arm themselves and defend their rights and freedom against a tyrant.

Although other intellectuals disagreed with him over the issue of a Presbyterian Church governance, his book was dynamic. In the preface he wrote, 'Truth to Christ cannot be treason to

Caesar.' He believed that a biblical view of our constitution would bring the best form of government, even though this might also be tarnished by people's sinfulness. Rutherford promoted what he called 'a sweet mixture' for the best possible government in Britain: a constitutional monarchy, an aristocracy represented by the House of Lords, and a democracy in the House of Commons that fairly represented the voice of the whole nation. All of this, he said, should be under Christ's authority and be based on biblical values, for he believed that a democracy without this biblical structure would eventually end up in anarchy, as Plato had rightly predicted about Athens in *The Republic*.

It was this very structure that Rutherford outlined, which Britain eventually came to develop, something which would be envied by much of the world for centuries. *Lex Rex* had a direct influence on such political activists as the Levellers in the 1640s in London. The leaders of this Christian movement pressed for free elections, influenced by the Presbyterian ideal, but also, in reaction to a more rigid Presbyterian stance, they called for more religious tolerance. What had begun with the Covenanters was being taken by other Christians who would develop a national movement towards democracy and human rights. It was this movement that would in turn influence the philosopher John Locke, who in turn would influence many of the key thinkers of the Enlightenment in Europe, such as Rousseau with *The Social Contract*, Voltaire, Kant, Hume, Adam Smith, and key movers for the American Constitution, such as Thomas Jefferson.

The 1820 Uprising

On 17th September 2015, twenty-seven MSPs from the Scottish Parliament signed their names to an official UK Parliament document, which said:

> That this House recognises the sacrifice of the 1820 martyrs, who gave their lives in the name of equality and democratic reform at a time when ordinary people were denied the vote ... and believes Wilson, Baird and Hardie should be honoured across the UK for

making the ultimate sacrifice for the democratic rights and liberties of ordinary people.[20]

In his book, *The Fight for Scottish Democracy: Rebellion and Reform in 1820*, Murray Armstrong tells the story of a largely forgotten episode in our national history, and of the key people in it who played a significant part in forging democratic freedom for the common man. All over Britain unemployment and poverty stalked the land in the aftermath of the Napoleonic Wars, as the gloom of depression rested on much of the population. Increasingly, voices were being raised in protest at the inequality of a system which had begun to walk forward into a more democratic expression, but which was being crippled and chained back by the political power of the aristocratic élite.

In 1819 Britain was reeling in shock. Over 60,000 people had gathered to peacefully protest about the inequality they faced and to demand the right to vote. On the whole they were ordinary folk wearing their Sunday best with banners unfurled, bearing such captions as, 'The Royton Female Union – Let us Die like Men and not be sold as Slaves,' 'Liberty and Fraternity,' 'Unity and Strength,' and 'Suffrage Universal.' On government orders the cavalry charged into the crowd, hacking and slashing with their swords. After the cavalry had left, the weeping and moaning of the victims could be heard. At least fifteen lay dead, and over six hundred wounded. The Peterloo massacre in Manchester became a byword for tyranny in our history.

In Scotland a strong movement of protest grew, especially in Glasgow, as the people stood with their fellow English. Understandably, some of the protesters began to plan armed self-defence, even as the Covenanters had done almost two hundred years before. The radicals who called for political reform were in two camps: the revolutionaries who believed in a violent overthrow of government, as had happened in the French

20. Official: UK Parliament, Early Day Motions, EDM 485: tables on 17th September 2015, https://edm.parliament.uk.

Revolution, and the constitutionalists, who believed in using educational and political pressure, without violence.

On Easter Sunday that year, posters appeared all over west Scotland entitled, 'Address to the Inhabitants of Great Britain and Ireland.' Crowds of locals gathered to read of the grievances of the masses, of repeated and failed petitions to Westminster, and of the need of a better constitutional government. The constitution, which was promoted, had been 'purchased with the Dearest Blood of our ANCESTORS,' and that it was founded on the Magna Carta and Bill of Rights. This constitution, it was claimed, would bring about the freedom the masses desired and their 'equality of Rights'.[21] It is clear that the Scottish people viewed this movement as a continuation of the Covenanters before them; if aristocratic tyranny had been removed from the church through the sacrifice of the Covenanters and Puritans, then it was now the turn of aristocratic tyranny to be removed from political government.

The three martyrs of the democratic cause in Scotland, who were recognised and celebrated by the twenty-seven MSPs, were James Wilson, John Baird and Andrew Hardie. They were also the main driving force behind this movement. All three were executed by hanging for high treason, and then beheaded: Wilson in Glasgow, and Baird and Hardie in Stirling. Wilson was not a Christian, but was inspired partly through the stand of the Covenanters, and partly through his reading of Thomas Paine's *Rights of Man*. However, it has often been forgotten that Baird and Hardie were Christians. Whilst being held in prison at Stirling they spent much time in prayer and reading their Bibles, encouraging each other in their faith.

As John Baird stood by the scaffold, he spoke to the watching crowd:

'What I would wish particularly to direct your attention to,' he said, 'is … God who is the judge of all mankind, and of all human actions, and to Jesus Christ the saviour of men…. My friends, when you go

---

21. M. Armstrong, *The Fight for Scottish Democracy: Rebellion and Reform in 1820* (London: Pluto Press, 2020), p. 157.

from this place, I entreat you not to go to change-houses, but to go home and take up your Bibles, not as a ballad or as a production of men, but as the work of God Almighty.'[22]

Hardie boldly walked to the front of the scaffold to address the crowd with a similar request. 'Countrymen!' he shouted, 'I declare before God I die as a martyr in the cause of truth and justice .... I recommend it to you not to think of us, but to be peaceable and pay attention to your Bibles, and in place of going to change-houses to drink to the memory of Baird and Hardie, to retire to your devotions.'[23]

As they were hanged together Baird held his New Testament, and Hardie a white handkerchief, as a symbol of approval of the Bible being their inspiration for a just and democratic society.

Voice for the Common Man

In 1848, much of Europe was engulfed in revolutions. Wave after wave of discontent broke out, as the masses, particularly of the poor, had had enough of their treadmill existence under the hand of oppressive regimes. Democracy, liberalism, socialism and nationalism were the key words of the rising generation.

In Britain, the Chartist Movement had been calling the government to pursue a policy of justice and equality. In 1838 the People's Charter was drawn up, largely by William Lovett of the London Working Men's Association. The movement for full democracy was seeing a marked progression since the early days of the Scottish reformers and Covenanters who had influenced the Puritans and Levellers in London. At this time only eighteen per cent of the male adult population could vote, so the People's Charter was seen as a Magna Carta of the people. The document contained six main points:

1. Universal Voting Rights: for all men over twenty-one, except for criminals and the insane.

---

22. ibid., p. 204.
23. ibid.

2. Removal of the Property Qualification: the system only allowed men who owned property up to a certain value to be potentially elected as members of Parliament. This excluded the majority of men in Britain and kept power in the ranks of the landed gentry.

3. Annual Voting in Parliament: rather than every five years, in order to break down power bases in government.

4. Equal Representation: the Chartists proposed dividing Britain into three hundred electoral districts, each with an equal number of inhabitants, with only one MP for each district. Again, the purpose was to promote fairness and equality, and reduce strongholds of power in certain places.

5. Paying MPs: those elected to Parliament were appointed at their own cost, being wealthy gentlemen and able to do so. By far the majority of men in Britain were unable to do this, because they had to work to provide for their families. If payment was given to MPs, then a level playing field for all men would potentially open up.

6. Vote by Secret Ballot: traditionally men raised their hands to vote and the numbers were counted. However, if the employers or landowners saw their staff or tenants voting against their preferences, they could fire or remove them. Posting a vote in a secret ballot would prevent this abuse.

When the People's Charter was launched on 21st May 1838, on Glasgow Green before a crowd estimated to be about 150,000 people, its influence soon spread far and wide throughout Britain. The mass rally had been organised by Glasgow's trade unions, with the two main speakers being Thomas Murphy and Rev. Dr Arthur Wade. When Rev. Wade held up the document and announced, 'I hold in my hand a charter – the People's Charter,' he expected a great cheer, but instead he was met by silence, just as the great Sarah Siddons had been in her premier performance as Belvidera, in *Venice Preserv'd* at Edinburgh's Theatre Royal during the previous century. But soon the

Scots were buzzing as they understood the significance of the moment. It was two centuries since the Scots had supported another Magna Carta for religious freedom, when they had raised their hands, tears streaming down their faces, and signed the National Covenant of 1638.

Wade had been chosen by the London Working Men's Association to represent them and the People's Charter. Admiration had accompanied him from the disenfranchised masses since he had led the peaceful protest with Robert Owen and had stood, fully regaled in his clerical and scholar's gown, at the great Tolpuddle demonstration in 1834. Out of Wesley's revivals in England had come the class meetings, in which rich and poor, common and aristocratic, had sat side by side as equals before Christ to study the Bible. From this Methodist movement had sprung the Tolpuddle Martyrs, a group of six men, mostly Christians, who were led by the Methodist preacher George Loveless.

Surrounded by poverty caused by the abusively small wages given to them by their landowners, they set up the first Trade Union, called The Friendly Society of Agricultural Labourers, and soon their catchy slogan was being heard by many: 'A fair day's wage for a fair day's work.' They were shipped off to Australia as criminals by the government, but in their absence Rev. Wade, Robert Owen, and others stood for them, organising a national petition for their release and for fair pay. With 250,000 signatures presented to Parliament and an army of 30,000 peaceful protesters lined up in London, the government backed down, enacted a law to protect workers, and brought back the 'criminals' to a heroes' welcome. Rev. Wade was highly esteemed by the working classes and non-conformist Christians for his brave stand; but many of his fellow Anglican clergy in England spat out their hatred and vitriol, the bishop even banning him from preaching.

Out of the Trade Union movement grew the Chartist movement, and several philosophies grew side by side in the progress towards freedom: Christian Socialist; Marxist, and others. Most followed Rev. Wade's desire for a peaceful and constitutional transformation of our system of government; yet others would seek a more violent response to speed up the change. In Scotland there were even twenty Chartist churches by 1841.[24] It was clear though that such a transformation would not come easily, because most of the aristocrats and landed gentry would oppose it all the way. The first petition in 1839 for the People's Charter was presented by Thomas Attwood to the House of Commons with almost 1.3 million signatures, but was rejected. A second attempt was made in 1842 with a petition containing three million signatures, but again it was turned down. On 10th April 1848, a mass gathering appeared on Kennington Common in south London. Although there had been some violent scuffles with the police by some of the more extremist Chartists in various parts of Britain, leading to some deaths, the organisers of the Great Gathering had made their intention clear. The handbill for the peaceful protest of about 150,000 people said:

Chartist Demonstration! 'Peace and Order' is our Motto.

We and our families are pining in misery, want and starvation! We demand a fair day's wage for a fair day's work! We are slaves of the capital – we demand protection to our labour. We are political serfs – we demand to be free.

Although the protesters were surrounded by police, everything was done in a peaceful and orderly way. Understandably, Parliament was deeply worried about an uprising in Britain, for they had watched nation after nation embroiled in revolution and death in Europe as the underclasses strove to shake off the shackles of monarchies and controlling systems to bring about democracy and equality. But yet again, the petition for the People's Charter was rejected. By the 1850s the Chartist movement began to die down, but their legacy stirred others to press on with transformation.

First came the Reform Act of 1867, with only partial success; then the Reform Act of 1884, by which time about sixty per cent of men could vote. But it would not be until 1918 that five out of

---

24. Tom Devine, *The Scottish Nation, 1700–2000* (Penguin, 2000), p. 279.

the six proposals of the People's Charter would be accepted and implemented by Parliament: the proposal of an annual election being rejected. With the reform in 1918 would also come the victory for the Suffragettes, and for the first time, women could be elected as MPs, with full voting for all men and women by 1928.

Deliverance from Revolution

The question often asked by historians is: Why did Britain not erupt into a bloody revolution, like many other nations in 1848? In *The Guardian* newspaper archives there is an entry, written on 7th October, 1848. It simply says that Britain avoided revolution due to 'the instinctive good sense and practical turn of mind of the English nation'.[25] Lord Shaftesbury, 'the Poor Man's Earl,' held to a different conclusion, based on accumulated knowledge of what was really going on below the surface. At the Annual Meeting of Edinburgh City Mission at Wemyss Bay, he gave an extraordinary speech to the missionaries and their supporters in 1874:

> 'Were it not,' he said, 'for the London City Mission, and other kindred associations, I really know not what would be the condition of the metropolis of London. But I am certain of this, that if God had not put it into the heart of excellent men like David Nasmyth, of whom all Scotsmen may well boast, some five and thirty years ago, to found and carry on the London City Mission, and kindred institutions, the metropolis of London, and a very large proportion of the empire of Great Britain would have been totally uninhabitable by anyone who pretended to civilization, morality and religion.... I remember the great Revolution of 1848, when, as you know, every throne was in the dust .... I remember, after that day, talking with M. Guizot, who had been Prime Minister of France, when he said, "I will tell you what saved your empire. It was not your constables; it was not your army; it was not your ministers, it was the deep, solemn, religious atmosphere ... it is the religion of England that saved the empire of Great Britain." He was right ... Sir George Grey

---

25. Richard Nelsson, *The Guardian 1848: Europe's year of revolution – from the archive*, Friday, 18th May 2018, quoting from *Editorial: Social Duties and Political Rights*, 7th October 1848.

said to me, "I am satisfied, as Secretary of State, that London could not have been kept in order, had not the state of mind been prepared by the operations of associations such as these."[26]

So much of our history lies buried in the dust; we forget so easily. Most of us in Scotland have never even heard of David Nasmith, the Scottish Christian pioneer from Glasgow. Donald Lewis, in his revealing book, *Lighten Their Darkness: The Evangelical Mission to Working-Class London, 1828–1860*, has with scholarly integrity mounted the evidence for a transformation of London through the evangelical Christian movement. Spearheading the charge to reach the poor was the London City Mission (LCM), established in 1835 by David Nasmith. Following Dr Thomas Chalmers' strategy, the swelling ranks of missionaries focused their efforts on the underbelly of a rotting society never seen by the average Londoner; it was an underground network of degradation, drunkenness, and despair: a cauldron of seething hatred and anger towards the system that held them captive. Few seemed to care; few tried to understand them; few would risk life and limb to operate a rescue mission within a metre of hell. And then God sent a Scotsman.

Lewis records that by 1848 there were two hundred and one LCM missionaries working amongst the warrens of darkness in London, and that they were assisted by thousands of volunteers. By 1860, LCM employed three hundred and seventy-five missionaries.[27] These agents of mercy shared the hope of Christ; clothed the naked; fed the hungry; restored the alcoholics, prostitutes and criminals, through God's help. They became the bridge between the disenfranchised and the Christian reformers in Parliament who worked on their behalf, like Shaftesbury and Buxton. Lord Shaftesbury himself addressed the LCM Annual Meeting, just weeks after the great Chartist gathering on

26. Speech of the Earl of Shaftesbury at Wemyss Bay, autumn, 1874, ECM Annual Report, 1874: pp. 11-12.

27. Donald M. Lewis, *Lighten Their Darkness: The Evangelical Mission to Working-Class London, 1828–1860*, Appendix B (Greenwood Press, 1986).

Kennington Common in 1848, when Parliament was trembling at the thought of revolution in London:

> 'I am here,' he said, 'to bear my testimony to the very great debt which the public owes to you, and to your missionaries, for having developed to the world a state of things, of which nineteen-twentieths of the educated and easy part of this great metropolis were just as ignorant as they are of what is going on upon the left horn of the moon .... They [the LCM missionaries] have proved to us that there are thousands and tens of thousands living in the courts and alleys of this great metropolis, in a condition disgusting to every sense, and ten times more fearful when contemplated in a spiritual aspect. For years and years these people continued to live and to multiply, and yet their existence was just as much unknown as are the inhabitants of many an undiscovered island at the present moment .... I will not hesitate to say, it is my firm belief, that in the late confusion and difficulty which seemed to hang over this metropolis, the agency of the London City Mission, along with other bodies of like character, did most materially contribute to keep the whole metropolis at peace. Large masses of this community have learned that they are really cared for, and that there are persons who make it their constant and unceasing business to consider their temporal and eternal welfare. I do not believe that ten years ago this town could have withstood the mighty shock that came from the Continent.'[28]

One contemporary journalist wrote that 'Clerkenwell [in London] ... is the locality of dirt, and ignorance, and vice – the recesses whereof are known but to the disguised policeman ... or the poor, shabby genteel City Missionary, as he kneels at midnight by the foul straw of some convulsed and dying outcast.'[29] It was this Christian love that softened the hearts of a desperate people and helped save our nation from a bloody revolution.

---

28. ibid., pp. 168 and 172, quoting from *LCM Thirteenth Annual Report in LCM Magazine* (June 1848), pp. 126-28.

29. ibid., p. 128, quoted from *Illustrated London News*, 22nd May 1847, cited by R. W. Vanderkiste, *Notes and Narratives of a Six Year Mission*, London, 1852, p. 5.

Keir Hardie and the Labour Party

When the American evangelist D. L. Moody embarked on his Glasgow tour, seeing revival and the transformation of thousands of lives as he preached the gospel, a teenage son of unbelieving parents listened raptly in Lanarkshire. Three years later, in 1877, this young man wrote in his diary, 'Today I have given my life to Jesus Christ.'[30] His name was James Keir Hardie, and he would go on to become the founder of the Labour Party, and the leading voice for the common man in Britain. The prayers of his ancestor martyr, Andrew Hardie, were being answered.

As with many evangelical Christians of the time, Keir Hardie pursued a Christian worldview, which, for him personally meant living out his faith in the world of politics and social action. It was this faith that carried him through the rough sea of politics and burned brightly in him right to his death, causing him to write in 1910 that 'The impetus which drove me first of all into the Labour movement and inspiration which carried me on it, has been derived more from the teachings of Jesus Christ of Nazareth than all other sources combined.'[31]

It was when the Labour Party finally came into being in London in 1900, that our British political constitution was forged as we now know it, bringing the vital pressure on Parliament for the voice of the common man to be heard. It had been a long and complex journey from when another Scottish Christian, Rev. Samuel Rutherford, had published his *Lex Rex* in 1644, but what had now been established peacefully became the envy of much of the world.

Democracy to the Nations

In 2012 a ground-breaking article was published in the *American Political Science Review*. Robert Woodberry, then the Associate Professor at the University of Singapore, submitted his thesis that

---

30. Lennie, *Scotland Ablaze*, pp. 523-24, quoted from Donald Carswell, *Brother Scots* (London, 1927), p. 164.

31. ibid., p. 524, quoted from Stephen Timms, MP, *Christianity and Politics*, cited from *The Bible in Transmission*, autumn 2001.

Protestant Christian missionaries had been the main contributing factor to the rise of modern democracy in much of the world. Building on the work of previous scholars, he opened his thesis with the following words:

> This article demonstrates historically and statistically that conversionary Protestants (CPs) heavily influenced the rise and spread of stable democracy around the world. It argues that CPs were a crucial catalyst initiating the development and spread of religious liberty, mass education, mass printing, newspapers, voluntary organizations, and colonial reforms, thereby creating the conditions that made stable democracy more likely. Statistically, the historic prevalence of Protestant missionaries explains about half the variation in democracy in Africa, Asia, Latin America and Oceania and removes the impact of most variables that dominate current statistical research about democracy. The association between Protestant missions and democracy is consistent in different continents and subsamples, and it is robust to more than 50 controls and to instrumental variable analyses.[32]

As he dug back into history, Woodberry soon realised that the Calvinistic/Presbyterian Christian democratic model was responsible for shaping the rise of modern democracy, rather than the Athenian Greek model. '[M]ost Enlightenment democratic theorists came from Calvinist families or had a Calvinist education,' he wrote, 'even if they were either not theologically orthodox or personally religious (e.g., John Locke, Rousseau, Hugo Grotius, Benjamin Franklin, John Adams, Patrick Henry, James Madison, and Alexander Hamilton) ... and they secularized ideas previously articulated by Calvinist theologians and jurists. For example, Hobbes' and Locke's social contracts are secular versions of Puritan and Nonconformist covenants, and Locke's ideas about the equality of all people are explicitly religious.'[33]

---

32. Robert Woodberry, *The Missionary Roots of Liberal Democracy*, American Political Science Review, Vol.106, No.2 (May 2012), p. 244. Robert Woodberry is now the Senior Research Professor at Baylor University.

33. ibid., p. 248.

Roderick Graham, an Edinburgh historian, wrote the ground-breaking work, *John Knox: Democrat*. Bucking the trend of contemporary critics of Knox, he concludes his thought-provoking book with the words:

> The reformed Church was a democratic Church. Knox's ideal state was democratic. John Knox was a democrat. The ideal he gave Scotland as a legacy was of a democratic state, caring for its weakest members, with free education available to all, fiercely independent and with its own voice in Europe. Time will tell what we have done with that legacy.[34]

---

34. Roderick Graham, *John Knox: Democrat* (London: Robert Hale Ltd, 2003), p. 354.

CHAPTER 7

HUMAN RIGHTS

'Britain is the most racist country in the world,' the Sudanese man explained to me near the University of Edinburgh. 'Seriously, you have to do something about this systemic racism and appalling human rights in this country; it's terrible.' I stood looking at him speechless and paralysed by his statement. He had come from a nation which has undergone some of the worst atrocities in the world this century during the civil war, but he seemed blind to this. The government there has also been implicit in the genocide and ethnic cleansing of the people of Darfur. This man's extraordinary and unbalanced statement demonstrated that he was the victim of Critical Race Theory.

In September 2019, student activists held a conference at the University of Edinburgh called 'Resisting Whiteness', implying that whiteness in Scotland is an evil to be opposed. During question time white people were prohibited from asking any questions, because the event was labelled a 'safe space' for ethnic minorities. Such an event is also the fruit of the Critical Race Theory, the belief that white people are born with racism and that racism is 'systemic' in white-based cultures. This movement is being led by such academics as Robin DiAngelo, bell hooks (her grammar), Derrick Bell and Kimberlé Crenshaw, whose dogma is spreading throughout all areas of Western life. DiAngelo in her book *White Fragility* (2018) makes sweeping statements, such as 'all white people are racist' and that whiteness means 'white supremacy'. Apparently, all white people are born with the sin of racism and are hopelessly enslaved by it. Worse still, white people are the root cause of all racism in history and the world.

It is a freezing winter's day, and yet another boat, almost sinking under the weight of refugees, arrives in Britain. The shivering and desperate people disembark, rejoicing that they have arrived safely after many harrowing ordeals. Many are Iraqis, Syrians, Africans, Iranians, Afghans and others. Why have they made these dangerous crossings? What has driven them to such an extreme course of action? Some are seeking a better economic life in the West, but most have come with horrendous tales of atrocities experienced in their own countries, where human rights do not exist for so many. They have fled to the West and to Britain to escape brutality and to be treated as human beings. For them issues of equality, freedom, rule of just law and human rights are the reason why they have left everything and faced so many dangers and trials to arrive here.

The Western model might not be perfect in its human rights, but it offers the best available system in a sinful world. Why else would 330,000 immigrants seek to enter the European Union without authorization in 2022, besides the millions of others who have fled to Europe looking for freedom during the last few years? Why would 504,000 more immigrants arrive than emigrants leave in the United Kingdom in the same year?[1] Why would 45,756 come illegally here by small boats, risking their very lives?[2] Are so many really choosing to come to Britain knowing that the human rights here are apparently the 'worst' in the world? Why don't they flee to China or North Korea? Thus, we see the strange world of Critical Race Theory in the cold light of hard reality.

Scotland's Magna Carta?

At an early hour it seemed that the whole city of Edinburgh was astir and moving en masse. They came in small groups and crowds,

---

1. Office for National Statistics: Long-term international migration, provisional: year ending June 2022.

2. *The Guardian*: 'Channel Crossings: 45,756 people came to UK in small boats in 2022,' Jessica Elgot, Sunday 1st January 2023.

converging on Greyfriars Kirk. Some were chatting excitedly, but others were deep in their own thoughts. Over the next few days, it was estimated that about 60,000 people had come to support this special event,[3] a remarkable number since the population of the city was only about 40,000 in those days.

Of all the milestones in the history of Scotland, 28th February 1638 stands out as being one of the most important: it was the date of the signing of the National Covenant in Greyfriars' Kirk, Edinburgh. This document has been called the 'Magna Carta' of Scotland by some,[4] and the 'Phanatical covenants' by others.[5] Enshrined within its text is a covenant of the Presbyterians to God that they would stand for their faith. It was the first time in history that a large part of a nation had covenanted with God, with the exception of Israel. Those who signed it were called Covenanters, and by doing so they were reaffirming their Reformed Faith, at the same time as sending out a petition to the king and authorities for freedom of faith and conscience in Scotland. It would trigger off a movement towards human rights, but the path ahead would end up being one of the darkest periods in our history. For Archibald Johnston, the lawyer who worked with Rev. Alexander Henderson to draw up the document, it was the 'gloriest day that ever Scotland saw since the Reformation.'[6]

---

3. Alexander Peterkin, 1780–1846; Andrew Dickson White, 1832–1918. *Records of the Kirk of Scotland: containing the acts and proceedings of the General Assemblies, from the year 1638 downwards, as authenticated by the clerks of assembly: with notes and historical illustrations*, p. 14, by the Church of Scotland, General Assembly (Edinburgh: John Sutherland, 1838).

4. *The Letters and Journals of Robert Baillie*, Principal of the University of Glasgow, Vol. I, p. 38, Letter to his cousin William Spang, 7th December 1637, Bannatyne Club, 1841, David Laing.

5. Sir George Mackenzie, *A Vindication of the Government in Scotland during the Reign of King Charles II against Mis-Representations made in several Scandalous Pamphlets to which is added the method of proceeding against criminals, as also some of the Phanatical Covenants as they were printed and published by themselves in that reign*. First printed in London in 1691 and reprinted in Edinburgh by James Watson in 1712.

6. *Diary of Sir Archibald Johnston of Wariston (1632–1639), edited from the original Manuscript with notes and Introduction*, 27th February 1638, p. 322, by

In Britain we have tended to focus on the vital milestones towards human rights, such as the Magna Carta (1215), the Petition of Right (1628), Habeas Corpus (1679) and The English Bill of Rights (1689), but have often left out the special place the Scots played in this development, especially in the seventeenth century. It would be the Scottish influence that would have particular relevance for the American Declaration of Independence (1776), and, surprisingly, the French Declaration of the Rights of Man and the Citizen (1789), and the American Bill of Rights (1791), all of which would have a huge impact on shaping the United Nations Charter for Human Rights (1948).

In order to understand the necessity of the National Covenant and its subsequent developments, we will need to retrace our steps back to the time of King Henry VIII, so that we can appreciate the background for such a document. Henry VIII was desperate for a son as his heir to the throne, but his marriage to Catherine of Aragon did not produce the desired outcome. Pretty Anne Boleyn had already caught his attention, so he sought to divorce the forty-year-old Catherine and marry Anne, but Pope Clement VII rejected this. Henry, used to getting his own way, broke from Rome, and in 1534 he became the Supreme Head of the Church of England through the Act of Supremacy. At one time he had been awarded the title of Defender of the Faith by Pope Leo X for his work called *Defence of the Seven Sacraments*, in which he defended the supremacy of the pope against Luther, but now he ceased to be a *Roman* Catholic, but remained a Catholic in his beliefs. In effect, Henry VIII had now removed the pope and had become the King-Pope of the Church of England.

Most people were too frightened to speak out against what he had done, and if they did, they were imprisoned or executed, as in the case of the Observant Friars and Sir Thomas More. Many of the Protestants thought it would be safer under Henry

---

George Morison Paul Ltd, Edinburgh, printed at the University Press by T. and A. Constable for the Scottish History Society, 1911.

than under the pope, and they hoped for further reformation in the church, but many of them were also imprisoned and treated cruelly. Unfortunately, the Bible translator William Tyndale was supportive of Henry's unbiblical position,[7] along with Archbishop Thomas Cranmer, and many others, but it is easy for us to be critical today, having hindsight and not realising that the Reformation was a work in progress. We must also bear in mind the atrocities that Protestants had received from the papal system, so for the English people who were developing a more Reformed view, Henry was still better news than the pope.

The egotistical nature of Henry VIII shone through during his reign. Between 1536 and 1541, during the Dissolution of the Monasteries, the huge income and wealth in assets was stripped from the Roman Catholics and given to feed his own greed, and that of his nobles, and to fund his military campaigns in the 1540s.

Besides the killing of many Roman Catholics, Henry set about exterminating Protestant reformers who dared to distribute Tyndale's English New Testament and preach the gospel and Reformed views. Among them were Frith and Lambert, the friends of Patrick Hamilton the Scottish Reformer, who, as with Hamilton and others, were burnt alive. People were even imprisoned for teaching their children the Lord's Prayer in English.[8] In 1539, Henry's Parliament passed The Six Articles, which was called by the reformers 'the whip with six strings'. In an attempt to force uniformity Henry, as 'by God's Law Supreme Head' of the church, compelled people to accept the following: the Roman Mass and transubstantiation; a reversion back to celibacy of the priests, meaning that married clergy had to dispose of their wives, or leave the church; private Masses; and

---

7. William Tyndale, *The Obedience of a Christen man, and how Christen rulers ought to govern, wherein also (if thou mark diligently) thou shalt find eyes to perceive the crafty convience of all iugglers*, section 38 forward, published in 1528.

8. John Foxe, *Foxe's Book of Martyrs*, J. Milner and I. Cobbin (London: Morgan Scott), p. 324.

auricular confession.[9] By law, those who disagreed with these articles, 'shall suffer ... imprisonment and make such fine and ransom to the King our Sovereign Lord ... shall suffer pains of death and lose and forfeit all his ... goods, lands, and tenements, as in cases of felony.'[10]

When therefore Henry VIII's descendants came to power they inherited such a tyrannical system against the reformers. His beloved son, Edward VI, showed from such a young age an acute interest and desire for a genuine biblical faith as England's first Protestant king, but he was a candle that burned brightly for a short while before being snuffed out, leaving the power in the hands of his half-sister, Mary Tudor. Mary sought to bring England back to Rome and had almost three hundred reformers burnt at the stake, including three bishops, and Archbishop Thomas Cranmer.

James VI and the Union of Crowns

When Mary, Queen of Scots, had a son called James, who was born in Edinburgh Castle, he would be destined to the throne after his mother had been forced to abdicate. Being brought up in a very Protestant environment, and being tutored by the Reformer-scholar George Buchanan, meant that he would grow up with a well-educated background and with a Reformed opinion. At the age of only fifteen he signed what was called *The King's Confession*, or *The Negative Confession* (1581), which was a covenant drawn up with his agreement, supporting the Reformed 'Kirke of Scotland ... as more particularly is expressed in the Confession of our Faith [1560], stablished, and publicly

---

9. Auricular Confession means the practice of a priest hearing the confession of sin from a person in private, and having the power to absolve or forgive that sin. Although private confession of sins to trusted persons was practiced in the early church (James 5:16), the reformers believed that the Roman Catholic papal system had gone too far in giving power to the priests to forgive others' sins when the people needed to go to their High Priest, Christ Himself.

10. The Six Articles of 1539 can be found in the *Documents of the English Reformation*, edited by Gerald Bray, Series: Library of Ecclesiastical History, edition 3, The Lutterworth Press, James Clarke & Co Ltd, 1994.

confirmed by sundry Acts of Parliament, and now of a long time has been openly professed by the King's Majesty, and the whole body of this Realm both in borough and in land.'[11]

The 'negative' part of the document highlights the reformers' rejection of Roman Catholicism with its 'Roman Antichrist' and 'All his tyrannous laws ... against our Christian liberty,' and 'His erroneous doctrine against the sufficiency of the written word, the perfection of the law, the office of Christ, and his blessed Evangel [gospel].' There then follows a list of practices which have been rejected by the Scottish Reformed church: the Mass; purgatory; praying to the saints, and so on. They also rejected the pope's 'worldly monarchy and wicked hierarchy', meaning the cardinals and bishops who ruled in their palaces as lords and oppressors over the people.

Embedded in this covenant are the words 'Christ our head', and the binding agreement, 'that we shall defend his person and authority [the King of Scotland], with our gear [possessions], bodies, and lives, in the defence of Christ's Evangel [gospel], liberty of our country, ministration of justice, and punishment of iniquity against all enemies, within this realm or without.'

The 'Confession of our Faith' referred to above was the Scots Confession of 1560, which had been legally ratified by the Scottish Parliament, and sealed by King James himself. In the Scots Confession it clearly states that 'Christ Jesus [is] ... the only Head of his Kirk .... In such honours and offices, if man or angel presume to intrude themselves, we utterly detest and abhor them, as blasphemous to our Sovereign and supreme Governor Christ Jesus.'[12] With this, there came the solemn pledge 'to save the lives of innocents, to repress tyranny, to defend the oppressed ...'[13]

Again, in the Scots Confession it is clear that the church must not rebel against the king and authority: 'Therefore we confess

---

11. *Scots Confession*, 1560 and *Negative Confession*, 1581, with an introduction by Professor G. D. Henderson of Aberdeen University, Church of Scotland Committee on Publications, Edinburgh, 1937, p. 103.

12. ibid., 1560: Article XI, p. 59.

13. ibid., Article XIV, p. 65.

and avow that those who resist the supreme powers, *as long as they are acting in their own spheres*, are resisting God's ordinance and cannot be held guiltless. We further state that *so long as princes and rulers vigilantly fulfill their office*, anyone who denies them aid, counsel, or service, denies it to God, who by his lieutenant craves it of them [my emphasis in italics].'

The Second Book of Discipline, compiled in 1578, made the distinction between Christ as Head of the Church and an earthly leader or king so clear that nobody could have mistaken it:

> For this ecclesiastical power flows immediately from God, and the Mediator Jesus Christ, and is spiritual, not having a temporal head on earth, but only Christ, the only spiritual King and Governor of his kirk. It is a title falsely usurped by Antichrist to call himself head of the kirk, and ought not to be attributed to angel nor man, of what estate that ever he is, saving to Christ, the only Head and Monarch of the kirk.[14]

In short, the Church of Scotland was legally bound to honour Christ as the only Head of the Church, and no religious leader, king, or even an angel, should take Christ's rightful place. The people must also defend the king, as long as he was not oppressing the people and acting in tyranny over them, or usurping the place of Christ. They would not accept the Romanist style of popes, cardinals, and political bishops. To this covenant the Scottish Parliament and King James VI were also legally bound. It would be these very issues that would cause deep conflict in the years to come.

At the time when King James VI signed *The Negative Confession* in 1581, Scotland and England were separate countries with their own kings and parliaments. This all changed with a single blow at the Union of Crowns, when in 1603, King James became the VI of Scotland and I of England. The Scots were delighted that a Stuart king would come to such a prominent position and they celebrated, believing that peace between the two nations had been achieved, with their freedom being honoured.

---

14. *Second Book of Discipline* (1578), 'Of the Kirk and Policy Thereof in General, and Wherein it is Different from the Civil Policy,' 1:5-6.

However, James was also appointed as the Supreme Head of the Church of England. Most of Scotland was not impressed, but they had their own independent church and their own church constitution, which was legally binding. James showed great support of the church in England, being the patron of the team of scholars who translated the Bible in 1611 from the ancient Hebrew and Greek into the English of the day, something which gave huge benefits for many nations in the centuries to come. But another thought was nagging away at him: if he were the Supreme Head of the Church of England, why could he not also make the church uniform and become the Supreme Head of the Church of Scotland as well?

In 1610 King James was overreaching himself, seeking to raise finance without parliamentary consent, leading to a disagreement between them. The Puritan lawyer, Sir Edward Coke, later raised the concerned cry of many, 'I must fly to Magna Charta [sic] ... the Charter of Liberty,' he said. 'When the king says he cannot allow our liberties of right, this strikes at the root.'[15] Coke and others resisted the king on this matter and drew up The Case of Proclamations, in which the king was not allowed to be above the law and proclaim what he wanted. It was summed up in the following line: 'the King by his proclamation of other ways cannot change any part of the common law, or statute law, or the customs of the realm.'[16] Not only was the church on a collision course with the Crown, but Parliament as well, on both sides of the border.

Black Saturday

King James, egged on by his bishops, decided he would muscle in and force the Presbyterians to submit to him as Head of the Church, and do away with their democratic system, imposing

---

15. C. D. Bowen, *The Lion and the Throne, the Life and Times of Sir Edward Coke 1552–1634* (Hamish Hamilton Publishers, 1957), p. 453.

16. Neutral Citation Number: [1610] EWHC KB J22, 77 ER 1352, (1611) 12 Co Rep 74, November 1610, England and Wales High Court (King's Bench Division) Decisions, Open Law, JISC, Bailii.

instead his bishops – his religious and political statesmen. The word 'tyranny' was beginning to be whispered in the corridors; but very few spoke boldly against him. With the Five Articles of Perth forced upon the Church of Scotland in 1618, it effectively became Episcopal against the will of most of the people. The assembly met at Perth, the diocese of Archbishop Spottiswoode, with him acting as Moderator. The assembly was deliberately filled with bishops and supporters of the king. Voters were told that if they voted against the Five Articles, they would be reported to the king. When voting took place, the Presbyterians lost. King James convened Parliament in Edinburgh three years later, when the government made the Episcopalian Church law in Scotland so that King James could control the church through his bishops. Some ministers were imprisoned, or forced out of their churches for protesting. It was known as Black Saturday in Scotland.

King Charles I: The Noose of Tyranny Tightens

When King James VI and I died in 1625, his son, Charles I, ascended to the throne over the three nations of England, Scotland and Ireland. In that same year he married Henrietta, the devout Roman Catholic daughter of King Henry IV of France and Marie de Medici. Such a marriage was bound to send shock waves throughout the Protestant world. The St Bartholomew's Day massacre of thousands of Protestants in 1572 in France was still fresh in the minds of many, and Catherine de Medici, a relative of Marie, was attributed as being the person behind this. Moreover, Henry IV's first wife, Margaret de Valois, was the daughter of Catherine de Medici and sister of Elizabeth de Valois, wife of King Philip II of Spain, who had commanded the Spanish Armada against England in 1588.

Apart from the genuine Protestant fear of being taken back to Rome, the parliamentarians also began to face growing tyranny from King Charles I. In 1627, in breach of the law, he tried to raise money for the war against France through a forced loan, a tax levied without Parliament's consent. The following year the Puritan Sir Edward Coke drew up *The Petition of Right* in London, challenging King Charles' autocratic behaviour. The House of Commons stood against the king to stop him: a) levying taxes without Parliament's consent; b) imposing martial law on civilians; c) imprisoning people without trial; and d) quartering soldiers in people's homes. Charles I was furious at what he thought was the meddling of Parliament with his right as a king to do as he pleased, and in 1629 he dissolved Parliament for eleven years, as well as imprisoning nine members of the House of Commons. By now there were deep concerns that England would lose its Magna Carta freedom and return to the days of absolute monarchs.

With the Parliament in Westminster gagged, Charles decided not only to challenge the law, but the church too. He appointed the Anglo-Catholic William Laud as Archbishop of Canterbury and gave him instructions to conform the Church of Scotland to his preference. When he was crowned King of Scotland in Edinburgh's St Giles in 1633, Charles made a point of having the ceremony performed by a bishop who would provide an Anglo-Catholic service. Charles I also supported Archbishop Laud's move in 1637 to have the Anglicised Book of Common Prayer read out in St Giles, without the consent of the Church of Scotland, or the Scottish Parliament. Kirk sessions and presbyteries established by Parliament in the Presbyterian Great Charter of 1592 were abolished and called 'conventicles' and became outlawed, clandestine meetings.

Of the fourteen bishops introduced, nine of them were part of the king's Privy Council, thus combining leaders of religion and politics under the headship of Charles I. It was what Peterkin called 'a conclave of despotism, entirely subservient to the king.'[17] Peterkin continues: 'The new order of things, therefore, was not a mere institution of Episcopacy, in which only spiritual jurisdiction was conferred ... but it was palpably a political engine, incompatible with the existence of civil liberty or freedom

---

17. Peterkin et al, p. 6.

of conscience in matters of religion; and this innovation became universally obnoxious to the whole nation.'[18]

This, then, is the backdrop to the signing of the National Covenant of 1638. As we can see, the growth of oppression against freedom of conscience and speech, whether in religion or politics, was a slow process: for the Reformed Protestants there was the fear of being forced back under the tyranny of Rome with the dire consequences of the kind of massacres seen in France and Europe, and for the parliamentarians there was the fear of being forced back under the yoke of the medieval feudal system under the tyranny of the king, who himself would bow in allegiance to the pope. It was this deep concern of both Reformed Protestants and parliamentarians that would drive them together as they faced a common enemy. It would be this combination, largely inspired by the Presbyterian democratic practice, which would eventually lead to a movement for democracy and human rights based on a Christian foundation: but its journey would be long, complex, and costly.

'Villain! Daurst Thou Say the Mass at me Lug!'

On 23rd July 1637, St Giles was packed to overflowing. Tension in the High Kirk was already tangible. As the Dean of Edinburgh read out the new liturgy from the Anglicised Book of Common Prayer, anxiety filled the minds of many. The city was filled with murmurings about the enforced policies of Charles I, about his Romanist wife, and growing fears of a return to Rome. All it would take would be a small match to be lit and the nation would be ablaze with contention. Dean Hannay, hoping that the people would allow him to lead the service peacefully, was just getting to the bit about church communion, when all of a sudden, a woman got up and shouted, 'Villain! Daurst thou say the Mass at me lug!'

---

18. ibid. It is to be noted that not *all* of Scotland disliked the policies of Charles I. He had his followers among the nobility and others, and particularly among the Episcopalian and Roman Catholic population in the Highlands and Islands.

('Dare you say the Mass in my ear!'). Throwing her stool at the Dean in the pulpit, she was joined by others with shouts and with the casting of sticks and objects at the poor man. The fire had been lit. It is difficult to know whether there was a woman called Jenny Geddes, who according to tradition, was the person mentioned above, but certainly a riot broke out in St Giles.[19]

Robert Baillie, a contemporary and later Principal at the University of Glasgow, recorded the event: 'The serving maids began such a tumult, as was never heard of since the Reformation in our nation .... The rascal multitude .... There was great fear for the King's wrath: the town and country did quake.'[20] The women, in particular, seemed to be irate. Baillie tells us that about nine o'clock that night, whilst Bishop Annan and some minister friends were walking in the Old Town, 'some hundreds of enraged women, of all qualities, are about him, with knives, and staves ... they beat him sore.'[21] In his view, Baillie thought these protesters were 'possessed with a bloody devil'.[22] The mood of the nation, however, was full of foreboding, as Baillie expresses: 'The whole people thinks popery at the doors .... The barricades of Paris, the Catholic League of France, is much before my eyes; but I hope the devil shall never find a Duke of Guise to lead the bands .... I think I may be killed and my house burnt upon my head.'[23]

Petitions came streaming in from diverse places: from Ayr, Fife, the Lothians, Stirling, and elsewhere, as people sought justice from their leaders in the Scottish Parliament and Council in Edinburgh. Everything was so chaotic and fragmentary. Sensing the need of a calm, peaceful, legal and united petition

---

19. Rosalind K. Marshall, *St Giles': The Dramatic Story of a Great Church and its People* (Saint Andrew Press, 2009), pp. 82-84. Marshall says that the woman may have been called Barbara Mein. There was a Jenny Geddes who sold fruit in the Royal Mile in the 1660s, but there is no eyewitness reference to her.

20. Baillie, *The Letters and Journals*, p. 18.

21. ibid, p. 21.

22. ibid., p. 23.

23. ibid., pp. 23-24.

for freedom of faith and conscience, some of the nobles and clergy met together to discuss drawing up a national covenant to present to the king and his authorities. It was decided at the General Assembly of the Church of Scotland in Glasgow in 1638 that Rev. Alexander Henderson should be chosen to put together such a document, for 'he was incomparably the ablest man of us all, for all things.'[24] Archibald Johnston of Warriston was also chosen as an able lawyer to put together the legal part of the document.

The National Covenant of 1638

Even though Henderson and Johnston were the key people in producing the National Covenant, it had to go through a process of being affirmed by the supporting nobles, then by a group of over two hundred church ministers, and then ratified by the Scottish Parliament. The actual document was produced on vellum and is in three parts: 1. The Negative Confession of 1580–1, copied word-for-word from the original, which had been signed by King James VI (and I of England), by the nobles and political leaders, and by the church leaders; 2. The legal backing of the Presbyterian Church, which had been ratified 'by manifold acts of Parliament'[25] which had been put together by Johnston; 3. The reasons for the Covenant, for which people would stand, agree upon, and sign: this last section was produced by Henderson.

In the last part, Henderson recalled the vow made by monarchs at their coronation, that they would 'serve the same Eternal God to the uttermost of their power, according as He hath required in His most Holy Word, contained in the old and new Testament ... and shall abolish and gainstand all false Religion contrary to the same.' Henderson then pointed out the 'foresaid crimes' of Charles I in 1633 at his coronation. This is followed by the oath of the nobles, barons, burgesses, ministers and common people who are concerned about 'the danger of the

---

24. ibid., p. 121.

25. The National Covenant of 1638, reproduced by Hugh Watt, Professor of Church History, New College, Edinburgh University, from his *Recalling the Scottish Covenants*, Appendix (Thomas Nelson and Sons Ltd, 1946), p. 100.

true reformed Religion ... the King's honour, and ... the publick peace of the Kingdome [being destroyed].' They were determined to defend their freedom of church and parliamentary assemblies which had been ratified by Acts of Parliament, and to stand against 'Popish Religion and Tyranny' and 'the ruine of our true Reformed Religion, and of our Liberties, Lawes and Estates.' They vowed to defend their king, provided he stood by these same freedoms.

The first covenant was signed by the nobles, led by the Earl of Sutherland on the afternoon of 28th February inside Greyfriars' Kirk,[26] and then by the barons. Emotional scenes accompanied this, and elsewhere, as copies of the documents were signed. Archibald Johnston makes it clear that this was no fanatical rebellious action by a bunch of religious zealots, but something that was carefully and thoughtfully decided upon by many respected leaders of the nation. One of the issues that repeatedly came to the fore was the sense of their previous sins of compromise, for which they grieved before God deeply; another issue was the seriousness of the situation if the king reacted badly to their Covenant and petition for freedom of conscience.

Johnston himself agonised in his soul as he prepared the legal part of the document. In his diary on 10th September 1637, we read that 'for one and a half hours with great abundance of continual gushing of tears' he confessed his shortcomings, his 'hypocrisy ... atheism ... infidelity.' He knew the cost of what would come, for he wrote that 'My wife and I discoursed upon the hazards was [sic] likely to follow one in this business .... The Lord makes me to apprehend that this clear day will have a dark night, and this fair calm will have a foul storm.'[27]

He describes similar phenomena experienced by the packed churches of people who signed the National Covenant. One

---

26. There are legendary accounts of multitudes signing the Covenant in the graveyard of Greyfriars Kirk, and even using their blood as ink. However, the eyewitness accounts know nothing of the blood-signing.

27. *Diary of Sir Archibald Johnston of Wariston (1632–1639)*, ibid, 10th September 1637 and 23rd April 1637, pp. 268 and 252-53.

of those churches that he remembered most was St Giles in Edinburgh on 1st April 1638. After the National Covenant had been explained and read out, the people were asked to stand up and the lords Loudon, Montrose, Boyd and Balmerino put up their hands to sign it. When the congregation did the same, 'There arose such a yelloch [loud yelling], such abundance of tears, such a heavenly harmony of sighs and sobs, universally through all the corners of the church, as the like was never seen nor heard of. The Spirit of the Lord so filled the sanctuary, warmed the affections, melted the hearts, dissolved the eyes of all the people, men and women, poor and noble, as for a long time they stood up with their hands up unto the Lord.'[28]

Johnston was overwhelmed by such an event in the church where John Knox had preached. He wrote: 'The Lord make us never forget his presence in it, but rather make us tell it to our posterity, and make us walk worthy of it, and within the compass of this Covenant .... O Edinburgh, Edinburgh, never forget this day of April, the gloriest day that ever you enjoyed.'[29]

The National Covenant had been signed secondly by the church ministers in the Tailors' Hall in the Cowgate before this, on 1st March, and next the local community signed it on 2nd and 3rd March, so the signing in St Giles was later. The scribes were very busy in copying out the document and despatch riders took copies over most of Scotland, with the exception of the Roman Catholic and Episcopalian areas. Peterkin wrote: 'No one who is versed in the elements of the British Constitution, or imbued with the spirit of genuine freedom, can hesitate to admit that, in adopting the covenant, the people of Scotland were, at the time, not only fully justified, but were imperatively constrained to do so by every motive which can influence Christians, patriots, and brave men.'[30]

During this time, information had reached the Covenanters that King Charles I was preparing to 'crush Scotland by force of

---

28. ibid., 1st April 1638, p. 330.

29. ibid., p. 331.

30. Peterkin et al, p. 9.

arms'.[31] The Marquis of Hamilton came from court on a pretended friendly mission as King's Commissioner, but was shocked by what he saw, for 'He was received at his entrance, by 60,000 of his Majesty's Scottish subjects, including nearly all the nobility, gentry, and 600 clergymen, in a body, whose line extended from Musselburgh to the outskirts of the Metropolis.'[32] The result of this peaceful protest was that Charles I backed down with a sort of amnesty, 'without one drop of blood being shed.' But this was only the first round.

'The Bishops' Wars'

When the General Assembly of the Church of Scotland met in Glasgow in 1638 and voted that the Episcopalian system and bishops should be removed from the church, Charles I reacted with wrath, appealing to his 'divine right' and calling the National Covenant 'a conspiracy'. In January 1639, Scotland began to prepare itself for an invasion by the king's army from England, with his Scottish and Irish allies. There were some skirmishes in 1639, but Charles I was shocked at the superiority and strong support of the covenanting army and withdrew, agreeing to hold negotiations in person at Berwick with Lord Rothes, Alexander Henderson and Archibald Johnston. The Covenanters pressed for the king to ratify that the Scots themselves should be responsible for their own church and civil rights in Parliament, and that all armies sent against Scotland should be returned. Although Charles I agreed to some of their demands, he would not relinquish his 'divine right' and Episcopalian position over Scotland. Charles I left for England, smouldering with a desire for revenge.

In the short ensuing lull, Charles I met with Sir Thomas Wentworth and prepared for another invasion, but again his army was ill-equipped, and to make matters worse, he sought to extract money for the war from the Parliaments in England and Ireland by force. The royalist army was again defeated in

---

31. ibid., p. 14.
32. ibid., p. 14.

1640, leaving Charles I to eat humble pie and agree the next year to give freedom to Scotland and to abolish episcopacy from the Presbyterian Church.

For the Covenanters, this was a great victory. They seized the opportunity to send a delegation to London to spread the Presbyterian democratic ideal of church government. All the way from Newcastle to London people came in their droves to hear the scholars Robert Baillie, Alexander Henderson, Robert Blair and George Gillespie, who came with three earls, three barons, and three burgesses. In London 'Thousands upon thousands, Sunday after Sunday, flocked to hear them,' wrote John Cunningham, formerly Professor of Church History at Edinburgh's New College. 'Those who could not find room within besieged the doors and clung to the windows, anxious to catch the faintest echoes of their northern eloquence .... Most of the Puritans were Presbyterians.'[33] In the same year 15,000 Londoners, stirred by the Scottish commissioners, signed the Root and Branch Petition, which they presented to Parliament. In this petition they requested that the politicians should abolish the tyranny of the bishops, which had brought so much corruption, and replace this with a Presbyterian style of church government.

Following this, during the Long Parliament, the House of Lords largely supporting the king, clashed with the House of Commons, which opposed the despotic tendencies of Charles I. By abolishing the Crown's right to raise money for its own ends, Parliament, led by John Pym, took the necessary steps towards the establishment of a constitutional monarchy and parliamentary democracy. Charles I retaliated in 1642 by illegally invading Parliament whilst it was in session, to try and arrest the five ringleaders, who had escaped just in time. The King and his royalists were now on a collision course with their own Parliament in what would lead to the Civil War between 1642 and 1651.

---

33. John Cunningham, *Church History of Scotland*, Vol. II, second edition (Edinburgh: James Thin, 1882), pp. 33-38.

The Solemn League and Covenant

The beleaguered parliamentarians, engaged in a civil war with the royalists, needed help in the fight for civil liberty. Eyes turned naturally to Scotland and to the Covenanters. John Pym, the Puritan leader, who with John Hampden, Edward Coke and other Puritans, had spearheaded this movement, appealed to the leaders in Edinburgh. The English wanted the military backing of Scotland, and a more democratic parliament, but the Covenanters were more interested in a Reformed religious bond between the nations, with a Presbyterian Church government, which itself was democratic. In the end, another document was drawn up by Rev. Alexander Henderson in 1643 called the Solemn League and Covenant. After some tweaking by the Scots and English, it was accepted by Westminster, and so we saw the beginning of a democratic movement in both Church and State.

In an extraordinary way, Presbyterianism from Edinburgh had triumphed, and crowds flocked to sign copies of this second covenant in England, Scotland and parts of Ireland. Robert Baillie, the Scottish scholar and eyewitness, was overwhelmed. 'Such stories lately told,' he wrote, 'would have been counted fancies, dreams, mere impossibilities, yet this day we tell them as deeds done, for the great honour of God, and, we are persuaded, the joy of many a godly soul. If any will not believe our report, let them trust their own eyes; for behold here are the warrant of our words, written and subscribed by the hands of the clerks of the Parliament of England, and the scribes of the Assembly there.'[34]

The actual document reiterated the biblical beliefs of the National Covenant of 1638, but also included the statements that this was for 'Scotland, England and Ireland ... being of one reformed Religion ... to preserve the Rights and Priviledges of the Parliaments, and the Liberties of the Kingdoms.'[35] Thus we

---

34. Baillie, ibid, Lii, on his return from London.

35. *Solemn League and Covenant*, 1643, from Hugh Watt's *Recalling the Scottish Covenants* (Thomas Nelson and Sons, Ltd, 1946), pp. 106-7.

see the civil rights of the Parliaments and the people embedded in this document.

For Robert Burns, Scotland's National Poet, this document 'sealed freedom's noble cause';[36] for others, this was a move from Christian democracy to Presbyterian democracy. The Covenanters just wept for joy. With it came greater freedom in many ways, but also a restrictive, legalistic attitude that was intolerant of others, such as Baptists and Independents. If the Presbyterians *began* the process of human rights on a national scale, the Independent Christians were those who developed it with greater grace, as Baillie himself says: 'It is usual to assert that the first correct notions of toleration or religious liberty [for all] originated with the Independents.'[37]

The Great Sin of Scotland

With the combined strength of the parliamentarians and covenanting armies, Charles I was defeated. To the shock of most of the Scots, the English Parliament decided to behead him as a tyrant in 1649. Their love, though, of the Stuart blood blinded them to their next action, which has been called 'Scotland's great sin'. After much discussion the Scottish leaders decided that they would approach Charles I's son, who was in exile in Holland, and try and convince him to agree to the National Covenant and Solemn League and Covenant; if he did so, they would support him in his effort to retake the throne, as long as his powers were reduced and he did not interfere with the church and Parliament. Thus, in 1650, the Scottish delegation met in Breda with Charles II,

---

36. ibid., p. 66.

37. Baillie, ibid, Liv. An example of this is one of the co-pioneers of the Baptist Church, Thomas Helwys, who suffered in prison for his faith. He wrote: 'If the King's people be obedient and true subjects, obeying all humane lawes made by the King, our Lord the King can require no more: for men's religion to God is betwixt God and themselves; the King shall not answer for it, neither may the King be judge between God and man. Let them be heretics, Turks, Jews or whatsoever, it appertains not to the earthly power to punish them in the least measure.' From *A Short Declaration of the Mistery of Iniquity*, 1612, en.wikipedia.org › wiki › Thomas_Helwys.

Prince of Wales. Things were about to go horribly wrong. The king was preached to and harangued for ages by preachers and the nobility, who pressed him to sign his agreement to the Covenants, which he finally did. Alexander Jaffray, one of the eyewitness delegates, was horrified. He wrote in his diary:

> But, being again sent by the Parliament, in the year 1650, for that same business, we did sinfully both entangle and engage the nation and ourselves and that poor young prince to whom we were sent, making him sign and swear a Covenant, which we knew from clear and demonstrable reasons, that he hated in his heart ... finding that upon these terms only, he could be admitted to rule over us (all other means having failed him) he sinfully complied with what we most sinfully pressed upon him: – where, I must confess, to my apprehension, our sin was more than his .... I spoke of it to the king himself, desiring him not to subscribe the Covenant, if in his conscience he was not satisfied – and yet went on to close the treaty with him, who, I knew so well, had for his own ends done it against his heart.[38]

With a feigned acceptance of the Covenants, Charles II was duly crowned at Scone as King of Scotland on 1st January 1651. At his coronation he made the following oath before God and the nation:

> I, Charles, King of Great Britain, France and Ireland, do assert and declare, by my solemn oath, in the Presence of Almighty God, the Searcher of Hearts, my Allowance and Approbation of the National Covenant, and of the Solemn League and Covenant .... I for Myself and Successors shall consent and agree to all Acts of Parliament enjoining National Covenant and Solemn League and Covenant, and fully establishing Presbyterial Government .... I shall never make Opposition to any of these, or endeavour any change thereof.[39]

---

38. *Diary of Alexander Jaffray Provost of Aberdeen, one of the Scottish Commissioners to King Charles II, and a Member of Cromwell's Parliament,* John Barclay, second edition, London, published by Darton and Harvey, Grace Church St, 1834, pp. 33-34.

39. Johannes G. Vos, *The Scottish Covenanters* (Blue Banner Productions, 1998), pp. 65-66, citing from James King Hewison, *The Covenanters: A History of the Church of Scotland from the Reformation to the Revolution,* Vol. II, 1908 (Alpha Editions, 2019), p. 27.

The bitter fruits of this huge blunder would remain with Scotland for centuries to come. Knowing what had happened at Breda, the Covenanters became divided: some supported the king; others wanted nothing to do with what they saw was worldly compromise and perjury, a manipulation of Charles II by their leaders, and a double-tongued monarch. The nation became divided essentially between three parties: the Protesters, who stood firmly to the Covenants, believing that an oath before God and the nation must be honoured; the Resolutioners, who sought a compromised position; and the Malignants who compromised so much that they joined the Episcopalian/Roman Catholic group.

Such a divided nation would collapse under Oliver Cromwell's army, and for a time we would be ruled under his Commonwealth government. However, when he died and his son Richard ruled in his stead, the Commonwealth itself was plagued with divisions. Frustrated and desperate, the people called for the restoration of Charles II, and he returned to London where he was welcomed as King in 1660 amidst great pomp and celebrations.

It seemed to the Presbyterians in London that their hour had come. The 'sweet mixture' that Samuel Rutherford had written about in his *Lex Rex* (1644), in which he promoted a government comprised of a constitutional monarch, a House of Lords, and a House of Commons with a majority voice of the people, all under the authority of Christ, was now becoming a reality. The Presbyterians were about to get the shock of their lives.

Having secured his power over Parliament, the next step of Charles II was to control State and Church and reverse all that had gone before since 1643. In one fell swoop, in total defiance of both the parliamentarians and Scottish and English Covenanters, he committed perjury by having copies of the Solemn League and Covenant publicly burnt by the hangman. In 1662, King Charles II's Parliament passed the Act of Uniformity, which meant that all Puritans, Presbyterians and Independents were forced by law to submit to the authority of the archbishops and bishops in the Church of England, who in turn were under the king as Head of the Church. They were compelled by law to submit to the Church of England liturgy and Book of Common Prayer, and were not allowed to defend themselves against the king's power.

The church ministers also had to reject the Solemn League and Covenant. If they did not obey these rules, they would be deprived from their parishes as rebels, and their salaries would be forfeited. Many compromised under pressure, but about two thousand church ministers in England refused to dishonour their oath, and were removed, and about four hundred in Scotland, leading to a great persecution by the king's men, including eventual prison, torture and death for some. Thus, despite his oath before God and Scotland at Scone twelve years before, Charles II reversed everything to conform Britain to Episcopacy, and then married Catherine of Braganza, a Roman Catholic and daughter of King John IV of Portugal. Again, subdued whisperers in the corridors feared that his intention was to bring Britain back to Rome.

The Scottish covenanting contingent in London watched what they thought was a triumph when the King was crowned in Westminster Abbey, after having previously agreed to the Covenants, now turn into a nightmare. A month before Charles II's coronation in 1660 their joy knew no bounds; after the gaining of the support of both Parliaments in Scotland and England, as well as the Divines at the Westminster Assembly, they were now on course for the last piece to fit their dream: a king who would bring his support to them as well. A letter from Rev. Robert Douglas to Rev. James Sharp expressed his initial delight on 4th March 1660:

> Whereupon the motion was stated, that the Solemn League and Covenant should be revived, and an order made for printing it, and setting it up in all the churches of England and Wales, and the doors of the Parliament House, to which none in the House offered to make any contradiction. And this day the League and Covenant, in great Lombard paper, is to be sold in all the shops of London .... Waristoun hath been with me.[40]

---

40. Robert Wodrow, *The History of the Suffering of the Church of Scotland from the Restoration to the Revolution*, p. 10, Letter of Robert Douglas to James Sharp, 4th March, 1660, Vol. I, Blackie, Fullerton and Co., Glasgow, 1828.

How dramatically and swiftly the situation would turn around: James Sharp would go on to betray many fellow Covenanters to death when he became an archbishop; Warriston, or Archibald Johnston, the lawyer of the National Covenant, would be executed, and anybody standing for the Covenants could be killed. By March 1660, the king's men were referring to a 'Presbyterian Empire' and most of the faithful 'dare not press the voting for Presbyterian government.'[41] On 31st March, Douglas wrote delightedly to Sharp about the English Parliament's decision to revive the Solemn League and Covenant,[42] but after Charles II's coronation in Westminster in April, everything had changed. Sharp dejectedly wrote to Douglas in June: "There are many nominal, few real Presbyterians. The cassock men do swarm here; and such who seemed before to be for Presbytery, would be content of a moderate Episcopacy ... the design is to overthrow all since the year 1640, and to make the king absolute .... I now begin to fear the long contended for cause is given up ... none of the Presbyterian way here oppose it, or do anything but mourn in secret.'[43]

An anonymous letter from some leaders in Scotland was sent to the authorities in England calling for the Parliament to uphold 'a threefold freedom' which did not allow any power, whether king, dictator, or general, to be absolute over it, and for a democratic voice of the people, so that 'there be a Freedom in their voicing, without being overawed ... to present their desires and overtures for the government.'[44] The group of anonymous men respectfully reminded the authorities that 'The people of Scotland have all this.' Such a petition would be like a whimper in the wind to those in power.

---

41. ibid., Letter of James Sharp to Robert Douglas, 1st March, 1660; Letter of James Sharp to John Smith, 4th March 1660.

42. ibid., Letter of Douglas to Sharp, 31st March 1660.

43. ibid., Letters of Sharp to Douglas: 2nd June; 10th June; and 23rd June 1660.

44. ibid., Lii–Lv, 'The Judgment of Some Sober-minded men in Scotland, concerning the Settlement of the Government in the Three Nations,' 1660.

In London, on 8th July, the soldiers arrested the covenanting leader, the Marquis of Argyll, and tried also to arrest Archibald Johnston, Lord Warriston. Rev. James Guthrie and nine other ministers, along with some gentlemen and elders, were meeting in Robert Simpson's house in Edinburgh to draw up a letter congratulating the king on his coronation, but respectfully reminding him to honour the Covenants, which he had sworn by oath before God and the nation to do. All of a sudden, there was a thumping at the door and the king's soldiers came in to arrest them and put all but one of them in Edinburgh Castle's prison. The day that they were imprisoned was 24th August, on the 100th anniversary of the Scottish Reformation. As Protesters they were behind *The Remonstrance* of 1650, a document which had been sent to the king expressing their disapproval of his feigned acceptance of the Covenants, and which also explained why, for this reason, they could not support him against Cromwell. Charles II had nursed his anger against them for ten years, and now it was time for vengeance.

On the same day that the Protesters were thrown into prison the Committee of Estates in Edinburgh ruled against 'all unlawful and unwarrantable meetings and conventicles [illegal gatherings] ... [and] all seditions, petitions and remonstrances.'[45] Following this, a copy came to the church leaders condemning all who sided with Guthrie and the Protesters as rebels and enemies of the king. Just a few weeks later, on 19th September 1660, a proclamation was published against two books: Rutherford's *Lex Rex* and what was believed to be a book by James Guthrie called *The Causes of God's Wrath*. All copies were called in by the government by 15th October, and if anybody dared to be found with these seditious books, that person would be regarded as an enemy of the king and would be subject to severe punishment. The hangman burnt the books at Mercat Cross by St Giles, but as Wodrow shrewdly noted, 'It was much easier to burn those books, than to answer the reasonings and facts in them.'[46]

---

45. ibid., p. 9.
46. ibid., p. 16.

Church presbyteries were only allowed to meet if approved by the king; sermons were monitored and restricted, as were prayers. What was even more heartbreaking for many of the faithful Covenanters was the fact that James Sharp had gone to London to represent them, and they had naively trusted him. Just a week after James Guthrie and his friends had been imprisoned, he arrived in Edinburgh with the king's letter commanding that the Episcopacy should be restored. Later, he would be enthroned as the Archbishop of St Andrews: all along he had been plotting in secret to overthrow the Presbyterian constitution and become the new leader of the Episcopal Church under Charles II.

The Drunken Parliament

On 1st January 1661, the Scottish Parliament met in Edinburgh. The Earl of Middleton had been appointed by King Charles II as his Commissioner in Scotland. The Scottish Parliament, like the English, was disillusioned by the previous Civil Wars, and by now it was full of those who had rejected the Covenants, many being Malignants. It was time for them to overthrow the National Covenant, and instead of making a pledge by this document, they swept it aside and replaced it with a new oath supporting the king's supremacy with the words, 'By this my solemn oath, that I acknowledge my said Sovereign, only Supreme Governor of this kingdom, over all persons, and in all causes.'[47] Thus King Charles II became the tyrant of Scotland, as well as England. The sad thing about all this is that many of the leaders of the nation who agreed with this autocratic kingdom were in a drunken stupor at the time, hence the name 'The Drunken Parliament'. Sir Walter Scott wrote that they were often 'under the influence of wine, and they were more than once obliged to adjourn because the royal commissioner [the Earl of Middleton] was too intoxicated to behave properly in the chair.'[48]

---

47. ibid., p. 23.
48. Chris Bryant, *Parliament–The Biography: Reform*, Vol. 2 (Transworld Publishers, part of the Penguin Random House group, 2014), p. 309.

Despite the pleading and reasoning of the Earls Cassilis and Melville, and others, the Scottish Parliament ploughed on with their Act 3: 'That no subject question or impugn anything in this Act or do anything contrary thereto, under the pains of treason.'[49] With this came Acts 4 and 5, that no covenants were allowed without the king's permission; that subjects acting in self-defence would be committing high treason; and that no meetings would be allowed without the king's permission. Reformation was now viewed as rebellion against the King's Majesty. All the painstaking decades of carefully building the Presbyterian Church and a fairer, more democratic government, now lay in ruins, like a shattered pane of glass on the floor. With the Act of Rescissory the clock had been turned back to 1633, for in one stroke of the pen all of the previous acts and laws of Parliament became as if they had never been. If the pro-king and Episcopalian party celebrated, the reformers wept. In deep gloom many feared that all freedom would be lost and that the nation would be forced back to papal power. The 'Bishops were the fountain of all our mischiefs,' mourned Robert Baillie. 'Tis a scorn to tell us of a moderate Episcopacy, a moderate Papacy!'[50]

The Killing Time

Between 1661 and 1688 was Scotland's darkest period. The kings, with absolute power, did as they pleased and those who opposed them were targets of persecution. Many Presbyterians crumbled under pressure, and those who stood became seen as 'fanatics' committing high treason. John Howie estimated that 'above 18,000 people, according to calculation, suffered death, or the utmost hardships and extremities.'[51] Among them he listed the following: 1,700 were sent as slaves to America; 750 were banished to the remote northern islands of Scotland; 3,600

---

49. Wodrow, ibid., p. 23.

50. ibid., Letter of Robert Baillie to the Earl of Lauderdale, 16th June 1660, p. 136.

51. John Howie, *The Scots Worthies* (John McGready, 1781), pp. 626-27.

were imprisoned, or outlawed and sentenced to be executed when caught; 680 died as a result of battles when acting in self-defence; 7,000 fled Scotland as refugees; 362 were executed following court procedure; 498 were killed without due course of law; and the number of those who died by other means, such a starvation, hypothermia, torture and hardships, adds up to the 18,000 estimation. Torture to extract information or to get the faithful to renounce the Covenants was common, and heads and hands of the victims were often impaled by the soldiers on spikes at various points in Edinburgh and elsewhere. Rev. James Guthrie's head was attached to a spike in Edinburgh for twenty-seven years because he had called Charles II to repent from perjury.

The Glorious Revolution

With James VII, the next king, determined to reset Britain and bring us back to Rome, even the liberals had had enough. When the seven bishops in England, who had opposed the king because of his tyrannical policies, were tried for seditious libel, imprisoned in the Tower of London, and acquitted by the court on 30th June 1688, anti-Catholic riots kicked off in England and Scotland. A group of politicians and religious and military leaders banded together and invited William of Orange to come over and intervene with his army. He was married to Mary Stuart II, the oldest daughter of James VII, and they had been following her father's rule carefully from Holland. For years, they had been regularly informed by worried English and Scottish leaders about where the people were being led, and now the time for revolution had come.

When we hear the word 'revolution', we tend to think of the French Revolution, which saw terrible atrocities and the deaths of 200,000 people, or of the Bolshevik Revolution, which saw about 100,000 people executed. The Glorious Revolution, by comparison, was almost free of any bloodshed at the beginning. Accompanied by Rev. William Carstares, a Covenanter who had been tortured for his faith, William of Orange landed with his forces at Brixham, Devon, on 5th November. As the army of

14,000 proceeded to march to London, James VII's nobles and soldiers deserted him en masse. In a panic, James VII and his family fled to France under the protection of the dissolute and tyrannical Roman Catholic, Louis XIV.

Here in Scotland, the nation was incensed. Students at Glasgow University burnt an effigy of the pope, along with those of the Archbishops of Glasgow and St Andrews. In December, a mob got into Holyroodhouse in Edinburgh and ransacked the king's private chapel. Taking away images of the saints, rosary beads and crucifixes, they piled them in a heap and publicly burnt them. Over two hundred Episcopalian clergymen were driven out of their manses by the mob, leaving them to plead for help from the Presbyterian Church for aid for their families, but as Professor John Cunningham says, 'Still no life was lost. The only martyrdom these men went through was a little rough usage from an ignorant rabble, and the loss of their livings,'[52] which had been raised through tyrannical taxes. It is an extraordinary fact, that after twenty-eight years of cruel oppression of the people by the State and fawning clergy, that nobody murdered their opponents. Even the rough handling of the Episcopalian clergy by some over-zealous Presbyterians was strongly condemned by the majority.

A new day had dawned for England and Scotland. The Glorious Revolution would see the process started through the Reformation, and through the stand of the Covenanters, advance to an era of growing freedom and democracy through a biblical Christian understanding. It would be a movement from which our British constitution would develop and eventually be the envy of many nations.

The English Bill of Rights and Scottish Claim of Right

With the tyrant King James VII in exile, the leaders in London had to move quickly to make sure an orderly joint coronation of William, Prince of Orange, and his wife, Mary Stuart, the

---

52. John Cunningham, p. 53.

daughter of James VII, could go ahead. As her uncle, Charles II, had had no legitimate heirs, she was next in line to the throne after her father. We had learnt our lessons: tyrant kings were not a good idea; neither was the divine right of a king as a controlling Head of the Church.

Before William and Mary were co-crowned in Westminster, they had to sign a vital document drawn up by the Houses of Lords and Commons, which would become enshrined as a pillar of our UK constitution, alongside the Magna Carta. On 13th February 1689, they dutifully signed the English Bill of Rights, which stated that the 'late King James the Second [of England, and Seventh of Scotland], by the assistance of divers evil counselors, judges and ministers employed by him, did endeavour to subvert and extirpate the Protestant religion and the laws and liberties of this kingdom …. All which are utterly and directly contrary to the known laws and statutes and freedom of this realm…'

Through this document, a free Parliament was reinstated, and absolute monarchy was abolished, as was the monarch's interference in matters of Church and State. A cause of even greater joy to the persecuted Presbyterians and Puritans was clause 5, which said 'That it is the right of the subjects to petition the king, and all commitments and prosecutions for such petitioning are illegal.' Protestants were now legally allowed to act in self-defence, and free election of members to Parliament was made law, as well as freedom of speech and open debate in Parliament. Only on accepting the English Bill of Rights, could William and Mary be crowned as 'king and queen of England, France and Ireland.' They were then crowned as King William III and Queen Mary II, on 11th April, 1689.

The Scottish people waited with bated breath for their own Scottish Claim of Right Act, produced by their own people. When it came out, its grievances against James VII were more than that of the English Bill. It stated that this king did 'Invade the fundamentall Constitution of this Kingdome and altered it from a legall limited monarchy to ane Arbitrary Despotick power.' It furthermore described him as a papist who became king without obedience to the law, and imposed Roman Catholicism in Scotland, according to his own whims, with 'subversione of the protestant religion and the violation of the lawes and liberties of the Kingdome, inverting all the Ends of Government wherby he hath forfaulted the right to the Croune and the throne is become vacant.'

In the Scottish document, freedom of faith and Parliament in Scotland are side by side. The Scottish Bill says, 'That Prelacy [bishop-statesmen] and the superiority of any office in the Church above presbyters is and hath been a great and insupportable greivance and trouble to this Nation and contrary to the Inclinationes of the generality of the people ever since the reformatione (they haveing reformed from popery by presbyters) and therfor ought to be abolished.' The Scots called for the freedom to protest peacefully against unjust laws, and to petition government without facing imprisonment, as well as there to be 'freedom of speech and debate to the members' in Parliament.

On 11th May 1689, the day of freedom had finally come for the suffering Covenanters, when William and Mary complied with the Scottish Claim of Right Act, and received the crown of Scotland. The very principles for which the faithful Covenanters had been tortured and hunted out like animals, and labelled as 'fanatics', would become enshrined in law.

With the peaceful enthronement of King William and Queen Mary, after they had agreed to the English Bill of Rights and Scottish Claim of Right, the clergy in Scotland focused their attention on the re-establishment of the Presbyterian Church. Back in 1592, Scottish Parliament had ratified the Presbyterian Church by law, in what was endearingly called the 'Magna Carta of Presbyterianism', with its roots in the 1560 Reformation. Now, almost a hundred years later, after so much suffering, this right would again be ratified in what was called The Revolution Settlement of 1690.

On 7th June, Parliament passed an 'Act Ratifying the Confession of Faith and Settling Presbyterian Church Government'. The Episcopalian system was overthrown in the Church of Scotland

and Presbyterianism was accepted as 'the government of Christ's church within this nation, agreeable to the Word of God, and most conducive to the advancement of true piety and godliness, and the establishing of peace and tranquility within this realm.' The ministers were welcomed back to their parishes in a legally accepted Presbyterian Church, and the church leaders met freely in the restored General Assembly on 16th October. Professor G. N. Collins notes that 'The old aim emerges clearly, the determination to preserve inviolate the democratic government of the Church under the sole Headship of Jesus Christ.'[53]

It was the despised Covenanters, who had stood through unbelievable suffering and misrepresentation, who have been vilified and dragged through the mud, that had been the harbingers of our human rights process, which in turn would lead to the Bills of Rights in England and Scotland, with their inspiration for the human rights movements in America and France, culminating in the UN Charter for Human Rights in 1948.

---

53. G. N. M. Collins, *The Heritage of our Fathers* (Edinburgh: The Knox Press, 1974), p. 38.

CHAPTER 8

PLIGHT OF THE POOR

In March 2022 the nation was outraged. P&O Ferries made eight hundred of its staff redundant through a Zoom call, without warning. Admittedly, the company had been running at a loss of £100 million 'year on year', and drastic action had to be taken, but this was appalling. P&O Ferries had been bought by DP World in 2019, which had been covering the severe financial haemorrhage. DP World is based in Dubai and is owned by the government of the United Arab Emirates, with the Vice-President and Prime Minister Sheikh Mohammed bin Rashid Al Maktoum in control of it. A few days later the union, working on behalf of the redundant staff, was horrified to learn that they were being replaced by '£1.81-an-hour workers from India, Philippines and Ukraine', a huge saving compared with the British minimum wage of £8.91 at that time.[1]

The reasoning from the point of view of the Sheikh was simply pragmatic: he needed to save a sinking ship by making drastic cuts, and as DP World owned the company in Dubai, he saw himself beyond British jurisdiction. For those who are concerned enough to peer beneath the opulence of Dubai, another scene emerges: one of horrendous exploitation, abuse, and what is virtually slave labour of the poor. Human Rights Watch issued a report in 2006 of the plights of 250,000 foreign labourers there, who live in conditions which are 'less than

---

1. Dan Sales, *Daily Mail*, 21st March, 2022. The actual figure was £1.82.

WHAT HAS CHRISTIANITY *EVER* DONE FOR SCOTLAND?

humane'. Britain was simply seeing first-hand what really goes on in a culture founded on the *kafala* system of private ownership of workers, which operates outside of government control and which is rife with exploitation of the worst kind.

It was this kind of abuse going on with our British workers that made Sir Keir Starmer's 'blood boil'. As leader of the Labour Party today he represents a party that has a long history in seeking to bring justice to the poor and oppressed and, through the vehicle of the Trade Unions, workers' rights have been upheld, with the accompanying cry of 'a fair day's work for a fair day's pay.' However, most of us do not stop to reflect from where this rallying call came. For this we have to dig back into our own past, in which wealthy British landowners exploited their workers, driving them into poverty and great hardship. It was the voice of the Tolpuddle Martyrs in Devon that caught the national attention, for it was their own cry for justice. George Loveless, a local Methodist preacher, led a band of five ringleaders, all of whom, except for one, were Methodist Christians. The authorities came down on them with an iron fist, exiling them as convicts to Australia, but the peaceful protests of many thousands led to their triumphant return. Out of this grew the Trade Union movement, which would later have a voice for the eight hundred workers ruthlessly sacked by Sheik Mohammed.

The Servant-Queen

It is not often that a queen washes the feet of the poor in her castle. Nor is it usual for such a person to impact a nation through her godliness, practical kindness and love, so that Scotland produced its golden age of kings because of her example.

When Turgot, Bishop of St Andrews, was requested by Matilda, the wife of King Henry I, to write a biography of her saintly mother, Queen Margaret, he compiled *Life of St Margaret, Queen of Scotland*, between seven and fourteen years after she had died in 1093. As Queen Margaret's private confessor, he knew her better than anyone. He tells us 'God is my Witness and my Judge – that I add nothing to the truth.'[2] Having a deep dislike of embellishing a biography for sensational purposes like some monks, his account is deliberately downplayed for fear that he might be charged with 'decking out the crow in the plumage of a swan'.

Margaret, whose grandfather was Edmund Ironside, the King of England, would have preferred to have lived the life of a nun. She was destined, however, to affect the course of Scotland. When King Harold fell in the fields of Senlac at the hands of William the Conqueror, Edgar Aetheling was chosen as the next king, but despite resistance by the bishops, William was crowned King of England. Fearing for their lives, Edgar fled England to King Malcolm in Scotland, with his mother Agatha and sisters Margaret and Christina. Malcolm fell in love with Margaret at first sight, but she deterred him, preferring the life of a celibate Christian. With much persuasion from her family, she finally married Malcolm. Thus begins an extraordinary account.

Turgot writes, 'When she went out of doors … crowds of poor people, orphans and widows, flocked to her, as they would have done to a most loving mother.'[3] Often she would greet them at a rock near Dunfermline where she would be available for counsel, prayer and practical help. Every morning she fed nine orphans with her own silver spoon. Regularly, three hundred of the poor would dine with her and King Malcolm, and she would wait on twenty-four poor people every day, serving them food and drink, even washing their feet as a sign of servant-leadership. Besides this, she sent spies throughout Scotland to report where the English were enslaved by cruel owners, so that they could be ransomed and set free. Often, she would visit hermits and monks to find out where the poorest people were, so that they could be helped.

Margaret's motivation was a deep love for Christ. She repeatedly asked Turgot to rebuke her if he found any sin or worldliness in

---

2. Turgot, *The Life of S. Margaret, Queen of Scotland*, Prologue, contained within *Lives of the Scottish Saints*, translated by W. M. Metcalfe (Llanerch Enterprises, 1990), p. 46.

3. ibid., 3:18, p. 59.

her; her desire was to be humble and virtuous, hating flattery and greed. 'In the house of God ... she was there simply to pray, and in praying to pour forth her tears,' said Turgot.[4] Her passion for God was demonstrated, too, in the building of Dunfermline Abbey and other churches, financial assistance of monasteries and the church, and her pioneering work of establishing a free ferry to enable the pilgrims to cross the Forth estuary on their way to St Andrews. Today, both South Queensferry and North Queensferry are named after her.

One of her enduring feats was to restore the abbey at Iona, which had been sacked by the Vikings. These cruel and fierce Scandinavian pirates began ravaging the coasts of Scotland from about the year 794, murdering, looting and raping the locals. The Orkneys and the Shetlands became their northern stronghold, after they had driven out the Picts. From this base they sallied forth to plunder the islands and coastline. The monasteries, being wealthy and unprotected, were easy targets for them. In 802, the monastery at Iona was raided again, but this time the Vikings burnt it; this was followed by the slaughter of sixty-eight monks four years later. By 825 the monks had abandoned Iona after a second massacre; settling at Kells in Ireland, they named their Gospels after this place. At a similar time, monks on St Ninian's Isle in the Shetlands had hurriedly buried twenty-eight items of silver under a slab of stone to avoid Viking pillaging. The fact that the silver hoard lay buried until its discovery by a boy in 1958 is a silent witness to the fact that the monks never returned – presumably they had been killed. Queen Margaret, appreciating the spiritual significance of Iona, restored the abbey with her husband King Malcolm in 1072. By this time the Vikings had been largely Christianised.

Queen Margaret is often depicted with her gem-studded Bible, which had been produced by her doting husband. She was scholarly, whereas he was illiterate; she promoted peace and healing; but he was a warlord. Often, she would help herself to his

---

4. ibid., 3:17, p. 58.

gold coins for the poor, whilst he smiled with affection. Her great passion for the Bible meant that when she discovered that parts of the church were out of tune with the Scriptures, 'with apostolic faith she laboured to root up all weeds which had lawlessly sprung up.'[5] At times she summoned a church council to solve issues, taking a full part in the discussions herself, freely referring them to the Scriptures and the Church Fathers, so that 'no-one on the opposite side could say one word against them.' Her promotion of education is shown today by the later founding of Queen Margaret University, named after her.

Her Christlike example had such an impact on the nation that the nobles and knights began to emulate her, so that 'when she saw wicked men she admonished them to be good, the good to become better, and the better to strive to be best.'[6] Her virtues were also accompanied by a sharp brain and a shrewd business sense, for she administered laws on behalf of her husband and encouraged merchants to travel by land and sea to increase trade, thereby introducing unknown wares to the Scots. With this came fashion, elegance and the arts. Her Christian faith was not drab and miserable, but full of life and colour, and 'her chamber was ... a workshop of sacred art.'[7] She believed that her role as helpmate to her husband meant that their castle should be adorned with dignity, beauty and the wealth necessary to reflect the king's position, yet this had no hold on her, and on her love for the poor.

On 16th November 1093, she lay on her deathbed in Edinburgh Castle. One of her sons came to her chamber, distraught with bad news. Her husband and eldest son had been killed in battle in Northumbria. The broken-hearted queen, not letting bitterness rule her heart, called for the Black Rood – a golden crucifix with a splinter of Christ's cross inside – and prayed. Her last request to Turgot concerned her children, that he should 'lavish [his]

---

5. ibid., 2:13, p. 54.

6. ibid.

7. ibid., 2:11, p. 53.

affection upon them' and 'teach them before all things to love and fear God.'[8] She was made a saint in 1250, one of the few in Scottish history, but it was her love of the poor which made her stand out.

Christ and the Poor

A long time ago, God spoke through Moses, saying, 'You shall open your hand wide to your brother, to your poor and needy, in your land' (Deut. 15:11). Rejoicing deeply, Hannah could cry out that God 'raises the poor from the dust and lifts the beggar from the ash heap, to set them among princes and make them inherit the throne of glory' (1 Sam. 2:8). God comes down very heavily on those who abuse the poor, and rewards those who show kindness to them. In a sublime and radical statement, the apostle Paul wrote: 'For you know the grace of our Lord Jesus Christ, that though He was rich, yet for your sakes He became poor, that you through His poverty might become rich' (2 Cor. 8:9).

Right from the beginning, Christ's love for the poor, abused and downtrodden was a flame of passion in His followers. Feeding and caring for the widows, orphans and the poor was an essential ministry of the church, and in a real way they developed a welfare system that stunned the ancient world in its radical and unselfish way, appointing deacons for this practical task. Although there were acts of charity and care for the poor in some ways in Pagan cultures, nothing had ever been witnessed that was as revolutionary as Christianity. William Lecky, Professor of History at Trinity College, Dublin, could write that 'the active, habitual, and detailed charity of private persons, which is such a conspicuous feature in Christian societies, was scarcely known in antiquity.'[9]

Rodney Stark, Professor of Sociology and Comparative Religion at the University of Washington, is even more gushing. 'Christianity revitalized life in Greco-Roman cities by providing new norms and new kinds of social relationships able to cope with

---

8. ibid., 4:27, p. 65.

9. W. Lecky, *History of European Morals*, 2:78, cited by Alvin J. Schmidt, formerly Professor of Sociology at Illinois College, in *How Christianity Changed the World* (Zondervan, 2001), p. 128.

many urgent problems,' he says. 'To cities filled with the homeless and impoverished, Christianity offered charity as well as hope. To cities filled with newcomers and strangers, Christianity offered an immediate basis for attachments. To cities filled with orphans and widows, Christianity provided a new and expanded sense of family. To cities torn by violent ethnic strife, Christianity offered a new basis of solidarity. And to cities faced with epidemics, fires, and earthquakes, Christianity offered effective nursing services.'[10]

The Early Church and the Poor

Emperor Julian in the fourth century hated Christians, and his hatred deepened when he realised that they not only cared for their own poor, but for the Pagan poor as well. It was this example that drove him to try and start a welfare programme to compete with the church. By the fifth century, Christians were even operating care homes for the frail and elderly, believing that people should be honoured and cared for from the womb to the grave. Every local church collected money regularly to assist the orphans, widows, sick, elderly and the poor and needy, so with the spread of Christianity such a welfare programme began to gradually change the culture, wherever it went. This pattern can be seen in the second century practice:

> And they who are well to do, and willing, give what each thinks fit; and what is collected is deposited with the president, who succours [gives help to] the orphans and widows, and those who, through sickness or any other cause, are in want, and those who are in bonds [in prison], and strangers sojourning among us, and in a word takes care of all who are in need.[11]

Even more radical than this was the fact that many Christians followed Jesus' injunction to the rich young man, to 'sell whatever you have and give to the poor, and you will have treasure in heaven;

---

10. R. Stark, *The Rise of Christianity* (New Jersey: Princeton University Press, 1996), p. 161.

11. Justin Martyr, 'The First Apology,' Chapter LXVII, *The Ante-Nicene Fathers*, Volume 1 (Edinburgh: T&T Clark; Grand Rapids: William B. Eerdmans Publishing Company, reprinted 1996), p. 186.

and come, take up the cross, and follow Me' (Mark 10:21). Such an extraordinary transformation was expressed in the early church, when the believers sold possessions and gave to those in need.[12] Eusebius tells us that even in the period after the apostles 'very many of the disciples' distributed their possessions among the needy, left their homes, and established churches.[13] The aristocracy and royal families began to display unusual kindness to the poor, providing for their needs and caring for their people in a way hitherto unknown.

In reaction to the growing power and wealth of the bishops and church hierarchy in the medieval period, the monastic orders, which often took a vow of poverty, laboured to elevate and assist the poor and needy in their communities, seeking a purer form of Christianity, until the aristocracy wormed their way into the orders seeking self-interests.

The Reformation and the Poor

With the growing stranglehold of the unconverted people of the aristocracy running the church, what should have been a representation on earth of Christ had become a system of control, wealth and oppression. The reformers were outraged at the behaviour of the ruling bishops 'who tyrannically have empired above the poor flock of Christ Jesus'.[14] They were determined to see transformation here too amongst their social reforms. Their passion for the poor speaks loudly:

> The streets shall be cleansed of the cryings and murmurings of them; as we shall no more be a scandal to other nations, as we have hitherto been, for not taking order with the poor amongst us, and causing the word which we profess to be evil spoken of, giving occasion of slander to the enemies, and offending the consciences of the simple and godly.[15]

---

12. Acts of the Apostles 4:32-37.

13. Eusebius, *The History of the Church*, 3:37 (Penguin Classics, 1989), p. 100.

14. *First Book of Discipline*, 1560, The Conclusion: *Works of John Knox*, edited by David Laing (Edinburgh: James Thin, 1895), Vol. 2, pp. 183-260.

15. *Second Book of Discipline, 3:13, 1578: David Calderwood's History of the Kirk of Scotland, edited* by Thomas Thomson (Edinburgh: Wodrow Society, 1843), Vol. 3, pp. 529-55.

At the settlement of the Reformation, Knox and his supporters hoped for the government to plough the money back into the church and education, for the welfare of the genuinely poor and needy. Instead, they received a slap in the face with the Lords and gentry fighting over material gain to the neglect of those in real need. Although Parliament had approved *The First Book of Discipline* in 1561, with the Duke of Châtelherault and almost all of the Lords signing the agreement in Edinburgh's Tolbooth, when it really came down to it, they valued their own self-interests above all else, and they did not seal it with their actions. Knox tried to stand up for the principles in *The First Book of Discipline*, but was mocked and left heartbroken. It would take centuries for the reformers' vision to be implemented socially in Scotland because of the greed of the aristocracy, but their passion to care for the poor was the heart of our national Scottish welfare; eventually its lifeblood would run through its veins to every part of our nation. However, discernment needed to be shown in helping the poor:

> Every several kirk must provide for the poor within itself; for fearful and horrible it is, that the poor, whom not only God the Father in his law, but Christ Jesus in his evangel, and the Holy Spirit speaking by Saint Paul, has so earnestly commended to our care, are universally so contemned and despised. We are not patrons for stubborn and idle beggars who, running from place to place, make a craft of their begging, whom the civil magistrate ought to punish; but for the widow and fatherless, the aged, impotent, or lame, who neither can nor may travail for their sustenance, we say that God commands his people to be careful. And therefore, for such, as also for persons of honesty fallen in[to] decay and penury, ought such provision be made that [of] our abundance should their indigence be relieved. How this most conveniently and most easily may be done in every city, and other parts of this realm, God shall show you wisdom and the means, so that your minds are godly thereto inclined.[16]

---

16. *First Book of Discipline*, 1560: 'The Fifth Head: Concerning the Provision for the Ministers, and for the Distribution of the Rents and Possessions Justly Appertaining to the Kirk, Works of John Knox,' edited by David Laing (Edinburgh: James Thin, 1895), Vol. 2, pp. 183-260.

New Lanark – a Model Village

The walk from New Lanark Mills to the Falls of Clyde is one of breathtaking beauty. Walkers begin at the World Heritage Centre, a series of buildings from the eighteenth and nineteenth centuries, where they can read some of the amazing history of what happened here. Usually, the socialist Robert Owen is rightly lauded for his extraordinary philanthropic work, which he harnessed together with his very lucrative business in the cotton mills there. Owen combined a rare talent of hard-nosed business with care for the children and employees who worked in his factories, setting a model for thousands of people to come and learn from what he had done, and then copy this model in their own nations. The part of the story that is usually airbrushed out of our history is the evangelical Christian preacher, David Dale, who pioneered this work.

David Dale was born in Stewarton, Ayrshire in 1739, and by 1783 he had become a leading figure in Glasgow as a merchant in textiles, and as a co-founder of the Glasgow branch of the Royal Bank of Scotland. One day he took a walk with Richard Arkwright, one of the pioneers of the Industrial Revolution in Britain, and one of its wealthiest men, and George Dempster. When they surveyed the land by the River Clyde, they all agreed that this would be the ideal site for a large cotton mill. Indeed, it would become one of Europe's foremost cotton mills.

By 1786 the mills were buzzing with life and Dale had become the sole owner. He soon realised that New Lanark was a bit remote for the workers to travel to every day, so he embarked on a building program to provide accommodation for them. By the 1790s a community and village existed with almost 1,400 people. The children were often from orphanages and had been transported to his village from Edinburgh and Glasgow – this was before Shaftesbury's breakthrough in Parliament, which enacted the law for children to receive an education and reduced hours of work, and for younger children to be able to go to school without factory work. Dale made sure that his workers were well looked after, and that the children received an education.

Word got out that something special and unusual was happening at New Lanark. Businessmen, scientists, politicians and statesmen poured in to learn from Dale how he had managed to establish such an innovative idea. For the first time in Britain somebody had pioneered a model incorporating a very prosperous business, with community care for his workers and education for the children. Amongst the visitors was a wealthy young Welshman named Robert Owen. Not only was he enraptured by what he saw there, but he was also enamoured by David Dale's eldest daughter. The two were married in 1799 and by 1800 Dale had sold the business to him. Owen saw New Lanark as an opportunity to pioneer a community based along socialist ideals. He began as a deist, and then transitioned to a more atheistic position, but towards the latter part of his life became a spiritualist. However, it was the Christian-based model that had been established first by Dale; Owen was inspired by it and simply took that model and adapted it to his own Utopian socialist ideal.

A Beautiful Field

Dr Thomas Guthrie peered down at the dismal scene below in the Cowgate. From his vantage point of George IV Bridge in Edinburgh, he could see the squalor and decadence of the poor. The putrid air from below rose to his nostrils, causing him to grimace. Again, he thought of his comfortable parish church in Arbirlot, with its pure country air. Now he had this. Suddenly he felt a hand on his shoulder and a friendly voice saying, 'A beautiful field, sir; a very fine field of operation.'[17] Looking round he saw the Luther-like face filled with holy zeal. It was Dr Thomas Chalmers, who was widely recognised as the nation's leading voice in the church.

Nineteenth-century Scotland saw an extraordinary movement forward in science, medicine, education and reform, but behind much of it was a church that threw off what Guthrie called 'the

---

17. Hugh M. Ferrier, *Echoes from Scotland's Heritage of Grace* (Stoke-on-Trent: Tentmaker Publications, 2006), p. 113.

drowsy, deadening reign of Moderatism'.[18] It was a period in which evangelical Christians rose up, cast aside compromise, lethargy and flowery niceties, rolled up their sleeves and laboured hard at the coalface of humanity, bringing extraordinary transformation. It was a movement that spread throughout most of the nation, but its epicentres were in Edinburgh and Glasgow.

When the evangelical Dr John Erskine had called out 'Moderator, rax [pass] me that Bible' in the General Assembly of the Church of Scotland in 1796, a new day for mission had begun. Contrary to Thomas Aikenhead's gloomy prediction in 1697 that Christianity would be 'extirpated' by the end of the nineteenth century, the very opposite happened: Edinburgh became the evangelical mission capital of the world. During the previous centuries the church had been through a gauntlet of reformation, covenanting agonies, and liberalism, so that few Christians had exercised their energies in promoting world mission, but now a new day was dawning.

The Rising Tide

The period between 1795 and 1825 saw a trickle of mission societies in Scotland rise to become a river, with over fifty-seven being established in Scotland. Dr Chalmers could write that 'There never was an age of the world in which a more effective machinery for conversion was, in the shape of schools and Bibles and missionaries, put into operation.'[19]

Dr Chalmers had been a liberal Church of Scotland minister who had combined God with social action, but did not know Christ for himself. In 1811 he was converted to Christ, largely through William Wilberforce's book, *A Practical View of the Prevailing Religious Systems of Professed Christians*, which had been written to disturb the middle and upper churchgoing classes, and shake

---

18. David K. Guthrie, and Charles J. Guthrie, *Autobiography of Thomas Guthrie and Memoir by his Sons* (New York: Robert Carter and Brothers, 1873), Vol. I, p. 234.

19. William Hanna, *Memoirs of Thomas Chalmers*, Chapter II (reprint by Nabu Press, 2011), p. 503.

them out of a cultural religion and into a vibrant, experiential Christianity. At once Chalmers began to preach the biblical gospel of salvation, but he was dismayed at the spiritual state of the Church of Scotland. Although the missionary movement was underway, many of the clergy spoke against it. Chalmers, beside himself with frustration, wrote in 1815:

> [There was an] impetuous and overbearing contempt for every-thing connected with the name of missionary. The cause has been outraged by a thousand indecencies .... All the epithets of disgrace which a perverted ingenuity could devise have been unsparingly lavished on the noblest benefactors of the species .... A great proportion of our nobility, gentry and clergy, look upon it as a very low and drivelling concern; as a visionary enterprise, and that no good thing can come out of it.[20]

Increasingly though, more and more ministers in the General Assembly became evangelicals, so that by 1824 they were in the majority. In the ensuing debates about mission, leading liberal Presbyterian ministers like John Hope could complain that 'We had a doze [sic] of fanaticism such as I suppose has not been heard in the General Assembly since the restoration of Charles the 2nd.'[21] Again, it would be these 'fanatics' who would transform Scotland.

For some of the older liberals, sharing Christ's gospel of eternal salvation at home and abroad was too extreme, akin to the stand of the Covenanters in the seventeenth century. The lines at the 1824 General Assembly were drawn: on the one side were the Moderates who held to the belief that we just need to 'civilize' people and teach them good manners, educate them, and feed the poor, and that this effort should be focused on our home country

---

20. Thomas Chalmers, *The Utility of Missions Ascertained by Experience*, Works, 1815, vol. 11, pp. 232f., quoted from John Roxborogh, *Thomas Chalmers: Enthusiast for Mission: The Christian Good of Scotland and the Rise of the Missionary Movement* (Rutherford House, 1999), p. 179.

21. Letter of John Hope, 5th June 1824, NLS 11, ff.157-60, quoted from John Roxborogh, *Thomas Chalmers: Enthusiast for Mission*, ibid., p. 91.

of Scotland, rather than going off on some expensive wild goose chase to preach to 'savages' who would not be able to understand such a sublime message as the gospel.

On the other side were the evangelicals who stood for preaching the traditional gospel and taking this, along with practical care, to Scotland and the nations that did not know the good news of Christ. The evangelicals were convinced that genuine encounters with Jesus Christ would bring about the fruit of transformed lives and cultures, and in so doing would also raise the poor from their quagmire of hopelessness. This assembly was a watershed moment in Scottish church history, for the majority vote favoured the evangelical cause, leading to an extraordinary outburst of home and global mission.

Strategic Mission

Dr Chalmers was a multi-talented minister with the strategic brain of a military commander. In 1815 he left the small village parish of Kilmany, where he had desired to be the Professor of Mathematics at the University of St Andrews, and gave himself to serving the poor in the parish of the Tron in Glasgow. He soon realised that this parish had grown too large for a single church to manage, so he created the smaller parish of St John's and began his 'experiment'. He divided this parish into twenty-five districts with about four hundred people in each, and appointed two visitors to be responsible for each district: one an elder who would care for the spiritual needs of the people, and the other a deacon who would care for the practical needs of those in the district.

In this way the church made spiritual inroads among the poor as the elder set up a Sabbath school and a day school, as well as giving Christian teaching to the adults, and the deacon was responsible for ascertaining the greatest needs of the people in his district, and meeting their crises with the Poor Relief Fund from the church, as well as helping the locals to help themselves through employment.

By 1823, Chalmers' experiment in Glasgow had thrived and, even before that, his work had caused William Wilberforce, the great abolitionist, to write in his diary, 'All the world is wild about Dr Chalmers!'[22] Chalmers became something of a celebrity, even being asked to address Parliament in London about his work. People were split over his model: some enthusiastically embraced it and saw a great improvement in their parishes; others thought such a model would only work under the supervision of someone special like Dr Chalmers.

Chalmers was not content with the advances he was making though and pioneered the Church Extension campaign in 1834, which was an ambitious project to build hundreds of new churches in Scotland, with a slogan, 'A church and a minister within easy reach of every door.'[23] He also repeated the Glasgow experiment in Edinburgh in 1844 in the slums of the West Port, which had a population of about two thousand people, with a high proportion being paupers, thieves and prostitutes. Again, he was successful, leading to many ministers in both Scotland and England adopting his method.

City Missions

A young man in his twenties, who spent every available hour sharing the good news of Christ with the poor in Glasgow, heard of Chalmers' exciting project at St John's, and with remarkable entrepreneurship started up the interdenominational Glasgow City Mission in 1826. His catchy slogan was, 'May the glory of God and the salvation of souls be our chief – our only end!' David Nasmith only lived for forty years, but in his short and dynamic life he established about sixty city missions, not just in Britain and Ireland, but in America, and elsewhere. He worked out a blueprint in Glasgow, which would be copied by many other missions.

At the first Annual Meeting on 1st January 1827, in the Trades Hall, Glassford Street, Glasgow, the message to the first missionaries was:

---

22. William Hanna, *Memoirs of the life and writings of Thomas Chalmers* (Edinburgh: Thomas Constable, 1849–1852), p. 111.

23. John Nicholls, *Evangelising Our Cities – the Abiding Challenge of Thomas Chalmers* (personal copy of this article), p. 23.

You will convert the houses that were tenanted by men of the foulest passions, into churches of the Redeemer, where the Lord the Spirit will dwell and the God of Salvation will be loved and served. You will arrest the progress of vice and promote the interest of virtue. You will make our poor, our ignorant, our degraded population stand forth in all that freshness and fairness of moral and of spiritual excellence.[24]

The vision was to penetrate the darkest places and see transformation: an incredible challenge indeed! More than this, it would be a movement that would bypass church sectarianism and unite Christians for the task of the gospel. There were three revolutionary ingredients to Nasmith's vision. The missionaries would evangelize our cities:

1. When the churches mostly believed the lie that Britain was 'Christian', and didn't need missionaries.

2. Using ordinary men and women without theology degrees, which was unheard of.

3. Using evangelical Christians from all church denominations, when people said it would be impossible.[25]

In 1832, Nasmith set up the Edinburgh City Mission (ECM) in a shop opposite St Giles, at 375 High Street. Soon suitable missionaries were found and, following Chalmers' strategy of splitting the city into thirty districts, the work began to expand. As the missionaries wove their way through the worst slums, they began to reveal the shocking underbelly of the city. The alarm bell was being rung by ECM to the church: 'Oh! Professing Christians of Edinburgh, awake! No longer shut your eyes to this dismal state of things.'[26]

---

24. Delores Burger, *Practical Religion: David Nasmith and the City Mission Movement*, 1799–2000 (printer unknown), p. 28.

25. Paul James-Griffiths, *The History of Edinburgh City Mission: David Nasmith: A Dynamic Founder of Missions (1799–1839)* (Edinburgh City Mission, 2006), pp. 1-2.

26. ibid., ECM Annual Report: 1834–1835, p. 35.

The missionaries, who combined their roles as evangelists, social workers and medical assistants, began to share their findings:

> In looking over the names of those I have visited, I believe that one out of every five, is either much given over to intemperance [alcoholic addiction], or a confirmed drunkard.[27]

> When I went into the house, three of the children were lying on the floor, on a mattress, with scarcely anything to cover them, and all deeply afflicted with the loathsome disease [i.e. smallpox]; two of them were very ill, and one seemly dying. In a small closet on a wretched bed covered up with a few dirty rags, lay the body of the poor girl, who had died in the morning. I had seen her before, and a very blooming young person she then was; she was fifteen years old, but so malignant had been the disease, and so awfully brutal the treatment to which she had been exposed, that it was difficult to recognise, in the black mass of corruption that remained, the body of a human being. The mother was drunk – most disgustingly drunk. The poor girl it seems had been in place, and had come home, in the fever, which generally precedes small pox. The wretched parents made her lie on the floor, and the father kicked her, – kicked his dying child! The mother's conduct was worse still, – but let darkness cover it.[28]

It seemed like a hopeless work; a task too huge, heartbreaking, and humanly impossible to bring about the positive change desired. But the missionaries were not alone: following Nasmith's vision, they spearheaded cross-denominational bands of men and women who were passionate in united prayer, united evangelism, and united social action in their districts. With God they found they were in the majority. Encouraging stories began to come out of these human hell-holes, stories that kindled the heart with warm expectancy of further miracles. One missionary's report in 1834 said:

> Visited the reformed drunkard mentioned a few days ago; I scarcely knew either the house or the children. The change is indeed

---

27. ibid., p. 37.
28. ibid., p. 42.

wonderful – everything in the house is now scrupulously clean, and in its proper place. Everything before, was confused, filthy and abominable. When I went in, the eldest girl was preparing a substantial dinner; and the former gownless, ragged, wretched mother, was sitting at a table decently clothed, and making herself a new gown! The whole appearance of the family equally surprised and delighted me. 'Great and marvellous are all thy works, Lord God Almighty.' What pleased me most of all, was the quiet and humble deportment of the poor woman herself. She did not seem at all to expect praise, or to court condemnation, but with tears she remarked that she was now quite ashamed of her former conduct. She then proceeded to give the most horrifying description of the evils of intemperance, that I have ever listened to; and then she spoke (and it was delightful to hear her) of having won back the affections of her husband, and the confidence of her children – some of whom are grown up. A pale and sickly-looking young person was sitting in the corner of the room sewing. When I looked towards her, she turned aside her face. I thought who it might be, and spoke kindly to the poor wanderer, which seemed to melt the mother more than anything. It may be in the recollection of some readers of this journal, that about a year ago, I made mention of a woman coming into one of the meetings in a state of intoxication, and bawling out with fiendish glee, that she had a daughter on the street. Dear readers! This is the woman, and this is her daughter. So soon as the mother came to herself, she went in search of her erring child, whom she found, and now watches over with a mother's care.[29]

In the Annual Report of ECM for 1838–39 there was a real sense that something special was beginning to happen in Edinburgh, right in the heart of darkness. The churches too were waking up, as the enthusiasm for home mission spread for, 'In regard, indeed to the whole operations of the Mission, its indirect effects are at least equal to all the other good which it produces. Of these the most important is, that a missionary spirit has been excited in the city.'[30]

---

29. ibid., p. 44.
30. ibid., ECM Annual Report: 1838–1839, p. 11.

When ECM celebrated their thirtieth anniversary they rejoiced at the changes in the city, for when ECM began not one church employed a missionary, and mission itself was at a very low condition, with just a few men struggling in an overwhelming landscape of despair: by 1862 there were forty church-based missionaries, and a total of ninety-six full-time missionaries in the city.[31] Nasmith's trumpet call 'to unite all denominations of Christians, and by one strong effort, to pluck sinners as brands from the burning' had become a reality, breaking the church factions of the past.[32] There was good cooperation between churches and mission societies, resulting in an extraordinary holistic Christ-centred movement. Out of this love of Christ and unity came a love for the poor and needy:

> Many institutions are happily in operation, all more or less directly subsidiary to the great objects of the gospel ministry: the Bible Society; the Religious Tract and Book Society; the 'Monthly Visitor' Society; City, Country and Coast Missions; Sabbath Schools; Industrial Schools, Temperance Societies and Savings Banks; Refuges, Reformatories, and Hospitals; the Destitute Sick Society; the Societies for supplying the poor with cheap coals, clothing, meal, and bread; and to these may now be added the Society for teaching the Blind to read.[33]

Savings Banks and the TSB

As the mission movement spread to the poor, many Christians realised that practical help had to be given to those coming out of the mire. Although they might be converted to Christ, they also needed to be delivered out of financial debt and learn a disciplined way of dealing with money, and put savings aside for harder times. Seeing this need, Rev. Henry Duncan pioneered a savings bank for the poor in his parish, out of which grew a network of

---

31. ibid., ECM Annual Report: 1861–1862, p. 12.

32. Delores Burger, *Practical Religion: David Nasmith and the City Mission Movement, 1799–2000*, p. 46, from *The Manchester Guardian*, 3rd May 1837.

33. Paul James-Griffiths, ECM Annual Report: 1861–1862, p. 24.

other savings banks, including the national Trustee Savings Bank (TSB), based on his democratic and philanthropic principles.

In 2017, TSB celebrated the life of their founder by donating two copies of a book entitled *Minister of Money,* by Professor Charles Munn, to every library in Scotland. Charles Munn says that 'Reverend Henry Duncan's legacy stretches across the world. He may justly claim to have created the first "thrifty Scots" but within a few years of him setting up his bank in Ruthwell in 1810 savings banks were being established in the rest of the UK, Europe, USA and many parts of the world. And he spent the rest of his life providing advice and guidance to anyone who asked for assistance in setting up a savings bank.'[34]

Transforming the Poor

During this same period ECM was thriving, and an indifference to the things of God was being changed to a hunger, even desperation. One missionary could record in his journal that 'multitudes who would formerly have resented any direct inquiry respecting their state before God, began eagerly to court opportunities of being conversed with on this topic, and some would follow the missionary to his house, or accompany him in a walk to the country, pressing, in various forms, the momentous inquiry, "What must I do to be saved?"'[35]

Just twelve years later there was an evangelical high-water mark, which continued unabated for several decades. Another missionary wrote an astounding account, saying, 'I have seen more of the Lord's mighty doings during the past three months than I expected to see in this life .... Nearly a hundred persons have met around our tea-table for converse and Bible instruction, nearly all of whom profess to have got pardon through faith in Jesus.'[36]

---

34. *Scotland's Banking pioneer,* Henry Duncan, 'is celebrated on St Andrews's day by nationwide book donation,' 1st December 2017, TSB website: http://www.tsb.co.uk.

35. ECM Annual Report: 1861: p.15.

36. ECM Annual Report: 1873: pp.14–15.

The city mission movement in Edinburgh, as well as in Glasgow, London and elsewhere, was having a tremendous galvanising effect on the churches and seeing extraordinary transformations: it had won great respect from the popr to the nobility. Mission was no longer a 'low and drivelling concern', but something to be admired and supported. The leading lights of Edinburgh flocked to sign up as trustees, or as external advisors: among them in this period were the Duke of Argyll; three earls; ten lords; nine knights; a lady; and a host of provosts (mayors); sheriffs; baillies; professors; judges; scientists; and leading clergy. Lord Shaftesbury, that indefatigable Christian social reformer and politician in London, stated that if it had not been the deep work of societies like the city missions, particularly amongst the poor, then Britain would have been engulfed in revolution in 1848, like France. As an English earl he could celebrate 'David Nasmyth, of whom all Scotsmen may well boast.'[37]

The Monthly Visitor

Although ECM, following Chalmers' inspiration, cut a decisive and courageous furrow in Edinburgh's field of humanity, many

---

37. Speech of the Earl of Shaftesbury at Wemyss Bay, Scotland, autumn, 1874, ECM Annual Report, 1874: pp. 11–12. The relevant part of this speech is given here: 'Were it not,' says his Lordship, 'for the London City Mission, and other kindred associations, I really know not what would be the condition of the metropolis of London. But I am certain of this, that if God had not put it into the heart of excellent men like David Nasmyth, of whom all Scotsmen may well boast, some five and thirty years ago, to found and carry on the London City Mission, and kindred institutions, the metropolis of London, and a very large proportion of the empire of Great Britain would have been totally uninhabitable by anyone who pretended to civilization, morality and religion …. I remember the great Revolution of 1848, when, as you know, every throne was in the dust …. I remember, after that day, talking with M. Guizot, who had been Prime Minister of France, when he said, "I will tell you what saved your empire. It was not your constables; it was not your army; it was not your ministers, it was the deep, solemn, religious atmosphere … it is the religion of England that saved the empire of Great Britain." He was right … Sir George Grey said to me, "I am satisfied, as Secretary of State, that London could not have been kept in order, had not the state of mind been prepared by the operations of associations such as these."'

other societies played their part. One of these was very much a sowing ministry – of producing relevant Christian literature, or tracts, and raising up a team to regularly visit every home in the entire city to reach people with the message of Christ. Dr John Erskine had not only provoked the sleepy churches to prayer and mission; he led by example and pioneered some mission societies, including the *Edinburgh Society for Publishing Religious Tracts*, which was founded in 1793. Out of this inspiration grew the *Edinburgh Society for Monthly Distribution of Tracts* in 1833, with its eventually popular leaflet called the *Monthly Visitor*. In fact, the locals were so endeared by this society that they called it by the name of the tract – and so the society became known by that name.

At first missionaries recruited a host of volunteers to commit to this monthly visitation, and it was reported by the end of the first year that 9,882 people had received these gospel tracts, often regularly, amounting to a print run of 242,432 tracts.[38] They were also used at large open-air preaching gatherings, which drew large crowds as ministers from different churches took it in turns to preach, and typically between 10,000 to 12,000 tracts would be taken by people.[39] By 1874 the *Monthly Visitor* committee could report that no other English language periodical of any sort had been so widely distributed in the whole of Scotland than this series of gospel tracts, and that all over the nation 'not fewer than from seven to eight thousand Christian men and women are employed from month to month in this labour of love.'[40] The tracts were written in a range of styles to suit every type of person, from 'the peer in the palace to the beggar in the street.' By 1899, the report tells us that 55,281 tracts were distributed in Edinburgh every month, and that every family was being reached, with a total number of 663,376

---

38. *The Monthly Visitor*, Annual Report, 1833, p. 5.

39. The ECM Annual Report of 1856, reported 'the audiences were usually very large and exceedingly attentive. From 10,000 to 12,000 tracts were distributed on these occasions.' p. 21.

40. *The Monthly Visitor*, Annual Report, 1874, pp. 5-6.

tracts being annually distributed. There was a sense of triumph as the workers approached the twentieth century:

> The number of distributors engaged in the work exceeds 1000 [in Edinburgh]. We are gradually overtaking the whole of the city, and hope that we may be able to state that this has been done before the new century begins.[41]

Although the society could only point to a trickle of people directly converted to Christ through the tracts, they realised that the regular and abundant sowing of the message, which would constantly be read by masses of people, would prepare the city for a large harvest, and they were happy to be part of this process. By 1899 they could also celebrate 'the great army of 10,000 co-workers' across Scotland, and beyond that, that their eight hundred and ten titles of tracts were being distributed worldwide to millions.

It was obvious that Christians would see the potential of gospel literature in conjunction with their education and schools' movement; after all, what would be the point of giving Christian literature to people, if they could not read? Dr John Erskine was a key person in the dissemination of good Christian literature, and worked arduously for this cause. When a young man named David Bogue from Coldingham in Berwickshire came to study divinity at Edinburgh University, he was stirred by Erskine's passion for prayer, mission and Christian literature. Bogue himself would go on to be a key founder and mover in England behind the *London Missionary Society* (1795); the *Religious Tract Society* (1799); and the *British and Foreign Bible Society* (1804), later known simply as the *Bible Society*, all of which would go on to have a huge impact on the world.

The Bread-basket of Books

During the Enlightenment the city of Edinburgh was full of literati and books, a legacy of the Reformation. Amongst the leading

---

41. *The Monthly Visitor*, Annual Report, 1899, pp. 9-10.

publishers and booksellers in the city were several dedicated Christians. One was the Christian, William Creech, the son of Rev. William Creech of Newbattle, whose bookshop, just behind St Giles, was a hive of intellectual discussion and debate. In the same period Thomas Nelson founded what eventually became the largest publisher of Christian books in the world. He began as a second-hand bookseller in 1798, next to the Royal Mile at 2 West Bow, with his business taking off through publishing. Today Nelson Publishers is based in America, being a subsidiary of HarperCollins.

The latter publisher is one of the five leading giants in the world for producing English literature, beginning its life in 1819 in Glasgow with William Collins, a dedicated Presbyterian Christian, whose partner was Charles Chalmers, the younger brother of Dr Thomas Chalmers. If you look at the inside cover of many Christian books published between the 1790s and 1890s, you will often discover their Scottish, and especially their Edinburgh origin. Just as Dr Erskine had been an enthusiastic disseminator of Christian books throughout Britain and America, so too did the Christian publishers, having a huge impact on shaping world history. When UNESCO voted Edinburgh the world's first City of Literature in 2004 because of its plethora of famous authors, few people stopped to consider the vital part Christianity had played in this rise of literacy and publishing; even Scotland's first printed book to come off Myllar and Chepman's press in Edinburgh in 1510 was the *Aberdeen Breviary*, a Christian work. It was through this movement that the poor became educated, with Christians pioneering free loan libraries throughout the nation.

Conversation with an Atheist

The third-year sociology student was venting her frustration outside the University of Edinburgh library. 'I have researched Edinburgh's history and the work of alleviating the conditions of the poor,' she exclaimed, 'and all I find is the church!' Taking another drag on her cigarette, she exhaled nervously and continued, 'Why is it always the Christians? Where were the atheists?' Perhaps it could be argued that atheists have had quite a short history in Edinburgh, although their roots go back to the eighteenth-century Enlightenment. Social justice for the poor has now become a major preoccupation with our students, with protests and banner-waving, and reams of them volunteering for short-term mission overseas during the summer holidays, to help the poor and developing nations. Not many of them, however, stop to think where this movement came from.

CHAPTER 9

ABOLITION OF SLAVERY

With cheers of jubilation the crowd toppled Edward Colston's statue to the ground. Soon the protesters had attached ropes to it and were dragging the heavy object with great enthusiasm towards its destination – Bristol Harbour – where they unceremoniously dumped it. Some called it an act of vandalism, but for Black Lives Matter it was a just act, fuelled by the death of an American African, George Floyd, just two weeks before, which had opened up a deep well of hurt, rejection and anger.

When George Floyd lay on a Minneapolis street, crying out, 'I can't breathe!' because of a policeman's knee on his neck, nobody would have predicted the eruption over racism that would burst out from millions. On 25th May 2020, 'Big Floyd,' a criminal who had become a Christian and was struggling to leave behind his past and help others break free in the notorious Third Ward, died of asphyxiation.[1] The video of his death, filmed by bystanders, went viral in days, causing disenfranchised black Americans, together with many white and other racial groups in support, to protest en masse against racism during the following days.

On 7th June, tens of thousands of people came out to support Black Lives Matter, demonstrating on the streets of Britain. It was in the Bristol protest that Edward Colston's statue was brought down. Colston had been a wealthy merchant of the

---

1. Kate Shellnut, 'George Floyd Left a Gospel Legacy in Houston: As a Person of Peace,' from *Christianity Today*, 28th May 2020.

seventeenth and eighteenth centuries who had used £70,000 of his money – in today's sum, over eight million pounds – to support schools, build hospitals and houses for the poor. His statue had been erected by the town council of Bristol as a memorial to his great generosity and philanthropic work. So why should the protesters pull down his statue? Sadly, Colston was also a man of his age, who made great profits through the slave trade. Between 1680 and 1692 he was responsible for transporting 84,000 black African men, women and children, who had been forcibly captured, sold in the slave markets of West Africa, and would be shipped off to work the sugar and tobacco plantations in the Caribbean and the Americas. On the voyages from Africa over 19,000 of them died on board, in inhumane and despicable ways. In recent years a growing voice for the removal of his statue has been heard; now it was time for action. George Floyd's death had been the spark that lit a ready fuel pile, with a fire spreading here in Scotland, with crowds protesting and calling for the pulling down of statues connected with the vile slave trade.

It was January 1846 when Frederick Douglass arrived in Edinburgh. He had fled his homeland of America because, as a black abolitionist, he had had the courage to name and shame the white slaveholding owners in his autobiography. This former slave stirred many audiences in America with his great gift as an orator and preacher, being an evangelical Christian, and informed multitudes about the 'blood-stained hell of slavery'. Before he arrived in Scotland, he had changed his surname from Bailey to Douglass because of his hero James Douglas, who had sought to overthrow tyranny in Sir Walter Scott's book, *The Lady of the Lake*. Immediately on his arrival, Frederick Douglass was appointed as 'Scotland's antislavery agent'.

As Douglass toured Scotland speaking about abolition of slavery in America, he was amazed at the welcome he received as an equal everywhere. He loved living in this nation where there was 'scarcely a stream but what has been pouring into song, or a hill that is not associated with some fierce and bloody conflict between liberty and slavery.'² He revelled in the Covenanters' stand against despotic kings, and the Scottish resistance against English tyranny over centuries. But how was it that Scotland had broken free from slavery?

The Early Days of Slavery

When Christianity burst into life in the Roman Empire the believers read in the apostle Paul's letter that they had been liberated from the slavery of sin to follow Christ. They also rejoiced in how God had delivered His people from the slavery of Pharaoh in Egypt, so that the Israelites could return to their Promised Land. Furthermore, the apostle Paul encouraged emancipation of slaves with the words, 'Were you called while a slave? Do not be concerned about it; but if you can be made free, rather use it .... You were bought at a price [by Christ]; do not become slaves of men' (1 Cor. 7:21-23).

It is necessary to understand that most ancient nations used slaves; it was not just a black and white issue. Egyptians enslaved black Africans and Israelites; Romans enslaved white-skinned, blonde-haired, blue-eyed Angles; the Scots enslaved the English; black people enslaved other black tribes. In the eyes of the Pagan culture of the time a slave was simply a sub-human machine to get jobs done, irrespective of colour, or, as Aristotle put it: 'a slave is a living tool, just as a tool is an inanimate slave.'³

In the early centuries of Christianity many churches had redemption funds for ransoming people out of slavery. Chrysostom, the famous fourth century preacher, wrote that 'in Christ Jesus there is no slave .... Therefore, it is not necessary to have a slave .... Buy them, and after you have taught them

---

2. From the exhibition in the National Library of Scotland, Edinburgh, 4th October 2018–16th February 2019, *Strike for Freedom: Slavery, Civil War and the Frederick Douglass Family in the Walter O. and Linda Evans Collection, 200th Anniversary.*

3. Aristotle, Nicomachean Ethics 8:11, quoted from Alvin J. Schmidt's *How Christianity Changed the World* (Zondervan, 2004), p. 274.

some skill by which they can maintain themselves, set them free.'[4] This not only happened through the local church, but also through individual Christians too. For example, the historian, W. E. H. Lecky wrote:

> St. Melania was said to have emancipated 8,000 slaves; St. Ovidius, a rich martyr of Gaul, 5,000; Chromatius, a Roman prefect under Diocletian, 1,400; Hermes, a prefect under Trajan, 1,200. [And] many of the Christian clergy at Hippo under the rule of St. Augustine, as well as great numbers of private individuals, freed their slaves as an act of piety.[5]

Christians in the early church were so radical and counter-cultural that it shocked the Pagan world of that time. Clement, Bishop of Rome, writing in A.D. 95, relates that 'for our own people, we know that many have surrendered themselves to captivity as a ransom for others, and many more have sold themselves into slavery and given the money to provide others with food.'[6]

Thus, long before the abolition of slavery in the British Empire in 1833, which was spearheaded by evangelicals, like William Wilberforce and Thomas Clarkson, Christians had been at work. Right from the beginning we see the British Christians living in Scotland following their lead from the French Christians. Patrick, who was born near Dumbarton and had been enslaved by the Irish, became an apostle to these same people in the fifth century, and sought to mediate for the release of Irish slaves, who had been kidnapped by his own people, the Britons in Scotland.[7] Likewise, Columba mediated with the Pictish Pagan King Brude to liberate

---

4. Chrysostom, Homily 40 on 1 Corinthians 10, quoted from Alvin J. Schmidt's *How Christianity Changed the World* (Zondervan, 2004), pp. 274-75.

5. Schmidt, ibid, p. 274, quoting from W .E. H. Lecky, *History of European Morals: From Augustine to Charlemagne* (New York: D. Appleton, 1927), 2:69.

6. Clement, Bishop of Rome, Letter to the Church at Corinth:54, A.D. 95, from *Early Christian Writings* (Penguin Classics, 1982), p. 51.

7. Patrick, Letter to the Soldiers of Coroticus, Appendix VII, from John Healy, *The Life and Writings of St. Patrick, With Appendices, etc.* (Dublin: M. H. Gill & Son Ltd., and Sealy, Bryers & Walker, 1905, reprinted by Scholar Select), pp. 696-704.

an Irish slave girl.[8] In the eleventh century, Queen Margaret sent spies throughout Scotland to find the worst-treated English slaves, so that she could liberate them.[9]

Slavery still existed in Europe during the Reformation period, as can be seen by John Knox's own account in *The Reformation of Scotland*, when he was a galley slave for the French, and in his letter to Anna Locke he describes 'the torments of the galleys for the space of nineteen months' before he managed to escape.[10] During the seventeenth century many Covenanters were imprisoned, and then sent off to slavery in the Americas to work for white slave-holders.[11] It is not surprising, therefore, that the descendants of the Covenanters were among the first Christians in Britain and America to press for abolition of slavery. Robert Burns, Scotland's Bard, understood this link well when he met a man who sneered at the sufferings of the Covenanters for their conscience's sake, calling them ridiculous and fanatical. Burns' response was to write a short poem:

> The Solemn League and Covenant
> Cost Scotland blood – cost Scotland tears:
> But it seal'd freedom's sacred cause –
> If thou'rt a slave, indulge thy sneers.[12]

One scholar put it this way: 'Covenanters mounted a witness against the sin of slavery unlike any other. First, their antislavery

---

8. Adomnan, *Life of St Columba*, 2:33, trans. by Richard Sharpe (Penguin Classics, 1995), p. 181.

9. *Life of St Margaret*, by her confessor Turgot, trans. by W. M. Metcalfe, *Lives of the Scottish Saints* (Llanerch Enterprises, 1990), p. 60.

10. John Knox, *The Reformation in Scotland* (Banner of Truth, 2000), pp. 96-97, also quoting from Knox's letter to Anna Locke, 31st December 1559.

11. An example of this is the two hundred and fifty Covenanters who were put in the hold of the *Crown of London* in November 1679 and shipped from Leith to America to work on the plantations as slaves. The boat was shipwrecked off Orkney and only forty-seven managed to escape. Most of them were recaptured and sent as slaves to Jamaica and New Jersey.

12. *The Poetical Works of Robert Burns* (Edinburgh: William and Robert Chambers, 1838), p. 140.

ideals antedated even the Quaker abolitionist movement; Covenanters were some of the first people in Britain or America to take a public stand against the institution.'[13] It is not surprising too that Frederick Douglass, the American black abolitionist, made this connection in his love for Scotland.

'Am I Not a Man and a Brother?'

In 1769 David Spens, a slave in Fife, became a Christian and was baptised as a member of Wemyss Church. He stood for freedom and was supported by some church ministers, their congregations and some lawyers, until he was liberated. It was not long after this that the owning of personal slaves was prohibited in Scotland in 1778 after the trial of the black slave Joseph Knight in Edinburgh's Court of Session. It was there that Lord Auchinleck could declare that 'it may be the custom in Jamaica to make slaves of poor blacks but I do not believe it agreeable to humanity nor to the Christian religion. He is our brother, and he is a man.'[14]

It is not that Scotland turned its back on slavery completely at this time; although slave-owning was banned in this country, Scotland grew fat on the pain, suffering and anguish of countless slaves in the Caribbean and the Americas, which has now caused many to consider pulling down statues and street names in Glasgow, Edinburgh and elsewhere linked to the slave trade. Cotton, sugar and tobacco farmed by slaves was big business, and Britain led the world in this evil. It would take a huge effort, led by evangelicals, to topple this giant.

Nine years after Britain had banned slave-owning in this nation, Granville Sharp and eleven other abolitionists in London established the *Society for Effecting the Abolition of the Slave Trade*, which developed into the *Anti-Slavery Society* in 1823. It was a movement that was pioneered by nine Quakers and three

---

13. Joseph S. Moore, *Founding Sins: How a Group of Antislavery Radicals Fought to Put Christ into the Constitution*, 2015, published online by Oxford Scholarship, September 2015 (Oxford University Press, 2020).

14. Iain Whyte, *Scotland and the Abolition of Black Slavery, 1756–1838* (Edinburgh: Edinburgh U.P., 2006).

Anglicans. By gathering solid evidence on the mistreatment of slaves, and disseminating it through an amazingly successful campaign, they eventually saw this giant fall. In 1787 a first step was made by Granville Sharp when he managed to obtain support from the British Crown to set up the Province of Freedom in Sierra Leone for freed slaves.

In 1788, Rev. Robert Walker of Canongate Kirk in the Royal Mile challenged church leaders in Edinburgh, and they petitioned Parliament to abolish slavery. After former slave, Olaudah Equiano, gave his account to the Church Assembly in Edinburgh in 1792, Scotland sent one hundred and eighty-five petitions to Westminster. It was not until 1807 that international slave-trading was abolished in the British Empire through the Slave Trade Act. However, many slaves still worked for their masters abroad.

Among the key Scots who worked with William Wilberforce, the evangelical MP in London, to abolish slavery in the British Empire, were Zachary Macaulay, William Dickson, James Ramsay, James Stephen and Henry Brougham. Zachary Macaulay from Inveraray experienced an evangelical conversion in 1789, and went on to be the key founding member of the *Anti-Slavery Society* in 1823. His indefatigable work alongside Wilberforce and others to liberate slaves, has been celebrated in Westminster Abbey by a memorial showing the figure of a kneeling slave and the words 'Am I not a Man and a Brother' – seemingly taken from Lord Auchinleck's statement in Edinburgh in 1778. This became the motto of the abolitionist movement. James Stephen, who was born of Scottish parents and was educated in Aberdeen, was the architect of the Abolition Bill. It is also of note that the *Glasgow Anti-Slavery Society* was formed in 1822, rallying together as an abolitionist stronghold.

In 1830, Rev. Dr Andrew Thomson led the movement here to put pressure on Parliament to abolish slavery altogether. The politician Sir Henry Brougham from Edinburgh, worked hard in London to get laws passed against slavery. All of these Scots were key players in the victory over slavery with their fellow Christians in England, such as the evangelicals, Thomas Clarkson, William Wilberforce and others. It was through the untiring work of the Quakers and other evangelicals in England and Scotland that the social conscience was pricked, inspiring many influential people of the Enlightenment, such as David Hume[15] and Adam Smith, also to speak out. In 1833 the Slavery Abolition Act was passed by Parliament, outlawing slavery completely in the British Empire.

The Slavery Division

It should be obvious to the casual reader of the Bible that slavery is wrong. After all Jesus said that we should love people, so slavery stands in stark opposition to this. He cemented God's directives clearly with the statement: "'You shall love the LORD your God with all your heart, with all your soul, and with all your mind." This is the first and great commandment. And the second is like it: "You shall love your neighbor as yourself." On these two commandments hang all the Law and the Prophets' (Matt. 22:37-40). And yet there were those in society, and even in the church, who covered their ears to this, as they pursued material wealth. Some of them justified their actions by claiming that Jesus and the apostles were silent about abolition; others dragged out a few references from the Old Testament that appeared to condone slavery;[16] and others said that the apostle Paul wrote that slaves should remain 'in that state in which they were called' (1 Cor. 7:24,). This was generally the position of many liberals in the church, but there were evangelicals too, like the revivalist George Whitefield, who allowed slaves to work his

15. Presently there has been a debate in Edinburgh to have the David Hume Tower at the University of Edinburgh renamed, because Hume made some racist comments as a *'white supremacist'*. However, most people, even among abolitionists, could have been judged in the same way by twenty-first century views. The new name for the time being is the rather non-descript 40 George Square. See *BBC News*, 'Edinburgh University renames David Hume Tower over "racist" views,' 13th September 2020. Did King George say anything racist, I wonder?

16. See Exodus 21:21 and Leviticus 25:44-45.

land to support an orphanage in Savannah, Georgia. They may have been treated well by him, but it was still slavery.

The evangelicals who challenged this were clear: black Africans are made in the image of God, even as are white people; they are both equal before God. They focused on Paul's positive recommendation that 'if you can be made free, rather use it ... do not become slaves of men" (1 Cor. 7:21). In answer to the Old Testament references used to condone slavery, they explained that the Hebrew law concerned Hebrew people who had fallen into debt, who could be 'bought' for six years, not as chattel slaves, but as bondservants. Such bond-servants would work for the landowner and thus pay off whatever debt they had accrued. During this time, they must not be treated harshly. On the seventh year, the Year of Jubilee, the bondservant would be free to go, and the landowner would be responsible to help him with a generous provision. If he wished, the bondservant could stay on to work for his landowner. So instead of sending the debtor to prison for his debt, he had to pay it back by giving free labour to the landowner. This is totally different from African chattel slavery.

The non-Hebrews who were enslaved through times of war, particularly as women and children, were not left to look after themselves and be at the mercy of roving and merciless tribal groups, but rather became servants who worked free of charge, but were looked after.

The point that the abolitionists pressed home was that the Bible spoke clearly against stealing people from their homes to be used in trade in both Old and New Testaments. One of the references often used was 'he that stealeth a man, and selleth him, or if he be found in his hand, he shall surely be put to death' (Exod. 21:16, KJV). Kidnapping people from Africa to sell in the marketplace was an abomination to God, and to those who wanted to obey Him. It was this biblical view that prevailed eventually, bringing liberty to hundreds of thousands of slaves.

When Frederick Douglass came to Edinburgh, he was amazed to find how people rallied to the abolitionist cause, saying that 'Scotland is all in a blaze of antislavery excitement',[17] and yet he uncovered a stain on the Free Church, despite all of the extraordinarily good things these devout Presbyterians were doing. In the previous year he had named and shamed American slaveholders, but now it was the turn of Dr Chalmers and the leaders who had received money from American slaveholders for their philanthropic causes. He publicly condemned them in May 1846, and the abolitionist leader George Thompson urged the audiences to put pressure on the Free Church to send the money back; he even said that the words 'Send the money back' should be inscribed into the Salisbury Crags near Arthur's Seat. Frederick Douglass literally took him up on this, as *The Fife Herald* relates:

> Mr Frederick Douglass … immediately hied, spade in hand, accompanied by two ladies belonging to the Society of Friends [Quaker Christians] … and began to carve this vulgar cry in graceful characters upon the great sward … we understand that Mr Douglas was immediately taken to task … upon which the philanthropic man of colour expressed deep contrition for the crime.[18]

Iain Whyte, in his *Send Back the Money! The Free Church of Scotland and American Slavery*, shows that Thomas Chalmers, William Cunningham and Robert Candlish sought to brush the issue under the carpet, whilst also speaking against abolition. Cunningham even defended some forms of slavery; Chalmers hoped for a more gradual, rather than revolutionary approach to abolition, particularly as he was concerned about the huge upheavals that had just broken out in Europe, leaving many dead. The actual money sent from American slaveholders to the Free Church amounted to about £3,000, a tidy sum in those days, but it was the principle that mattered.

---

17. Letter by Frederick Douglass, 28th April 1846, from the exhibition in the National Library of Scotland, Edinburgh, 4th October 2018–16th February 2019, *Strike for Freedom: Slavery, Civil War and the Frederick Douglass Family in the Walter O. and Linda Evans Collection, 200th Anniversary*.

18. *The Fife Herald*, 21st May 1846, from the Strike for Freedom exhibition.

The Free Church was also pressured to cease fellowship with churches in America with known slaveholders who were members. The Free Church had come from the same lineage as the Covenanters, some of whom had ended up in America. From the American Covenanters had come the first movement to abolish slavery there, and Rev. Alexander Macleod, the first leader of the Reformed Presbyterian Church in America, could write in 1802 that 'There is not a slave-holder now in the communion of the Reformed Presbytery.'[19] Abolitionists were indeed split on the best approach to abolition: gradual, or more revolutionary. In the end, Civil War broke out in America with the issue being fully resolved there in 1865 when total abolition of slavery was made law. The cost in human lives for such a victorious Civil War over slavery amounted to between 600,000 and 1,000,000, including about 80,000 slaves who had perished through it all. It was this kind of carnage that Dr Chalmers envisaged, and that caused him to prefer a more gradual approach of abolition.

---

19. Alexander Macleod, *Negro Slavery Unjustifiable: A Discourse* (New York, 1802).

CHAPTER 10

EMANCIPATION OF WOMEN

'The church in Scotland has oppressed women,' a young lady retorted angrily to me one day, 'It's got nothing but a record of abuse of their rights.' At the time I did not know what to do; the anger and bitterness that erupted that afternoon took me off guard, and I felt overwhelmed with a sense of numbing inadequacy. As the church, we do have to own up to our faults, weaknesses, and mistakes concerning the treatment of women, but it is only one side of the story.

I love the tender way in which Jesus treated women in the Gospels. He chose a former prostitute to be the first witness of His resurrection in a man's world in which a woman's testimony did not count for much. It was to her at that dawn on Sunday He appeared and said 'Mary!' causing her to swivel around and hug Him. She recognised the tender tone of His voice because it was so totally different to the many men who had abused her. God chose five women who had social stigmas attached to them to be Jesus' ancestors, according to His human ancestry recorded in Matthew's Gospel.

Jesus taught men and women together, side by side, when society segregated them; He and His disciples were financially supported by women. The men and women in the early church decided together who should replace the traitor, Judas Iscariot, as the next apostle. When the promised Holy Spirit was poured out, it was in fulfilment of the prophet Joel through whom God had said 'I will pour out My Spirit on all flesh; your sons and daughters will prophesy .... And also on My menservants and on My maidservants I will pour out My Spirit in those days" (Joel 2:28-29). Jesus' kingdom was radically different from the systems into which the gospel would spread in the ancient world, for the apostle Paul declared 'There is neither Jew nor Greek, there is neither slave nor free, there is neither male nor female; for you are all one in Christ Jesus' (Gal. 3:28).

My teenage daughter came home from school in Edinburgh one afternoon looking crushed. She knew Jesus, but her teacher had laid into the Christian faith (and no other religion) that morning by attacking Paul in front of a deeply offended class of young girls. 'Dad, is it true that women are not allowed to speak in church?' Miriam asked. Taking my Bible from the shelf I sat with her and we read the whole chapter from which her teacher had extricated one verse. Yes, there it was: 'Let your women be silent in the churches, for they are not permitted to speak' (1 Cor. 14:34). My daughter's look of consternation showed that, like her teacher, she had focused on just one verse, out of context.

'To whom is Paul speaking?' I asked. 'Look at verse 26.'

'The brethren,' she replied.

'Who are the brethren? Look at verse 23,' I continued.

'The whole church,' she said, looking up with a smile.

'That's right,' I affirmed. 'This means that men and women can do all these speaking things mentioned in this passage. So, what does Paul mean about women being silent in church?'

She shrugged her shoulders.

'Look at the passage again,' I said. 'What is the purpose of meeting together?'

'To build each other up in the faith,' she answered. 'To share the gifts God has given them with everyone, so that all can learn and be encouraged.'

'And how should this be done? Look at verses 33 and 40,' I said.

Miriam studied the verse and replied, 'In order, with peace and decency, and without confusion.'

'Yes, that's the point,' I responded. 'So there were some rude women who kept on interrupting the church meeting, causing chaos, speaking out of turn, with no sense of order, decency and peace. This chapter follows Paul's famous one on love. Do you think they should have been allowed to keep on interrupting and causing confusion? Is that love?'

'No,' she said, grinning.

Did you know that it is not just women who are told by Paul to be quiet in church, but also men? In the same chapter men and women are told to 'keep silent in church', if there is nobody to interpret the spoken gift of 'tongues', a supernatural gift. Again, the reason is love, for mutual encouragement, rather than for spiritual exhibitionism.

Critics of the New Testament have also brought up the verse that says 'wives should submit to your own husbands' (Eph. 5:22), as if this is clear evidence of misogyny. But they rarely bother to read the context, which is that Christians should 'submit to one another' out of reverence and love of God, and that husbands should lay down their lives out of love for their wives, as Christ did for His church. It is true that in God's order married men are the heads of their wives, and that elders of the church should only be men, but in both cases they are expected to serve in sacrificial ways, not lord it over people. In biblical understanding we see a picture of *equality* and *diversity* working together, rather than *uniformity* and control, which at times the church has got wrong.

The rise of feminism came about when people lost sight of this godly principle and women were wounded by men who oppressed them; unfortunately, when women try to be men it does not work either. Men and women are meant, in God's plan, to complement one another in teamwork, and not be in angry competition with each other. It is not surprising that women flocked into the church in the Pagan Roman Empire, because of its counter-cultural and revolutionary message. This is something which Rodney Stark, an agnostic and Professor of Sociology at the University of Washington, freely admits, as do many others who have studied the role of women in the early church. Professor Stark highlights the reasons for this massive movement of women into the church. 'This shift,' he says, 'was the result of Christian prohibitions against infanticide and abortion…. Christian women enjoyed substantially higher status within Christian subcultures than pagan women did in the world at large ... but women also filled leadership positions within the church.'[1]

In order to show how revolutionary and liberating Christ's teaching was for women in the first century, we will need to compare His model with the models of those of other contemporary cultures. Amongst the religious Jewish people, women were not allowed to give testimony in court (Talmud, *Yoma* 43b), whereas Jesus chose women to be the first witnesses of His resurrection. 'Let the words of the Law [Torah] be burned rather than committed to a woman,' says the Talmud (*Sotah* 3:4), 'If a man teaches his daughter the Law, it is as though he taught her lechery.' Jesus, on the other hand, taught women and men together. The Talmud states, 'He who talks with a woman [in public] brings evil upon himself' (*Aboth* 1:5). Remember that Jesus overthrew this taboo regularly, and we especially recall His tender conversation with the Samaritan woman at the well (John 4).

What about the Pagan world? Surely, Athenian democracy produced freedom for women? In this culture a woman was not allowed to leave the house unaccompanied by a male, and she was not allowed to eat with her husband's guests. The average woman had the social standing of a slave, with no voting rights, and no education. Aristophanes' chorus sang in *Lysistrata*: 'For women are a shameless set, the vilest of creatures going' (368–369). Typically, a woman's husband could have a mistress on the side and a young boy at the gym, whilst being married. Having a baby girl was an economic burden because of having to provide a dowry when she got married, whereas boys were preferable: this led to sex-selective abortions and infanticides, as happens in countries like India today. Roman and Greek cultures were similar. In the *Twelve Tables of Roman law*, the husband, as *paterfamilias*, had absolute rule over his wife and children. He alone could divorce his wife, whereas she was powerless. He could

---

1. R. Stark, *The Rise of Christianity: How the Obscure, Marginal Jesus Movement Became the Dominant Religious Force in the Western World in a Few Centuries* (Princeton University Press, Harper One, 1996), p. 128.

even have his wife and children executed for adultery in Caesar Augustus' *Lex Julia de adulteriis coercendis* of 17 B.C., yet he was free to live a life of loose sex.

It was through the gospel of Christ that multitudes of women in the ancient world were liberated. In more modern times, it was through the social action of Christians in India that the horrific Hindu practice of *sati* was banned, in which a widow whose husband died was expected to be burned alive on a funeral pyre. In China, the custom of foot-binding was banned through the work of Christians in 1912. In this practice small girls had their feet bound tightly, so that by the time they were women their feet had become totally deformed; many died of gangrene. Mary Slessor from Scotland led the movement in Nigeria to ban the practice of slaughtering the chief's wives after he had died.

Herodotus described a tradition in about 450 B.C. in Babylon, in which 'every woman who is a native of the country must once in her life go and sit in the temple of Aphrodite [the goddess of sexual love] and there give herself to a strange man.' The men would patrol the cattle market of women, each man selecting a woman, throw a coin in her lap, then say '"In the name of the goddess Mylitta" – that being the Assyrian name for Aphrodite.' After this, the woman had to go and have sex with the stranger to fulfil her duty to the goddess, before being free to be married at an auction to the highest bidder.[2] It was Christians who liberated these women through the law.

Today, millions of girls and women, in twenty-six countries, have to undergo the barbaric ritual of female genital mutilation: this involves having their clitoris and often the labia removed with a razor blade or knife, usually without any pain relief or anaesthetic. In Islam, the Qur'an teaches that 'Men stand superior to women.... But those whose perverseness ye fear, admonish them and remove them into bedchambers and beat them; but if they submit to you then do not seek a way against them'

---

2. Herodotus, *The Histories*, Book 1:194-199 (Penguin Classics, 1972), pp. 121-22.

(Sura 4:34). Jesus forgave the woman 'caught in the very act of adultery', rescuing her from those who would have stoned her to death, and told her to 'go and sin no more' (John 8:11).

Women's Voting and Scottish Christians

Who would have ever thought that women's suffrage, or voting as equals with men, would largely have arisen out of the Presbyterian Church in Scotland? Did not John Knox write that inflammatory book *The First Blast against the Monstrous Regiment of Women*? Yes, he did, but his axe to grind was against the three Marys: Mary de Guise, whose family slaughtered many Protestants in France; Mary Tudor, who had about three hundred Protestants burnt at the stake; and Mary, Queen of Scots, whom he deeply mistrusted.

We will need to explore what happened in the Presbyterian Church to discover how Christians in Scotland played a significant part in women's suffrage. For this I am indebted to Dr Eun Soo Choi, whose PhD at Glasgow University was entitled *The religious dimension of the women's suffrage movement: the role of the Scottish Presbyterian churches, 1867–1918*.

Dr Choi points out that, although many Christians in the Presbyterian denominations remained neutral, with some being antagonistic, there were also many who championed equal votes for women in national politics. It was their dogged determination and hard work which inspired a multitude at the beginning of the movement, and whose significant support contributed hugely to its ultimate success. Besides them, the Quakers and other Christians were instrumental in the long fight for freedom for women to vote.

Even though 1918 was the milestone in British history for the breakthrough for some women being allowed to vote, followed by full voting rights for adult women in 1928, we will have to look back to 1733 to see one of the significant roots of the movement. In 1712, Queen Anne's Parliament enforced the Patronage Act, in which churches in Britain, which now included Scotland, had to submit to the local landowner's choice of minister for the church. As we have seen earlier in this book, this meant the democratic voting for leaders by their congregations in the Church of Scotland was dismissed by the government. The national church again found itself in dispute over church polity. In 1733, a breakaway movement, led by the brothers Rev. Ebenezer and Rev. Ralph Erskine, left the Church of Scotland because this group was determined to be obedient to its Presbyterian democratic constitution. When their Secession Church was set up in that same year, a new freedom was introduced: women could vote for their leaders in church. Before this, only male heads of homes could vote. Their Associate Presbytery's Testimony of the Secession Church stated, 'That ministers and other office-bearers are to be set over congregations by the call and consent of the majority of the members in full communion with the church in her sealing ordinances.'[3]

One example, among many, of this equal voting system in the Secession Church can be seen in 1751 when Rev. James Erskine was called to minister at a church in Stirling, in which the call was signed by 826 male and female members of the church there.[4] Even Rev. Thomas McCrie, who spoke out against the female vote, accepted the call to minister in Davie St Church in 1836, in which the voting register had been signed by ninety-five men and one hundred and sixty-five women.[5]

The stand on women's suffrage (voting) by the Secession Church directly inspired the Free Church of Scotland, when it too broke away from the national church, chiefly over the same issue of patronage, at the Disruption of 1843. With over 30% of the ministers joining the Free Church, and all missionaries, except

---

3. J. M'Kerrow, *History of the Secession Church*, pp. 80-110; R. Small, *Woman's Vote in the Secession Church*, the United Presbyterian Magazine, April 1899, both cited by Choi in *The religious dimension of the women's suffrage movement*, 1996, p. 18.

4. R. Small, *History of the Congregations of the United Presbyterian Church*, Vol II (Edinburgh, 1904), p. 664; R. Small, *Women's Vote in the Secession Church*, p. 166, cited by Choi, ibid., p. 21.

5. D. Scott, *Annals and Statistics of the Original Secession Church* (Edinburgh, 1886), p. 324, cited by Choi, ibid., p. 26.

for one, throwing their lot in with them, as well as hundreds of elders, the impact on Scotland and Britain, and as far away as America, was colossal, because like the Secession Church, it was over the main issue of constitutional voting and democracy. Even at the first General Assembly of the Free Church in Glasgow on 24th October 1843, the subject of women's suffrage was discussed; by 1846, women were allowed to vote for their leaders in the Free Church. It was not until patronage was abolished in the Church of Scotland in 1874 that women could vote there as well, despite there already being a strong voice for women's suffrage within its ranks. By 1884, the chief leadership to support the women's political votes was found in the Free Church, followed by other Presbyterian denominations.

With such a groundswell for freedom for women to vote in the Presbyterian churches, as well as in the Quaker, Baptist, Congregational, and other denominations, it is not surprising that people began to press for women to vote alongside men for their political candidates as well. Rev. Dr Robert Wallace, the minister at Old Greyfriars Kirk in Edinburgh, and the former Professor of Church History at the University of Edinburgh, took it a step further. 'If women were allowed to exercise political privileges,' he said, 'where was the matter to stop? Why not permit them to enter Parliament itself?'[6] Being the editor of *The Scotsman* newspaper his call echoed throughout the nation. That was in 1870; the first woman parliamentarian would not be until 1919.

The Suffragists

Three women's suffrage societies were formed in 1867 in London, Edinburgh and Manchester, which came together under the banner of the *National Society for Women's Suffrage*. In Edinburgh we can uncover the strong Christian influence in this movement. Eliza Wigham and her stepmother, Jane Wigham (née Smeal), were the founders. Both were keen Quaker Christians who had fought for the emancipation of slaves, and now the victory had been won in

---

6. *The Scotsman*, 18th January 1870, cited by Choi, ibid., p. 71.

that arena, it was time to focus their energies on liberating women to vote in Britain. The key leaders of the Edinburgh branch were all dedicated Quakers: the first president was Priscilla Bright McLaren; the two secretaries were Eliza Wigham and Agnes McLaren, Priscilla's daughter; and the treasurer was Elizabeth Pease. When the first national suffrage gathering happened in Manchester at the Free Trade Hall in 1868, Priscilla Bright McLaren was its first presiding leader at this meeting. Their vision was to petition Parliament for women's votes, and to develop a supportive movement throughout Britain through education and a rigorous publicity campaign.

Priscilla Bright McLaren was surrounded by influential members of Parliament: her husband, Duncan McLaren, was a devoted Presbyterian Christian, and as a Liberal MP for Edinburgh his passion for all things Scottish had given him the endearing popular title of 'the Member for Scotland'. His hard work and support for the Free Church dissenters had gained a strong evangelical base, and his wisdom and skill in pulling Edinburgh out of bankruptcy, as well as promoting free schools for poor children, earned him great favour in Scottish society. Together with Priscilla's Quaker brothers John and Jacob Bright, who were both MPs, Duncan McLaren spearheaded this Christian political trio to press for women's suffrage in Parliament.

By the next year in 1868, the emancipation movement had grown rapidly in Scotland. Jane Taylour and Mary Burton, with Flora and Louisa Stevenson, criss-crossed the nation to speak at gatherings on behalf of the Edinburgh Suffrage Society. Louisa herself would also play a significant part in campaigning to see victory for women in education, when in the Universities Act of 1889 women were allowed to study as equals at Scottish universities. With the devout Episcopalian Christian, Guthrie Wright, she also co-founded the Edinburgh School of Cookery, from which grew Queen Margaret University in 1875.

One of Louisa's friends was Sophia Jex-Blake, another member of the Edinburgh Suffrage Society, who went on to lead the movement for emancipation of women in medicine. Through her efforts the 'Edinburgh Seven' became the first women to study medicine at a university in Britain in 1869. Jex-Blake was overjoyed and wrote to her friend Lucy Sewell: 'It is a grand thing to enter the very first British University ever opened to women, isn't it?[7] Jex-Blake went on to pioneer the first college for training women in medicine in 1886, called the Edinburgh School of Medicine for Women, but it closed in 1898 because of her ultra-disciplinarian approach. However, one of her pupils called Elsie Inglis was destined to develop a model that would last.

In 1889, Elsie Inglis co-founded the Edinburgh College of Medicine for Women, with the support of her father, John Inglis, and their friend Sir William Muir, the Principal of the University of Edinburgh. All three were evangelical Christians. The college began in 30 Chambers Street, opposite the National Museum in Edinburgh and the college eventually merged with the School of Medicine of the Royal Colleges of Edinburgh in 1916. The original building of Elsie's college was demolished in 1927 and a new building was erected as the Edinburgh Dental Hospital and College.

Although such victories for British women in education and medicine began in Edinburgh, the celebration of women's suffrage was still some way off. Meanwhile, the Edinburgh Suffrage Society was very busy, with *The Scotsman* covering the long campaign. By 1871 there had been six hundred and nineteen petitions to Parliament in which there were 186,000 signatures. Despite the growing groundswell of popular support in Britain through the multiplying suffragist societies, including the Christian Women's Union in Scotland, Parliament would still not budge. There was a great push behind the Woodall's Amendment to the Reform Bill in 1884, but again Parliament rejected women's suffrage. Increasingly the suffragists became frustrated at the slow progress in nearly forty years of campaigning for freedom. Out of this frustration emerged the more radical approach of the suffragettes.

---

7. Wikipedia, uncited source, under the entry *Edinburgh Seven*.

The Suffragettes

Christabel Pankhurst from Manchester had grown up in the suffragist movement with her mother Emeline, but by 1903 they had had enough and their patience was frayed. Emmeline pioneered a meeting in her home which became known as the Women's Social and Political Union (WSPU). They were tired of words; they believed that militant action was now required. Interrupting public meetings, heckling politicians, smashing windows, throwing stones, arson and hunger strikes became the methods of this breakaway group. This approach suited more the Marxist revolutionary style than that of the Christian-led peaceful lobbying movement of the suffragists. Unfortunately, the more aggressive the Pankhurst suffragettes became, the more they initially lost popular support. 'Violence answered our demand for justice ... better violence than jeers, sneers, or silent contempt,' came the war cry of Christabel Pankhurst. 'Where peaceful means had failed, one act of militancy succeeded and never again was the cause ignored by that or any other newspaper.'[8]

As the suffragettes became more frustrated in their passion to obtain the vote, they became more daring, and more extreme. After the Franchise Registration Bill was withdrawn in the House of Commons on 27th January, 1913, the suffragettes reacted with terrorism. Between April 1913 and August 1914, thirty-six buildings were destroyed or burnt down in protest.[9] When the suffragettes burnt down St Mary's White Kirk near Haddington, by using inflammable liquid and explosives to try and attract attention to their cause, most of the nation was horrified. This was a beautiful twelfth century medieval church with a fascinating history, and with priceless artefacts inside, such as the old White Kirk Bible.

---

8. S. Pankhurst, *Unshackled* (Hutchinson of London, 1959), p. 51, cited by Choi, ibid., p. 21.

9. Andrew Rosen, *Rise Up, Women!* (Routledge, 2012), pp. 192, 197, 201, 202, 222; L. Leneman, *A Guide Cause: The Women's Suffrage Movement in Scotland*, revised edition (Aberdeen, 1995), pp. 275-78; *The Suffragette*, 10th July 1914; *The Times*, 4th July 1914, all cited in Choi, ibid., p. 128.

Not surprisingly, the radical methods of the suffragettes estranged many Christian and other constitutional suffragists. The Haddington Church of Scotland Presbytery pulled out from supporting the suffragettes, and now churches were labelled as being 'anti-Christian' for not supporting the militant and revolutionary methods of the extremists. However, when one hundred and sixty-one police were sent to break up a suffragette meeting in St Andrew's Hall in Glasgow on 9th March, 1914, the brutal methods used by the force led to national protests in support of the women, and drew many church people back to stand with them because of their unfair treatment.

Although most Christians did not seem to be involved in the more extreme work of the suffragettes, they were also represented in their ranks. Even those who were not Christians often appealed to reformers like John Knox as their example of militancy against corruption. Lady Ramsay in the *Free Church Suffrage Times* could write that 'the movement is essentially spiritual ... it makes a special call to women. The Divine call has reached them, bidding them rise and do the work God requires of them; and everywhere throughout the world they are responding to the call.'[10]

Lady Ramsay was in both camps, being a suffragette member of the *Scottish Women's Social and Political Union* (WSPU), and the suffragist vice-president of the *Scottish Churches League for Women's Suffrage*, an inter-church movement. For her the two approaches, without extremism, were needed in what she saw was 'a Christian movement', and being the daughter of the dedicated Christian, the Duke of Argyll, she shared his active faith in seeking social reforms, by using her position in the aristocracy as a lever for suffrage amongst politicians. She worked closely with Millicent Fawcett, the first president of the *National Union of Women's Suffrage Societies* (NUWSS), who herself had been inspired to fight the women's cause through the preaching of Rev. Professor Frederick Denison Maurice, one of the founders of the Christian Socialists.

---

10. *Free Church Suffrage Times*, April 1913, cited by Choi, ibid., p. 76.

Helen Crawfurd, the wife of Rev. Alexander Crawfurd, minister at Brownfield Church in Glasgow, saw her work in both the suffragists and suffragettes as 'a holy crusade for the liberation of women'.[11] After praying one Sunday morning about whether to join the more militant suffragettes in their protests, she was inspired to do so through her husband's sermon a few hours later when he preached on Jesus Christ making a whip of cords and driving the money-changers out of the temple. Defending her more radical action she justified it by saying, 'If Christ could be militant, so could I.'[12]

Victory

Women worked so admirably during World War I, and in such vital roles, that many of those who had obstructed their right to vote equally with men were silenced. Amidst great jubilation, women over thirty, who met a property qualification, were given the vote in 1918; this was followed by the first woman MP in 1919, and the complete voting victory for all adult women in England, Scotland and Wales in 1928. Sadly, the very significant role that Christians from Scotland exerted in the process has been airbrushed from the story, leaving the bra-burning feminists of the 1960s in the limelight, alongside Pankhursts' suffragettes.

Simon Webb, in *The Suffragette Bombers: Britain's Forgotten Terrorists*, shows that the more radical and extreme suffragettes have been painted as heroines, but they ran a 'widespread and sustained bombing campaign' across Britain, causing havoc. Webb argues that it was this form of extremism that delayed the voting right of women, rather than accelerated it. Christabel Pankhurst, one of the core founders of the WSPU, became an evangelical Christian later, and expressed her regret at the more excessive use of violence used to achieve women's suffrage, wishing that they had followed a more Christlike approach.

---

11. Unpublished manuscript of Helen Crawfurd's autobiography, p. 228, cited by Choi, ibid., p. 89.

12. Helen Crawfurd, ibid., cited by Choi, ibid., p. 89.

As the twentieth century came to a close, Christians could look back with encouragement at the growth of world mission as a result of the revival movements in Scotland. They had also witnessed the implementation of such Christian ideals as a national education system, health system, modern democracy, and social reforms that had become deeply entrenched in our culture. In the nineteenth and twentieth centuries, Christian women would rise up and achieve phenomenal transformation under God.

Liberated Women Missionary Pioneers

As the Christian faith inspired and liberated women, some of them would go abroad from Scotland and see transformations in other cultures. Not many people have appeared on our national banknotes, but in 1997, to commemorate the courageous work of Mary Slessor, Clydesdale Bank printed the £10 issue with her image on it. This red-haired, blue-eyed, small fireball from an impoverished Dundee home had a huge impact on Nigeria. Her passion was to go where no missionaries had been, to love the tribes and share Jesus with them.

When Mary expressed her passion to reach the outlying villages further afield, Mrs Anderson, one of the missionaries, tried to dissuade her: 'Many are cannibals,' she said. 'When a chief dies, his wives and slaves have their heads cut off and are buried with him. A slave receives no more consideration than a pig. They sleep on the ground like animals and are branded with a hot iron. Many have their ears cut off, and the girls are fattened like animals and sold for slave wives.... And one of the worst customs is the treatment of twins.... The people fear twins worse than death.... They are not allowed to live. They are killed, crushed into pots and thrown into the bush. The mother is driven out. No one will have anything to do with her, leaving her to die in the forests or be eaten by the animals.'[13]

---

13. Basil Miller, *Mary Slessor: Heroine of Calabar* (Bethany House Publishers, 1974), pp. 23-24.

Instead of being scared off, Mary's love for these people kept growing. In particular, her motherly heart was broken by the plight of the twins in Nigeria. With tears in her eyes, she looked up at Mrs Anderson. With her resolute Scottish accent she declared, 'I shall fight this. It must be stopped .... I will never give up.' Through Mary, the tribal chiefs of Calabar agreed to pass the law banning the murder of twins. With much clapping and tears pouring down their faces the women gathered to celebrate. 'It was a glorious day for Calabar,' Mary wrote, 'I wept tears of joy.' A few days later, when the legal papers were signed, such a great noise of celebration erupted from the women that Mary asked the chief to stop it. 'Ma, how can I stop them women mouths?' he replied, 'How can I do it? They be women.'[14]

As she persevered, Mary began to see dramatic changes among the Okoyong people. 'Of results affecting the condition and conduct of our people,' she wrote, 'Raiding, plundering and stealing of slaves have almost entirely ceased .... No tribe formerly was so feared because of their utter disregard for human life. But human life is now safe. No chief ever died without the sacrifice of many lives, but the custom has now ceased .... In regard to infanticide and twin-murder, there has dawned on them the fact that life is worth saving, even at the risk of one's own.'[15]

In 1915, Mary lay dying. Her legacy: a field of changed lives, of social reforms, churches and schools. Above all, the people of Calabar knew her as 'the White Ma who loves babies'.

Minnie Watson

In the shadow of Mary Slessor is a largely forgotten woman, also from Dundee, who is regarded by 3.5 million Kenyan Presbyterian Christians as their spiritual mother. The BBC News featured this extraordinary woman in 2017 with the title: *Church Missionary Minnie Watson inspires millions of Kenyans*. After being married to Rev. Thomas Watson in Kenya in 1899, tragedy hit and her

14. Ibid., p. 34.
15. Ibid., p. 86.

husband died of pneumonia. The heartbroken widow continued the work of her husband and excelled, leaving a lasting impact. Her foundational work in planting churches, schools, healthcare and breaking the poverty cycle through agricultural industry has shaped the nation. Kenya's first President, Jomo Kenyatta, was a former pupil at one of the schools founded by Minnie and he was baptised in the Watson-Scott Memorial Church. In a very real sense, President Kenyatta was the founding father of the modern nation of Kenya. At the grave where Minnie and Thomas are buried is a Celtic cross and the inscription: 'They brought the light of God to the Kikuyu people.'

The First Woman Prime Minister

Our first-ever woman Prime Minister in Britain was Margaret Thatcher, who was of Methodist Christian stock. In a speech in 1988 she was unusually candid and reflective. 'We are a nation whose ideals were founded on the Bible,' she said. 'The truths of the Judaeo-Christian tradition are infinitely precious, not only, as I believe, because they are true, but also because they provide the moral impulse which alone can lead to that peace, in the true meaning of the word, for which we all long ... there is little hope for democracy if the hearts of men and women in democratic societies cannot be touched by a call to something greater than ourselves. Political structures, state institutions, collective ideals are not enough .... [Democracy requires] the life of faith ... as much to the temporal as to the spiritual welfare of the nation.'[16]

---

16. *Christianity and Conservatism*, the Rt Hon Michael Alison MP and David L. Edwards eds. (London: Hodder and Stoughton, 1990), pp. 337-38, cited from *The Book that Made your World: How the Bible Created the Soul of Western Civilization*, Vishal Mangalwadi (Thomas Nelson, 2011), pp. 161-62.

CHAPTER 11

SCIENCE

Ronald was irate. He was so steamed up that it seemed he could not
see through his own glasses. 'The church is the enemy of science,'
he shouted. Then he began to list the offences, ticking them off
with his fingers: 'Flat earth; Galileo; superstition; and the Dark
Ages.' I waited for him to calm down and gently reasoned with
him. Only two church scholars, Lactantius and Cosmas, had held
to a flat earth theory, whereas almost all of the church scholars
had understood that the earth is a sphere because of biblical and
ancient scientific reasoning. The idea that the sun revolved around
the earth was the belief of the Pagan Ptolemy, which became
accepted as an early scientific understanding in the Greco-Roman
world, and which the church and Islam largely followed until this
idea was challenged by Copernicus, Kepler and Galileo. Kepler
said, 'I had the intention of becoming a theologian ... but now I
see how God is, by my endeavours, also glorified in astronomy,
for "the heavens declare the glory of God".'[1]

It has been the fashionable opinion in our generation not to
let the divine foot in the door of science, for if we do, sceptics
believe, we shall be taken back to the Dark Ages. Such thinking
may be popular now, but it is totally untrue: most of our branches
of science were founded by Christians,[2] and in the Middle Ages

---

1. Ann Lamont, *21 Great Scientists who Believed the Bible* (Creation Science
Foundation Ltd, 1995), p. 15.

2. For further research: Ann Lamont, *21 Great Scientists who Believed
the Bible* (Creation Science Foundation Ltd, 1995); James Hannam, *God's
Philosophers: How the Medieval World Laid the Foundations of Modern*

it was the church that kept science alive and developed it, with the reformers setting a foundation of empirical testing that cast aside the so-called science of Aristotle and others. In the last ten years, more historians of science are beginning to realise that the Dark Ages is a myth of the Enlightenment. For example, James Hannam, who has a PhD in the history of science at the University of Cambridge, tells us that 'Popular opinion, journalistic cliché and misinformed historians notwithstanding, recent research has shown that the Middle Ages was a period of enormous advances in science, technology and culture.'[3] And then he goes on to uncover the list of medieval scientists from the church who advanced science, so that Isaac Newton and others could sit on their shoulders.

Professor Peter Harrison, whose doctorate was from the University of Oxford, is even more illuminating. Of the ten scientists who founded the Royal Society, seven were Bible-believing Puritans, and by 1663 the number of Puritans in the Royal Society was 62 per cent, even though Puritans were a minority of the population.[4] 'The modern approach to texts, driven by the agenda of the reformers and disseminated through Protestant religious practices,' he wrote, 'created the conditions which made possible the emergence of modern science.'[5]

Science (Icon Books Ltd, 2009); Peter Harrison, *The Bible, Protestantism, and the Rise of Natural Science* (Cambridge University Press, 1998) (Peter Harrison gained his DLitt from the University of Oxford, and his PhD from the University of Queensland. He was the Andreas Idreos Professor of Science and Religion at the University of Oxford, and is now Professor of Philosophy at Bond University in Australia); Christopher B. Kaiser, *Creation and the History of Science*, Vol. 3 (Marshall Pickering, 1991) (Christopher Kaiser has doctorates in astrophysics [Harvard and Colorado Universities], and also in Christian Dogmatics at the University of Edinburgh. His book won an award from the Templeton Foundation).

3. James Hannam, *God's Philosophers: How the Medieval World Laid the Foundations of Modern Science* (Icon Books Ltd, 2009), p. 5.

4. Peter Harrison, *The Bible, Protestantism, and the Rise of Natural Science* (Cambridge University Press, 1998), pp. 5-6.

5. Peter Harrison, ibid., p. 266.

At the beginning of Genesis chapter one God said, 'Let there be light.' This short phrase became the inspiration for the mottos of many famous universities which were founded by the church in Britain and America, but it also inspired many scientists who were passionate to find out how light works. In Scotland, particularly in Edinburgh, we saw the rise of some key scientists who explored the qualities of light, and who pioneered significant inventions. For them, their Christian faith and ground-breaking discoveries and inventions went hand-in-hand. They referred to two foundational books as their authority: the Bible and nature; as they focused their understanding of both, like with binoculars being adjusted, they saw science more clearly.

In the first three centuries of the church the Christian faith mushroomed through the ancient Greco-Roman world, despite at least ten cycles of systematic persecution. At Alexandria, the foremost bible school was established by Clement (c.150–c.215) who incorporated Greek philosophy and natural science as part of the students' curriculum. The scholars there realised that they needed to develop a strong Christian biblical worldview as they engaged with clever Pagan philosophers, and typically agreed with the philosophy that was in line with Scripture, but rejected contrary ideas. It was John Philoponus of Alexandria (490–570) however, who rose up as an intellectual Christian giant before the end of the sixth century. He took on Aristotle and others, by using the Bible and nature as his two sources. Three main ingredients emerged out of his understanding:

'The universe is the single creation of a single God and is not eternal.

'The heaven we see has the same physical properties as the earth.

'The stars are not divine [as Aristotle taught].'[6]

---

6. Dan Graves, *Scientists of Faith: Forty-Eight Biographies of Historic Scientists and Their Christian Faith* (Kregel Resources, 1996), p. 14.

Although most of his writings, as well as those of early medieval Christian thinkers, have been lost, a foundational work had been established in the scientific method for Islam and Europe.

John Duns Scotus (c.1265–1308)

Years ago, a naughty child who had misbehaved in class was sent to the 'Dunce's corner'; in earlier times the child sometimes even wore a 'Dunce's cap'. This unfortunate punishment travelled down through the centuries from the reformers who mocked John Duns Scotus, who came from Duns in Berwickshire, Scotland. The reformers particularly ridiculed his writings because of his Mariology and attempts at trying to prove the Immaculate Conception. Known as the 'subtle doctor' because of his sharp and inquisitive mind at both the University of Oxford and the University of Paris, his philosophical thinking, however, would influence others like William of Ockham, Descartes and today's Alvin Plantinga.

Like many of the leading thinkers of Europe, Scotus was received into the Order of the Friars Minor, with a Franciscan branch in Dumfries being in existence then. Cutting his philosophical teeth at Oxford and Paris, he went on to write his commentary on Peter Lombard's *Sentences*; it is this work that launched him into fame in the medieval world. Being influenced by the arguments for God by Thomas Aquinas and Anselm of Canterbury, he developed what he called 'Univocity of Being', or a rational argument for the existence of universals in our common experience, which also points to the existence of God and a rational universe.

The monastic orders in Europe may have sought, for the most part, a life of fraternity, equality, charity, poverty and prayer, but some of them were incubators of philosophy and science. Hannam remarks that 'the people of medieval Europe invented spectacles, the mechanical clock, the windmill and the blast furnace by themselves. Lenses and cameras, almost all kinds of machinery and the industrial revolution itself all owe their origins to the forgotten inventors of the Middle Ages.... Most significantly, the

Middle Ages laid the foundation for the greatest achievement of western civilisation, modern science.'[7]

John Napier (1550–1617), the Genius of Logarithms

The man with his bones was at it again. Laying out his ivory sticks on the ground, John Napier made some more markings, which he called integers, then took notes. Totally focused on his work, he ignored the rumours circulating in the Edinburgh area that he was a sorcerer. His razor-like mind was grappling with big numbers, really big numbers. His work in logarithms (1614) would lay the foundation in maths for our computers, with sums, quotients, products, and square and cube roots, and be a significant stepping stone for such great astronomers as Kepler.

John Napier's breakthrough in maths is so prominent that we have a university named after him, Edinburgh Napier University, based at Merchiston, which was his family home. The *Encyclopaedia Britannica* of 1902 states under his name that: 'There is no British author [scientist] of the time except Napier whose name can be placed in the same rank of those of Copernicus, Tycho Brahe, Kepler, Galileo, or Stevinus.'

Like Isaac Newton, another Christian, his passion for maths drove him to try and solve the mysteries of the Book of Revelation. Napier's *A Plaine Discourse on the Whole Revelation of St John* was one of the first Bible commentaries in Scotland. Today the remains of this Christian reformer are buried at St Cuthbert's, just below Edinburgh Castle, and a memorial about him can be found inside the church.

Thomas Young (1773–1829), the Polymath

As a teenager, I remember using the double-slit experiment to see how light behaves in physics; it is something that is part of the staple diet in the science department of our education system. The Englishman, Thomas Young, was a child prodigy: at the age of two

---

7. James Hannam, *God's Philosophers*, p. 5.

he had learned to read; by the age of four he had read through the Bible twice; and by the age of six he had already become a Latin scholar! He was so gifted that by the age of fourteen he had become a private tutor in the classics. Between 1792 and 1794, he went to the University of Edinburgh to study medicine, where he was known as 'Phenomenon Young' because of his unique genius, and later became a doctor at St George's in London and Professor of Natural Philosophy at the Royal Institution, focusing on physics.

It was while he was there in 1803 that he demonstrated before the Royal Society for the first time, that light behaves as a wave. Up until then scientists who followed Isaac Newton's work thought that light only behaved as a particle. This critical discovery of Young, through his double-slit experiment, meant that light is now understood to act both as a particle *and* as a wave, mystifying physicists who like to have everything working in a smooth, orderly and predictable way. It was this discovery of the duality of light that led to quantum physics, a branch of science pioneered by the German church deacon, Max Planck. Albert Einstein acknowledged Young in his preface to Isaac Newton's *Opticks* in 1931, expressing that the critical discovery of Young's wave-theory had to wait a hundred years.

Besides this, Thomas Young was one of the key scholars who began the process of decoding the Egyptian hieroglyphs after the archaeological discovery of the Rosetta Stone in 1799. This large slab of stone was found in Egypt with three languages: Egyptian hieroglyphs; Egyptian demotic script; and Greek: the latter, being a known language, was the key to unlocking the mystery of the ancient Egyptian languages.

As a Christian he was shy about sharing his faith. He grew up as a Quaker and later, through his marriage to Eliza Maxwell, joined the Church of England. However, he believed that God had given him a sharp mind to be used for science, to advance understanding for the benefit of his fellow human beings. Henry Brougham from Edinburgh criticised some of his work on physics, but Young's response was: 'For the talents which

God has not given me, I am not responsible, but those which I possess, I have hitherto cultivated and employed as diligently as my opportunities have allowed me to do; and I shall continue to apply them with assiduity, and in tranquillity, to that profession which has constantly been the ultimate object of all my labours.'[8]

The Christian physicist, Sir David Brewster, wrote in the *Edinburgh Journal of Science* that Young's 'religious sentiments were by himself stated to be liberal, though orthodox. He had extensively studied the Scriptures, of which the precepts were deeply impressed upon his mind from his earliest years; and he evidenced the faith which he professed; in an unbending course of usefulness and rectitude.'[9]

Sir David Brewster (1781–1868), Scientist of Light

David Brewster from Jedburgh went to Edinburgh University at the age of twelve. In 1813 he presented his paper to the Royal Society on various scientific instruments, and on the evidence of two hundred substances that can refract, or disperse light. As a result, he was welcomed into the Fellowship of this Society a few years later. During his life he won many top awards for his work in science. He invented the kaleidoscope and helped improve the stereoscope, but he is especially remembered for his work in optics, in which he discovered what became known as Brewster's Law. He demonstrated that 'a beam of light can be split into reflected and refracted portions at right angles to each other, both beams retaining full polarization.'[10] It was this discovery that was critical in the development of laser technology later.

Brewster worked with indefatigable energy to support the growth of empirical science, raising financial provision for

8. Alexander Wood, *Thomas Young: Natural Philosopher, 1773–1829* (Cambridge University Press), p. 173.

9. David Brewster, *The Edinburgh Journal of Science*. Vol. 8 (Blackwood, 1831), pp. 204, 207.

10. Dan Graves, *Scientists of Faith*, p. 94.

struggling researchers, editing and writing in the science sections of the *Encyclopaedia Britannica,* and co-founding the British Association for the Advancement of Science (BAAS) in 1831 with fellow Christians, Rev. Vernon Harcourt, Charles Babbage (Cambridge pioneer of the mechanical computer), William Whelwell, and James Finlay Weir Johnston, a Scottish Presbyterian and chemist who was sympathetic to the Free Church and was a Fellow of the Royal Society of Edinburgh. The agreed reason for the founding of the BAAS was to ensure that science moved forward using strict measures of empirical testing and rejected pseudo-science. Furthermore, its founders were determined to see the Christian democratic model being introduced into science to prevent the well-to-do set dominating the field, as in the Royal Society, and to encourage and welcome good scientists, irrespective of their class status.

Typically, at the time, these Christian founders of the BAAS believed, as Babbage expressed it, 'that the study of the works of nature with scientific precision, was a necessary and indispensable preparation to the understanding and interpreting their testimony of the wisdom and goodness of their Divine Author.'[11] It was the BAAS that also hosted the famous debate between Bishop Samuel Wilberforce and Thomas Huxley over Charles Darwin's evolutionary theory in 1860 at Oxford.

When the Free Church broke away from the Church of Scotland at the Disruption of 1843, Brewster joined the Free Church and was a licensed preacher. He would rise early to pray and study his Bible, believing that a thorough testing of all things with both Scripture and science was vital. Brewster spoke of his certainty of Christ and thought 'it can't be presumption to be SURE [of our forgiveness] because it is Christ's work, not ours; on the contrary, it is presumption to doubt His word and work.' Before he died, he reiterated his strong faith. 'I shall see Jesus,' he said, 'and that will be grand. I shall see Him who made the worlds.'[12]

---

11. Ann Lamont, *21 Great Scientists who Believed the Bible,* p. 109.

12. Dan Graves, *Scientists of Faith,* ibid., p. 95.

James Clerk Maxwell (1831–1879), Scotland's Greatest Scientist

Whenever the people of Scotland vote for the greatest scientist in their history, the name James Clerk Maxwell inevitably comes to the top of the pile. It is not just the Scots who celebrate his memory, for Albert Einstein, when asked whether he stood on the shoulders of Isaac Newton, replied: 'No, on the shoulders of Maxwell.'[13] Einstein placed Maxwell's photograph on the place of honour on his office wall and shared his gratitude for this Scottish scientist who was born in Edinburgh. Indeed, three scientists have been considered by almost everyone as the most important in history: Newton, Maxwell and Einstein.

Whether you are using an iPod, computer, mobile phone, X-ray machine, television, radio, or taking photos in colour, or discussing the special theory of relativity, quantum physics and the universe, you will find that all of these things find their history entwined with Maxwell. Despite dying at the young age of forty-eight, his impact has been colossal. He is called the Father of Modern Physics, and his Maxwell equations set the foundation for the theory of electromagnetism.

Maxwell went to the University of Edinburgh in 1847 and the University of Cambridge in 1850. Another Christian called Michael Faraday had invented the first electric generator in 1831, in which a moving magnet produced electricity. Faraday was convinced that the universe contained electromagnetic forces, and his field theory inspired Maxwell to research electricity and magnetism, leading to his four mathematical equations which described this reality. When calculating the speed of electromagnetic waves, he also found that the speed of light was the same and concluded that light was another expression of electromagnetism. From this work he proposed that other wavelengths would exist as well. It was this ground-breaking

---

13. 'Einstein Inspired by James Clerk Maxwell,' *The Guardian*, Tuesday, 8th December 2015.

proposal that heralded the invention of the radio in 1883 by the German Lutheran Christian, Heinrich Hertz. Out of Maxwell's theory others invented television (John Logie Baird from Edinburgh), radar and satellite communications.

In 1871 Maxwell became the Professor of Experimental Physics at the University of Cambridge, and it was here that he was asked to supervise the planning and construction of the Cavendish Laboratory. As a committed Christian he was keen to make sure that credit was given to God, so at his instigation Psalm 111:2 was inscribed above the door in Latin, with the translation in English being: 'Great are the works of the Lord, studied by all who delight in them' (KJV). It was the Cavendish Laboratory that produced J. J. Thomson, an Anglican Christian who discovered the electron, Ernest Rutherford, the agnostic who discovered the neutron, and the atheists Crick and Watson who decoded the DNA.

Maxwell was a church elder for much of his adult life, showing a humble and devout faith which was expressed in his regular and caring visits to those in hospital. This strong faith was reflected in a prayer which he had written for his personal use:

> Almighty God, who has created man in Thine own image, and made him a living soul that he might seek after Thee, and have dominion over Thy creatures, teach us to study the works of Thy hands, that we may subdue the earth to our use, and strengthen the reason for Thy service; so to receive Thy blessed Word, that we may believe on Him Whom Thou has sent, to give us knowledge of salvation and the remission of our sins. All of which we ask in the name of the same Jesus Christ, our Lord.[14]

He was repeatedly requested to become a member of the Victoria Institute, a society of Christian scholars and scientists. In March 1875 he received another request by the secretary, which again, he turned down. He stated in his reply: 'I think men of science as well as other men need to learn from Christ, and I think Christians whose minds are scientific are bound to study science

---

14. Dan Graves, *Scientists of Faith*, ibid., p. 208.

that their view of the glory of God may be as extensive as their being is capable of.'[15]

Today, his name is honoured with the James Clerk Maxwell building being part of the prestigious King's Buildings of the University of Edinburgh, and a statue of him was erected in George Street in this city.

William Thomson, Lord Kelvin (1824–1907), Formulator of Thermodynamics

Having been born in Belfast, Northern Ireland, William Thomson went on to study at the University of Glasgow, and then he ended up being Professor of Physics at the same university from 1846, where he remained for fifty-three years. His great contribution to science was the formulation of the Laws of Thermodynamics, and the development of the absolute temperature scale. In 1844, the American Christian, Samuel Morse, had invented telegraph communication. Thomson was appointed to supervise the laying of the first transatlantic telegraph cable to America, for which he was knighted in 1866 by Queen Victoria. Besides this, he also patented about seventy inventions. During his lifetime, he received twenty-one honorary doctorates and was appointed as President of the Royal Society in Edinburgh, with the later title of Baron Kelvin of Largs being granted to him in 1892. He is buried with honour in Westminster Abbey.

Thomson was a devout Christian who spoke out clearly against the rise of atheism in his day. As a Church of Scotland elder, he wrote in *The Times* newspaper on 2nd May 1903: 'Do not be afraid of being free thinkers. If you think strongly enough you will be forced by science to the belief in God, which is the foundation of all Religion. You will find science not antagonistic, but helpful to Religion.'

---

15. Lewis Campbell and William Garnett, *The Life of James Clerk Maxwell, With A Selection From His Correspondence and Occasional Writings, And A Sketch of His Contribution To Science* (MacMillan and Co., 1882), pp. 404-05.

Rev. Thomas Bayes (c.1701–1761): Father of Data Science

In 2018, the £45 million Bayes Centre building was opened by HRH The Princess Royal. The University of Edinburgh is proud of its new addition, bringing into this building a collaboration of scientists, business people and the public to pioneer advances in data science and artificial intelligence. The university website tells us that the Rev. Thomas Bayes was 'a statistician, philosopher and minister who came to Edinburgh to study logic and theology in 1719.' This Christian is 'famous for Bayes' Theorem, which provides an elegant and simple way of calculating how likely a certain hypothesis is, given some observed evidence.' The website goes on to say that Bayes' Theorem 'is considered by many to be that foundation of modern-day machine learning, one of the key methods used in Data Science and Artificial Intelligence.'[16] Bayes' Theorem has been vital, not only in data science, but in medical and weather predictions, and for the Stock Exchange.

Bayes was a modest Presbyterian who did not publish his papers. If it had not been for his friend and fellow church minister, Rev. Richard Price, who made Bayes' work public, his genius would have been buried. It has been suggested that Bayes was inspired by the logic of probability to try and refute David Hume's writings against divine miracles. Bayes' formula is found in his paper entitled *An Essay towards solving a Problem in the Doctrine of Chances*, and it is this which Rev. Price used as another arrow in his theological quiver against Hume's sceptical book, *Miracles*.

Rev. Alexander Webster (1707–1784): Father of Insurance Modelling

At one time Webster's Close used to exist in Edinburgh, near Castlehill, roughly where Boswell's Court is today. It was from a house in this close that the Rev. Dr Alexander Webster would sally forth to lead the charge of the High Flyers against the

---

16. The University of Edinburgh website for the Bayes Centre: https://www.ed.ac.uk/bayes/about/history

Moderates. Essentially, the High Flyers were the evangelicals and the Moderates were the liberals of the eighteenth century. Webster was so famous as a preacher in Edinburgh that it was said 'it was easier to get a seat in the Kingdom of Heaven than in the Tolbooth Kirk,' where he was the minister for forty-seven years (1737–1784). His magnetic preaching seemed to draw in the most unlikely visitors to his packed congregation, such as Robert Burns and David Hume.

It was Webster who invited the human fireball, George Whitefield, to preach in Edinburgh and Scotland, and who defended the Methodists. Organising the events through his considerable networks, he would accompany Whitefield as he preached to crowds said to be fifteen thousand strong in St Giles' churchyard (now a car park and buildings), in the King's Park (today's Holyrood Park), and in the grounds of the Trinity Hospital (today's George Heriot's School). On 15th August 1742, he was there on the green at Cambuslang near Glasgow, to take it in turns to preach alongside Whitefield and ten other ministers who witnessed an outpouring of the Holy Spirit on the estimated crowd of forty thousand, many of whom were 'bathed in tears'.

Despite his evangelistic fervour though, Webster was a known alcoholic who could drink any man under the table and still remain standing and fairly clear-headed. His craving for claret meant that he would even take his wine into the pulpit with him, so he could have a swig. Such a habit was viewed with mixed responses by the locals, from horror to amusement. You would have thought that his brain would have been fuddled with all that wine, yet he had such a sharp mind that the government called on his skill as a statistician to lead the census for Scotland's first population, resulting in a return of 1,265,380 people in 1755. Adam Smith, the author of the *Wealth of Nations*, could admit that 'of all men I have ever known, [Webster is] the most skilful in political arithmetic.' Webster also combined his mathematical aptitude with pastoral compassion, establishing, with another clergyman, Rev. Dr Wallace, the first proper insurance fund for widows of the clergy in Scotland, in 1748; it was his calculations and model that set a precedent for modern insurance companies to follow.

His indefatigable lifestyle meant that he was right in the heart of Edinburgh, being one of the key figures in advising magistrates about the development of the New Town. He seemed to pop up everywhere, influencing the city and nation for its prosperity, and being one of the movers and shakers of Scotland. It is a stark reminder to us that despite his weakness for wine, he was a vessel mightily used through God's grace.

Rev. Patrick Bell (1799–1869): Pioneer of the Combine Harvester

From time to time, I love to stop and watch a combine harvester at work. What an extraordinary machine it is! Just think of all the labour it saves, and the efficiency with which it serves us. Taking the history of the development of the combine harvester back to its beginning, we arrive at Rev. Patrick Bell, the minister of Carmyllie Parish Church in Scotland. Before his ordination he had worked on his father's farm in Auchterhouse in Angus where he invented what he called the 'reaping machine', which in those days was pushed along by horses. By 1828, his invention was being used successfully in this area of Scotland.

Bell was more eager to use his skills for the benefit of humanity than to make his name as an inventor; for this reason, he did not apply for a patent. It was the Americans, William Manning (1831) and Obed Hussey (1833) who copied Bell's invention, receiving patents, and Cyrus McCormick (1834), an evangelical Christian who developed the machine more effectively, putting this technology on the agricultural map before the invention of traction engines from 1858–1880s, when motors began to replace horses.

Robert William Thomson (1822–1873): Inventor of Pneumatic Tyres

Every so often there is a mad scramble for the credit to be given to an inventor of something. Here in Scotland, we tend to think of John Boyd Dunlop of Dreghorn in Ayrshire as the inventor of the pneumatic tyre, which he patented in 1888, but he was beaten to this invention by another Scot. Robert Thomson of Stonehaven received a patent for what he called the 'aerial wheel' in 1845, which was a hollow leather tyre surrounding a rubber tube filled with air. He demonstrated his invention in Regent's Park in London in 1847, but Dunlop's improved version proved to be cheaper. Both were Presbyterian Christians.

Robert Thomson's inventive mind was not just applied to the pneumatic tyre. Among his patents were the fountain pen; steam boilers; steam omnibuses; applying steam power in agriculture; elastic wheel tyres; road steamers; the ribbon saw, and a host of other inventions or developments.

Sir Henry Littlejohn (1826–1914): Father of Forensics

We have already met this Scottish surgeon and Edinburgh's first Medical Officer of Health, who revolutionised our sewage system, replacing open sewage and its attending plagues, with an underground network of pipes. This practical development quickly caught on across Europe, saving the lives of millions. Working together with his friend, the Lord Provost William Chambers, and the Edinburgh City Missionaries on the ground, evidence was accumulated showing that high mortality rates accompanied overcrowding in the slums and bad sanitary conditions. Implementing a new sewage system, along with demolishing the slums and building better housing for the poor, the Council under his guidance transformed Edinburgh, causing it to be a model for other cities.

According to an article by the Royal College of Physicians, 'The improvement of the health of residents of Edinburgh in the nineteenth century associated with Littlejohn's work was clearly demonstrated by the fall in mortality rates from around thirty-four per thousand in the 1860s to fourteen per thousand in the early twentieth century. Smallpox and typhus disappeared from the city. The main causes of these improvements were the environmental changes and sanitary reforms, to which Littlejohn was the major contributor.'[17] After his death, the British Medical Journal stated that 'Edinburgh's low death-rate is his great monument'.[18]

However, Littlejohn also pioneered forensics – the science of catching the criminal without having eyewitnesses present. In 1856 he began to lecture on forensic medicine in Edinburgh's Surgeons' Hall and became a Crown medical examiner in Edinburgh's courts. He soon became an expert in investigating deaths, whether they were accidental or by murder. He proved cases of poisoning, and other methods of murdering victims through a careful examination of the evidence or traces left behind, such as finger-prints. Among his students was Joseph Bell, both of whom were thought to be the inspiration behind Sir Arthur Conan Doyle's detective, Sherlock Holmes.

Sir Henry Littlejohn was an elder at St Giles' Kirk (Cathedral) who used to go to the daily prayers there. As a dedicated Presbyterian Christian, he always combined his faith with his pioneering work amongst the poor and with his passion to ensure that true justice was enacted.

James Braidwood (1800–1861): Pioneer of Modern Fire-Fighting

As the shrill siren sound echoed along the street everyone knew they had to clear a path for the fire engine. It roared along, red and furious, to fight the fire in a hotel. Its crew, qualified and equipped, were bursting with adrenalin, knowing that their training in the science of fighting fires would save the lives of many people in what otherwise would have been a total disaster.

As we look back at history, even the Romans had fire-fighting teams, but it was a Christian called James Braidwood who would turn this brave action into a scientific skill and thus save many

---

17. M. Bain, A. Bentley, T. Squires, *Sir Henry Duncan Littlejohn – A Dynamic Figure in Forensic Medicine and Public Health in the Nineteenth Century*, Proc R Coll Physicians Edinb, 1999; 29:248-52.

18. *British Medical Journal*, Vol. 2, No.2806, 10th October 1914.

lives. Braidwood, who was born in Edinburgh, would go on to pioneer the world's first municipal fire service in the city of his birth in 1824. Only six years later, after his team had battled the Great Fire of Edinburgh, he put together a manual on how to improve the methodology of fire-fighting, using the best available practice. It was this manual which would become the blueprint for the service in Britain and the world.

In 1832, he was given the task of heading up the London Fire Engine Establishment and would be called upon to lead the fight against the huge blaze at the Palace of Westminster shortly after. It was there that he established London's first full-time fire brigade. A memorial near St Giles in Edinburgh has a text with the words: 'This statue is dedicated to the memory of James Braidwood, a pioneer of the scientific approach to fire-fighting … he developed new fire-fighting techniques, many of which are still used today.' His book, which was published after he died trying to save lives in a terrible fire at Tooley Street in London, was entitled *Fire Prevention and Fire Extinction* (1866). He was so appreciated that his funeral procession was measured at about one and a half miles long.

James Braidwood was a dedicated Christian whose inspiration for fire-fighting came from the prophet Zechariah in the Bible, who spoke of Joshua the high priest as 'a brand plucked from the fire' (Zech. 3:1-2). For Braidwood, God's calling for his life was to save as many people as he could from the fires of destruction, just as he believed the gospel of Christ could save people from the fire of hell. Using his skill, he determined to develop the scientific understanding of fire-fighting to increase the success rates of the firemen. The text on his tombstone in London has a Scripture: 'Blessed are the dead which die in the Lord' (Rev. 14:13, KJV). His wife Mary, equally devout, chose the words of the famous hymn about Christ for when she would be buried alongside him ten years later:

> Just as I am without one plea,
> But that Thy blood was shed for me.
> And that Thou bidst me come to Thee,
> O Lamb of God, I come.

Braidwood, concerned with both the physical care of people and their spiritual wellbeing in this heart-breaking work, made sure that Christian chaplains from London City Mission would be appointed to come alongside those in need: including the firemen, their families, and the victims of fire who survived, as well as the grieving families who lost loved ones.

Every Spring, the Edinburgh Science Festival draws thousands with a love for science to this city. Amidst the excitement of the developing fields of genetics, computer technology, and many other areas, people are drawn to Scotland because of its rich pedigree in advancing science in major ways. Amongst the celebrities like John Logie Baird (pioneer of television), Alexander Bell (pioneer of the telephone), and others who were not Christians, there stands a crowd of dedicated Christians who were key harbingers of science, combining their skills with a love for God and compassion for the people.

CHAPTER 12

THE ARTS

The minibus pulled over to join a Conga line of cars parked at Loch Katrine in Perthshire. Out of the vehicle erupted a group of tourists, keen to stretch their legs and savour the dramatic natural scene. As they chattered with excitement, first one, then another, posed for a portrait photograph. Without realising it, they, and millions before them, were experiencing the work of key Scottish Christian pioneers from the nineteenth century.

Photography

It is so easy these days to take portrait photographs on our mobile phones and send them by WhatsApp to people all over the world, but the developing of photography as a science and art form was a major breakthrough in the nineteenth century. The Frenchman, Joseph Niépce, can be regarded as the first person to fix images properly to plates in 1826/7 with a simple camera, and by 1839 his colleague, Louis Daguerre, developed this further in what became known as the Daguerreotype. However, the English Christian, William Henry Fox Talbot's calotype process of fixing images on paper with silver iodide became far more practical in 1840 and superseded the Daguerreotype.

Talbot contacted his friend, Sir David Brewster, in Edinburgh who helped him refine the calotype process, and Brewster in turn encouraged David Octavius Hill, a member of Free St John's (now St Columba's Free Church), and his friend Robert Adamson, to produce photographs. David Hill, a noted artist who had pioneered the Royal Scottish Academy with Lord Cockburn in

1829, and was the secretary for the Royal Academy of Fine Arts, combined his creative gift with Adamson's technical skill, and so the first photographic portrait studio in the world called 'The Rock' was established in Edinburgh, near the foot of Calton Hill.

In the Free Church Presbytery Hall, located in the same building as Edinburgh Theological Seminary, hangs a famous painting of the Disruption. It took ten men to carry this huge work and lower it out of the building when a request came through for a loan to an art gallery. It took twenty-three years for David Hill to complete this historical painting and he can be seen in it, sketching pencil in hand, just above Robert Adamson with his early box camera. Part of the reason for the excessive time taken to finish the work is that the two men were capturing thousands of portrait photos, and that most of those portraits were copied by Hill and painted on to the canvas, so what you have instead is a nineteenth century collage of many of the movers and shakers of Scotland involved in the 1843 Disruption, all in one picture; an enormous and spectacular feat.

The Novelists

The tourists at Loch Katrine not only captured their memories on camera, but some of them read out from a well-known poem, *The Lady of the Lake*, and an extract from the novel *Rob Roy*, both of which are associated with this beautiful loch. The author was Sir Walter Scott, who combined history and fiction in his own romantic Scottish way, so that droves of tourists from Europe and America in the nineteenth century, who had read his Waverley novels and poems, came pouring into this nation. Scotland had been discovered as a tourist destination, and Walter Scott had been the pied piper: the father of Scottish tourism.

Sir Walter Scott, Writer and the Father of Scottish Tourism (1771–1832)

Walter Scott grew up in Edinburgh and went on to study law at the university there, but his burning passion was creative writing and history. Besides his very successful career as a novelist, whose books are full of Scripture,[1] he was also an antiquarian. Through his painstaking research he finally traced the Honours of Scotland – the lost Scottish Crown Jewels, which had disappeared and had been hidden during the time of Cromwell. The English Parliament had melted down most of the English Crown Jewels after the execution of Charles I in 1649, and had turned them into coins, so the Scots feared a repeat scenario here.

The Honours are the oldest Crown Jewels in Britain, being made in the fifteenth and sixteenth centuries, and are on display in Edinburgh Castle, alongside the Stone of Scone (now held in Perth since 2024). But it took a sharp mind like Scott's, with the royal warrant of the Prince Regent, and future king, George IV, to track them down. In 1818, Walter Scott and an excited group of officials were allowed to break down the wall of the Crown Room of Edinburgh Castle, to investigate whether the Honours were still in an old oak chest. With whoops of celebration, they uncovered the ancient crown, sceptre and sword, which had remained undisturbed since 1707. Scott's detective work had paid off, but what a strange journey the Honours had made when they were hidden. Firstly, they had been put in Dunnottar Castle, from which they were secretly removed during the besieging of Cromwell's army; then they had been kept under the floor of Kineff Parish Church, before being taken to their storage room in Edinburgh Castle.

Walter Scott had become doubly famous: firstly, for his books, which had put Scotland on the tourist map, and secondly for being the scholar who had rediscovered the lost Scottish Crown Jewels. Like Robert Burns, Scott was a key person in restoring Scottish dignity and its rich heritage after the Anglicisation following the defeat at Culloden in 1746, when wearing tartan was banned by the British government. When King George IV came on his historic visit to Edinburgh in 1822 dressed in a kilt, it was a celebrated moment. For the first time since 1651 a British monarch had come, and he had arrived dressed like a

1. Nicholas Dickson, *The Bible in Waverley: Or Sir Walter Scott's Use of the Sacred Scriptures* (Forgotten Books, 2018), reprint.

Scotsman. The person he most wanted to see in all of Scotland was Sir Walter Scott.

As he lay dying, Sir Walter Scott called out to his son-in-law, John Lockhart, 'Read to me out of the Book.' Lockhart, knowing Scott's passion for his extensive library at Abbotsford House, asked, 'Which book?' 'There is only one Book,' came the response, 'the Bible! The Bible is the Book to live by and the Book to die by. Therefore, read it to be wise, believe it to be safe, practise it to be holy. As another has said: 'Know it in the head, store it in the heart, show it in the life, sow it in the world.'[2]

Although Sir Walter Scott was famous for other reasons, his Christian faith has often been obscured. He grew up in a Calvinistic and Presbyterian home, and although he found Calvinism restrictive and dull, the example of Christian faith set by his parents became a strong part in shaping his life. He was ordained as an elder in the picturesque Duddingston Parish Church in 1806, where he served alongside his minister, Rev. John Thomson, a recognised and successful colour artist. However, Scott left the Church of Scotland and joined the Scottish Episcopal Church. As with many of this period he also combined his Christian faith with Freemasonry. His writing became the inspiration of many other novelists and composers like Rossini, Schubert, Beethoven, Berlioz and Hamish MacCunn. Today, Scott's huge, towering monument next to Princes Street demonstrates the affection and admiration of this nation for the scholar-writer.

Rev. George MacDonald, the Father of Fantasy Novels (1824–1905)

Among the many famous writers from Scotland, several others were dedicated Christians. The Rev. George MacDonald is not so well-known, but his genre of fantasy novels went on to inspire other world-famous writers like C. S. Lewis, J. R. R. Tolkien,

---

2. A. W. Pink, *The Divine Inspiration of the Bible*, Chapter Fourteen: 'Application of the Argument, V. It Has Unique Claims Upon Us,' Precept Austin, https://www.preceptaustin.org/the-divine-inspiration-of-the-bible-a-w-pink

Lewis Carroll, J. M. Barrie, W. H. Auden, Mark Twain, G. K. Chesterton, J. K. Rowling, and others. MacDonald grew up in Huntly and went to the University of Aberdeen where he graduated with an MA in chemistry and physics. However, he sensed God's calling to the ministry and was ordained as a pastor in the Congregational Church in England. His first appointment in 1850 was at Trinity Congregational Church at Arundel in Sussex. He struggled with Calvinism and preached that Christ offers his salvation not just to the elect, but to everyone. This resulted in MacDonald becoming a 'controversialist', and leaving Arundel three years later. After a short while serving a church in Manchester he left because of ill health, but recovered, and went on to teach at the University of London.

MacDonald's writing career began with *David Elginbrod* in 1863, but it was his other novels, such as *Phantastes*, *The Princess and the Goblin*, and *Lilith*, and his short stories, such as *The Light Princess* and *The Golden Key*, that would bring him success as the pioneer of modern fantasy writing. His desire was to write books which would be read and loved by children and adults alike, although many people of his time thought that this would not work as a specific genre. He and his children were just the encouragement that Lewis Carroll needed to risk publishing his famous *Alice in Wonderland*. MacDonald turned even the most mundane things into aspects of magic, bringing sparkle and vibrancy to the common objects of life. It was this sense that inspired fellow Scotsman, J. M. Barrie, to write *Peter Pan*.

C. S. Lewis, the atheist who was converted to Christ whilst being a professor at Oxford University in 1931, saw MacDonald as a key person in his conversion through reading his *Phantases* and *Unspoken Sermons*, alongside others like J. R. R. Tolkien, another Oxford professor, who was a devout Catholic and author of *The Hobbit* and *The Lord of the Rings*. Lewis wrote in the foreword to *George MacDonald: An Anthology*:

> I know hardly any other writer who seems to be closer, or more continually close, to the Spirit of Christ Himself .... In making this collection I was discharging a debt of justice. I have never concealed

the fact that I regarded him [MacDonald] as my master; indeed, I fancy I have never written a book in which I did not quote from him. But it has not seemed to me that those who have received my books kindly take even now sufficient notice of the affiliation. Honesty drives me to emphasize it.[3]

Whilst sipping a beer with my son-in-law in Oxford's *Eagle and Child* pub, we reminisced about the Inklings who had met in that very place last century. How we had wished to have been listening ears to this extraordinary group of cultured writers and scholars! The chief leaders were C. S. Lewis, whose *The Chronicles of Narnia* have inspired generations of children and adults alike, and J. R. R. Tolkien, who at times read out extracts from their own fledgling novels. Little did I know then of the huge debt they, and their little influential group, owed to George MacDonald – a Scottish Christian writer.

Robert Louis Stevenson, the Adventurer (1850–1894)

In the Writers' Museum in Edinburgh's Old Town, three of the city's authors are particularly singled out for celebration: Robert Burns, the National Poet; Sir Walter Scott, and Robert Louis Stevenson. RLS, as he is fondly known, was something of an adventurer, a student at Edinburgh University with a wild reputation. Later he would become the author of some of the best-loved classics in the world, such as *Treasure Island*, *Kidnapped*, and *The Strange Case of Dr Jekyll and Mr Hyde*. Not so well-known is the fact that his first published book, *The Pentland Rising: A Page of History, 1666*, was written to commemorate the 200th anniversary of the Covenanter history, written when he was only sixteen.

Stevenson's most famous book, *Treasure Island*, had been inspired by the Christian writer, R. M. Ballantyne, who had published his *Coral Island* in 1857. This Edinburgh-born man spent years in Canada and came back to write of his adventures.

---

3. *George MacDonald: An Anthology*, editor: C. S. Lewis, 1947.

He aimed in his books to feature godly Christian characters in particular, who were men of integrity and courage, in order to establish a good role model for the youth growing up. It was Ballantyne's sense of adventure that would inspire Stevenson, but towards the end of his life, Stevenson was on his own personal quest to find God.

Upolu was a far-flung island for a travelling Scotsman in the nineteenth century, and yet Stevenson and his family settled in this Samoan haven in 1890. He bought four hundred acres and set about building a house on his estate, which he named Vailima. Within a short time of their arrival, the family discovered that the natives were mostly Christians. The London Missionary Society had sent out missionaries to Samoa in 1830, and when they arrived, they found two of the main tribes engaged in a bitter, long war, from which they longed for deliverance and resolution. When the first missionaries preached the gospel of peace through Christ, there was a remarkable movement of God, leading to a rapid spread of Christianity throughout all the islands. By 1886, they had their own Samoan Bible and schools.

Stevenson, a cultural Presbyterian, found himself in the midst of this deeply spiritual situation in which he saw transformation of the locals before his eyes. He soon became part of it as requests came in for him to teach Sunday school children. He realised too that if he would be a good church teacher, he must be a good example to them by his behaviour. Soon this adventurer was on his last and most important adventure – to find God.

It is difficult to know exactly whether Stevenson became fully Christian, as he wrestled with the biblical concept of the Trinity, but by the time he had died he was at least a Unitarian. The last book he published in 1894, the year of his death, was co-written by him and his stepson, Lloyd Osbourne. This short novel called *Ebb-Tide* had been written in his Samoan home. It contains at the end of the book, in one of the last sections he ever wrote, a most revealing scene which seems to reflect his own personal spiritual struggle. Captain Davis is a wicked man in the book who intended to murder a Christian to obtain some pearls, but when the atheist Herrick comes upon him, he finds a transformed man. 'I found peace here,' said Captain Davis, 'peace in believing .... Why not come to Jesus right away, and let's meet in yon beautiful land [heaven].... Just say "Lord, I believe, help Thou mine unbelief!" And He'll fold you in His arms. You see, I know; I've been a sinner myself.'[4]

On my bookshelf is one of my favourite treasures: *Prayers Written at Vailima, by Robert Louis Stevenson*. After his death in 1894, Stevenson's wife collected his handwritten prayers together and arranged for the artist Alberto Sangorski to produce a stunning illuminated work in calligraphy, which was published in 1910. It is in these prayers that we find RLS pouring out his heart to God; how far he had come from despising his father's prayers in Edinburgh, to writing his own in Samoa.

Charles Dickens, Freeman of Edinburgh (1812–1870)

An unlikely writer to be associated with Edinburgh is the Englishman Charles Dickens, who along with Shakespeare, is frequently listed among the greatest of British writers. It was while the young struggling Dickens worked as a reporter in London that he met George Hogarth, the editor of *The Evening Chronicle*. Hogarth had studied law at the University of Edinburgh and had moved south. He spotted Dickens' talent as a novelist, and encouraged him to write some of his first original literary work, which was published in *The Evening Chronicle* under Dickens' pen name 'Boz'. From this, Dickens' career was launched, and he also married Hogarth's daughter Catherine in 1836.

When Dickens came up to Edinburgh with his Scottish wife in 1841, his fame had already gone before him with the publishing of his novels, *The Pickwick Papers*, *Oliver Twist*, and *Nicholas Nickleby*. A special dinner party was thrown for him, which was attended by two hundred and fifty of the Edinburgh literati, where he was made a Freeman of Edinburgh. Many of the good

---

4. R. L. Stevenson and L. Osbourne, *The Ebb-Tide: A Trio and a Quartette* (Heinemann [UK], Smith & Kimball [USA], 1894).

characters in his books reflected the evangelical workers among the poor in London, particularly the London City Missionaries, whose founder was David Nasmith of Glasgow. Whilst in Edinburgh, Dickens was shocked to witness the great poverty and squalor of the slums in the Old Town, but, as in London, it would be the evangelical awakening that would lead the movement to transform society.

One day, so the story goes, he was visiting Edinburgh, when he called in to see the graveyard at Canongate Kirk, near the bottom of the Royal Mile. There, before him, was a gravestone inscription: *Ebenezzer Lennox Scroggie – Meal man*. Dickens mistook *Meal man* for *Mean man*, and so the principal character, Ebenezer Scrooge, in *A Christmas Carol* became a household name for being miserly. This much-loved story appears every Christmas and ends with the conversion of a wealthy miser into a liberated philanthropist, who helps the poor. Dickens would be regarded as a liberal Christian of this period, whose moral inspiration in his classic books came clearly from the teachings of Christ. He once wrote to his son Edward: 'The New Testament … is the best book that ever was or will be known in the world.'[5]

Back to the Painting

One winter's day I had led a walking tour in and around the Royal Mile. When we came to the Presbytery Hall, I pointed out several well-known people from this nineteenth century Disruption collage painting. The pastor of the group was

---

5. Letter to 'Plorn', his son Edward, on 26th September 1868, cited from David Paroissien: *Selected Letters of Charles Dickens* (Basingstoke: Macmillan Press, 1985), p. 167. The full quotation from Charles Dickens is: 'I put a New Testament among your books, for the very same reasons, and with the very same hopes that made me write an easy account of it for you, when you were a little child; because it is the best book that ever was or will be known in the world, and because it teaches you the best lessons by which any human creature who tries to be truthful and faithful to duty can possibly be guided. As your brothers have gone away, one by one, I have written to each such words as I am now writing to you, and have entreated them all to guide themselves by this book, putting aside the interpretations and inventions of Man.'

transfixed, soaking up the information. A few days later he contacted me to see whether we could meet up to discuss some of these people in the painting. An hour became four as we pored over person after person who had been used to shape and transform our modern world.

The Disruption Painting reflects a galaxy of movers and shakers of the nineteenth century in Scotland, most of whom were dedicated Christians: Sir James Young Simpson, the father of anaesthetics; Sir David Brewster, co-pioneer of the British Association for the Advancement of Science, whose work was foundational in laser technology; Dr Thomas Chalmers, whose church and missionary models impacted Britain and much of the world; Dr Thomas Guthrie, pioneer of the Ragged Schools in Edinburgh and elsewhere; William Nelson of Thomas Nelson, one of the biggest Christian publishers in the world; Rev. Henry Duncan, founder of savings banks for the poor, which became the Trustee Savings Bank; Lord Brisbane, after whom Brisbane in Australia is named; Rev. Henry Beecher, whose abolitionist daughter, Harriet Beecher Stowe wrote the hugely influential book, *Uncle Tom's Cabin*; and many more.

On the far right of the painting, gathered around a map of Palestine, is a group of leading missionaries of the nineteenth century whose pioneering work has brought untold benefits to modern humanity. It is a painting that unlocks the door of Christian history in Scotland and introduces us to many of the nineteenth century's vibrant transformers of society.

CHAPTER 13

THE WAR YEARS

When German bombers rained down their cargo of destruction on the naval base of Rosyth on 16th October 1939, Scotland experienced their first casualties of the Second World War. It was the first bombing raid in the war as the German Axis began its long and bitter air campaign. For those in Scotland who had barely recovered from the First World War, another long, dark night of the soul was upon them.

During the two world wars Christianity was still strong in Scotland. Many dedicated Christians played their part against tyranny in the war effort, both at home and abroad, and the Scots were famous for their warrior courage and resilience. Here in Edinburgh, the missionaries were in great demand. The Edinburgh City Mission 1915 Report says that 'Never before have our City Missionaries won and held the confidence of the people to a greater degree than now amidst the widespread sorrow and anxiety consequent upon the war …. The Missionary in his daily round of visits has to lead sorrow-stricken ones into the deep heart of things – to the God of all comfort and compassion.'[1]

This was the general picture across all of Scotland, and also during World War Two as well. The industrial sites and key cities of Scotland were bombed by the Germans, such as Edinburgh, Glasgow, Clydebank, Greenock, Aberdeen and Dundee, leaving thousands killed. Today, if you go to Cramond Island near Edinburgh you can still see the ruins of where the gun emplacements would have been.

---

1. Annual Report of ECM, 1915, pp. 1-7.

During 1939 and 1945 every soldier was issued with a Gospel. Inside the book were the words: 'We commend the Gospel of Christ our Saviour for it alone can effectively mould character, control conduct and solve the problems of men and nations, and thus make life what it should be. Faith in Christ the Lord and loyal obedience to His Will as revealed in the Bible ensures peace of mind and brings satisfaction in service to God and man.'

To this was affixed the official names of the Admiral of the Fleet, Andrew Cunningham, who was the son of Scottish parents who lived in Edinburgh, and General H. R. Alexander, of Ulster-Scots descent, besides three other English leaders. During the war, several other key leaders of Scottish descent would play a decisive role in the war: Field Marshall Sir Bernard Montgomery of Alamein, the son of an Ulster-Scot, Rev. Henry Montgomery, and General Sir William Dobbie of Malta, a devout Brethren Christian.

News had emerged from Germany about Hitler and the Nazis, and Britain sought to stand against this tyranny, believing it was the righteous thing to do. The deeply upsetting fact, though, is that few influential church leaders in Germany or Italy stood up against the fascism of Hitler and Mussolini at first. Eventually the pope and his cardinals and bishops did try to intervene against Hitler because of the growing censorship of churches and the Nazi policy of euthanasia. In 1937, Pope Pius XI's letter called Hitler 'a mad prophet with repulsive arrogance'; the priests that dared read out this papal letter in their churches were imprisoned, with about four hundred being sent to Dachau.

Among the Lutherans, about 2,000 church leaders were either cowering in fear, or conditioned through the propaganda of eugenics and race hygiene, and were led by Bishop Muller in the new Reich Church. In contrast to this, an estimated six thousand Protestant pastors eventually took their stand as the Confessional Church against the Nazi regime's indoctrination, once they realised what was really going on. About eight hundred were sent to concentration camps.[2]

---

2. *BBC*, 'Control and opposition in Nazi Germany – CCEA: Opposition from the Churches,' bbc.co.uk. See also *The New York Times*, '6,000 Reich Pastors Defy Nazis, Saying They Will Not Be "Muzzled",' 8th January 1934.

Hitler sought to rally all of Germany to his cause, and this even meant making use of Luther's essay against the Jews, which he had written in a time of deep depression.[3] There were many evangelical Christians who did stand against the Nazis and who also hid Jewish people, but like those they protected, many lost their lives in the death camps, or were executed.[4] Indeed, Hitler's rage began to grow against these Christians, and if he had not lost the war when he did, there would have been a movement to exterminate them as well. He even forced churches to display the Swastika and gathered some liberal church scholars to produce a Nazi New Testament, with all references to Jews removed.

Righteous Among the Nations

On 3rd September 1939, when war broke out against Germany, Jane Haining, a missionary with the Church of Scotland in Hungary, rushed back to Budapest from her trip to Cornwall.

---

3. Martin Luther was for years a supporter of the Jews who disliked the papal policy of persecution against them. He wrote in 1523: 'If we really want to help them [the Jews], we must be guided in our dealings with them not by papal law but by the law of Christian love. We must receive them cordially, and permit them to trade and work with us, that they may have occasion and opportunity to associate with us, hear our Christian teaching, and witness our Christian life. If some of them should prove stiff-necked, what of it? After all, we ourselves are not all good Christians either' (Luther, essay in 1523: *That Jesus Christ Was Born a Jew*).

Luther changed his mind in 1543 when suffering from a severe bout of depression, three years before he died. The writing was also stirred up by their tenacious resistance because they would not convert to Christ. He wrote: 'What shall we Christians do with this rejected and condemned people, the Jews? ... First (to) set fire to their synagogues or schools and to bury and cover with dirt whatever will not burn, so that no man will never [sic] again see a stone or cinder of them. This is to be done in honour of our Lord and of Christendom, so that God might see that we are Christians, and do not condone or knowingly tolerate such public lying, cursing, and blaspheming of his Son and of his Christians .... Second, I advise that their houses also be razed and destroyed ...' (Luther: *The Jews and their Lies*, Vol. 47, The Christian in Society, IV, pp. 268-93).

4. For an account of the underground evangelical Christian movement in Germany that opposed Hitler, please see Eric Metaxas' *Bonhoeffer: Pastor, Martyr, Prophet, Spy* (Thomas Nelson, 2011).

The Mission Committee in Edinburgh pressed for her to return home the next year, but instead she was determined to continue her work as matron to the girls' boarding school, which was part of the Mission School of four hundred children. 'If these children need me in days of sunshine,' she said, 'how much more do they need me in days of darkness?'[5] When the German Wehrmacht invaded Hungary in 1944, the persecution against the Jews began immediately. Jane Haining had to comply with Nazi regulations and sew the yellow Star of David on each of the girls' uniforms to mark them out as Jews, but as she did, she wept, sensing the human tragedy that would surely come. She had exemplified Jesus in her teaching and lifestyle, modelling equality between Jew and Gentile, but such a concept would be anathema to the Nazis.

The pupils followed her example, with the Christian children choosing to stand in solidarity with their Jewish friends. 'Miss Haining sobbed and she walked with red eyes among us,' said Dr Ninon Leader, now in her eighties, as she looked back at her time in Budapest. This Jewish survivor and former pupil continued: 'I heard later that she had tried to refuse "to mark those children who were to be sent to the slaughterhouse". Acting in Miss Haining's spirit and personality, irrespective of their religion, every single boarder in the Mission Home sewed a yellow star on their uniforms. That's how we left our building for our daily walk to the Heroes' Square and back, hand in hand, as equals.'[6] On false accusations of espionage for the British and for the crime of caring for Jewish people, she was taken by the Gestapo, along with many Jewish children, to Auschwitz, where she died. Since then, she has been honoured by the Jewish people as one of the *Righteous Among the Nations.* She was one among many unsung heroes.

---

5. *The Scottish missionary who died saving Jewish children in WWII,* 16th September 2016, News, Christians United for Israel.

6. *Remembering the acts of defiance which made Jane Haining a Second World War heroine,* The Press and Journal, Neil Drysdale, 27th January 2020.

National Days of Prayer

The fact that King Edward VI and Parliament could call the country to national days of prayer shows the influence that the Christian faith still had in our culture at this time. Dr Victor Pearce kept a contemporary record of these momentous times and relates what happened in his book *Miracles and Angels*. The fact was that Britain was facing the darkest hours of its existence, with Hitler's belief that he could 'frighten the British people into surrender before the autumn' of 1940.[7] Even the sceptics realised that their great skills, strategies, technology and huge efforts would not be enough to defeat a German invasion of Britain, and a subsequent spreading of great darkness throughout the world. Even our British Bulldog, Winston Churchill, prepared to announce 'hard and heavy tidings,' and the Commander of the British Forces, Lt General Sir Frederick Morgan, said that only a miracle would save them.

When the call went out for a National Day of Prayer on 26th May 1940, the majority of people dropped everything and piled into churches everywhere, all over England, Scotland, Wales and Northern Ireland, queuing outside on the streets. The call to prayer was so strong and desperate that even the *Daily Express* ran an article entitled *How do you Pray?* and containing teaching about *how* we should pray – not for self-centred requests for the bombs to fall anywhere else 'but not on us'; rather for righteousness, truth and justice to prevail.

When the German war machine had defeated France, the British troops, with some allies, numbering 350,000, retreated to the coast at Dunkirk. Their situation was so serious that a mass slaughter was feared, ending the war in just months. As the nation prayed to God for deliverance, a call went out for every available sizeable boat to cross the channel to rescue the British and allied soldiers. The nation played its part in mustering hundreds of

---

7. Letter sent to the clergy and ministers by Duff Cooper, on behalf of The Special Secretariat for the Ministry of Information, Malet St, London, 21st June 1940, reproduced in Dr E. K. Victor Pearce's book *Miracles and Angels: Evidence for Faith*, Vol. 4 (Eagle Publishers, 1999), pp. 143-44.

private boats of all sorts, besides the naval vessels and fishing boats, to rescue 338,000 soldiers and bring them home between 27th May and 4th June, with a loss of only 12,000.

The courageous defence by the Royal Airforce against the German Luftwaffe was also vital. However, more was needed. What happened? The Germans should have destroyed the army either at Dunkirk, or on the sea. The crossing itself should have been disastrous because the weather forecast predicted severe storms. Several extraordinary things occurred: firstly, Hitler delayed in a full assault, the reason for which scholars still debate today, but it was seen as one of his great mistakes in the war; secondly, the weather dramatically and inexplicably changed, producing such a great calm, that the sea became like a millpond at just the right time to allow the hundreds of smaller boats to rescue the stranded soldiers.

The second Day of Prayer was on Sunday, 11th August 1940. The King called all the youth of Britain to gather to pray, with most of them responding. Again, the situation was grave, for this time Air Field Marshall Goering sent in a huge wave of bombers and fighter planes to bomb the nation into submission. In what was known as the Battle of Britain, our heroic fighter pilots in their Spitfires and Hurricanes defeated the attack, with great loss of life, bringing victory within the week. The British air commander said that apart from the skill and resolute action of the Royal Airforce, 'the rate of interception excelled by far anything that could be expected or explained by radar' or technology.[8]

Only a month later Parliament called for another National Day of Prayer, on 8th September, 1940. It was in August of the same year that some people claimed to see a vision of the crucified Christ and six angels at Firle Lewes in the sky above the Sussex Downs. In the *News Chronicle* we read that an excited shepherd, Mr Fowler, ran to the village to share with others what he had seen, only to be told by others that they had also seen

8. Pearce, ibid., p. 145.

the same apparition. Some of the eyewitnesses claimed that they 'could see the nail in the crossed feet of Christ, and one of the angels with arms outstretched appeared to be praying.'[9] This time, the Germans sent a second, larger wave of bombers and fighters; again, our brave fighter crews played their part, and the air attack was driven back. The newspapers of the time were not afraid to print a statement by Air Chief Marshall Dowding who has been credited with his brilliant skill in the Battle for Britain, but he said:

> I pay homage to those gallant boys who gave their all that our nation might live. I pay tribute to their leaders and commanders; but I say with absolute conviction that I can trace the intervention of God, not only in the Battle itself, but in the events which led up to it. *At the end of the Battle one had the feeling that there had been some special Divine Intervention to alter some sequence of events which would otherwise have occurred .... Humanly speaking victory was impossible!*[10]

This Scottish man, who was born in Moffat, later sadly turned away from conventional Christianity to spiritualism. Victor Pearce remarks on his notes taken at the time that Hitler was so confident the Luftwaffe would defeat Britain in the air, that he prepared his barges for the great invasion – but this never happened, as in what should have been the quietest time of the year, an unusual and terrific storm erupted in the English Channel and North Sea, which blew away the barges at Bremen, leaving Hitler having to postpone the invasion.

The next National Day of Prayer was called six months later by the King and Parliament on 23rd March, 1941. Britain did not know that Hitler had chosen this very day for his second attempted invasion, but 'a great earthquake created waves with terrific gales which blew Nazi ships 80 miles of [sic] course .... Hitler changed his plans entirely as a result of the submarine earthquake. He gave up invading Britain, and against all the advice of his generals,

---

9. Pearce, ibid., p. 138.

10. Pearce, ibid., p. 145.

he turned his attention eastwards to invade Russia. This was the turning point of the war.'[11]

Over and over again, top leaders of our armed forces recognised that something more than our courage, strong leadership under Churchill, intelligence and technology was at work in the battle against world tyranny. General Sir William Dobbie, a devout Christian of Scottish descent, tells of God's interventions in Malta in his book *A Very Present Help*, when he, his officers, and the people became accustomed to witnessing the miraculous as they held their ground against impossible odds. Lt General Sir Frederick Morgan, who was head of the British and American Planning Staff that planned the invasion, leading to Germany's surrender, was certain about God's intervention. 'Miracles happen still,' he wrote, 'How many of them have we not seen enacted before our eyes in these past few years?'[12]

The War Room of Prayer

Years ago, I had the honour to speak to the students at the Bible College of Wales in Swansea and meet Samuel Howells, the son of the founder, Rees Howells. Some dear elderly ladies proudly took me to the Blue Room, which they affectionately called 'the War Room'. It was here that Rees Howells, his staff, and the students wrestled in prayer for God's miraculous interventions during World War Two. The college itself stood as a testament to God's miraculous provision. Rees Howells, who walked closely with his Saviour, was convinced that God was guiding him to buy a mansion with large grounds to be a Bible college. There was only one problem: he had no money, and he struggled to believe that this would be possible.

Howells was invited to preach at a church in Anwoth, Southern Scotland. His host, a Mrs Stewart, told him that in front of his bedroom window scores of Covenanter Christians had been martyred in the seventeenth century. The next day he was taken to

---

11. Pearce, ibid., pp. 145-46.
12. Pearce, ibid., p. 154.

meet Sir William and Lady Maxwell at Cardoness House. He was shown one of the original documents of the National Covenant of 1638 and describes what happened. 'When I saw it,' he wrote, 'I changed altogether, and there wasn't one thing I wouldn't do to vindicate the Holy Spirit. I never felt anything like it before or since. I shed tears that night in my room. I said to the Holy Ghost, "If it costs my blood, I'll do this for You."'[13] From that night he believed with an unwavering faith that God would supply the money for the college, and he did, miraculously, so that when the Bible College of Wales opened in 1924, crowds pressed in to hear for themselves what had happened.

During the Second World War, the Blue Room was continually used for sacrificial and sustained prayer. From the records we can sense something of the significance of what was happening in this War Room of prayer:

> May 26 [1940] was the public day of prayer in Britain. As Mr. Churchill said of the May 26 Service of Intercession in Westminster Abbey: 'The English are loath to expose their feelings, but in my stall in the choir I could feel the pent-up passionate emotion, and also the fear of the congregation, not of death or wounds or national loss, but of defeat and the final ruin of Britain.'… All the leading people know to-day that unless God intervenes, we will be slaves …. We are going against this Beast [Nazism], as David went against Goliath.[14]

Miracle at Salerno

As they prayed, they witnessed miracle after miracle: often God would show them what to pray for, even before the official national news was released to the public. One such example of this was in September 1943. Rees Howells stood up before the prayer group, and with trembling voice, said, 'The Lord has burdened me between meetings with the invasion at Salerno [in Italy]. I believe our men are in great difficulties, and the Lord has told

---

13. Norman Grubb, *Rees Howells Intercessor* (Guildford and London: Lutterworth Press, first edition 1973, eighth edition 1983), p. 190.

14. Grubb, ibid., p. 254.

me that unless we can pray through, they are in danger of losing their hold.' Dr Symonds, who was present, says that 'The awe of God settled down upon us, for this came as a complete surprise, there having been no official news to this effect on the wireless [radio].' Immediately the group poured out their prayers to God for his intervention, and then there came a great sense of rejoicing as they all knew he was acting on behalf of the British forces in some miraculous way in Italy. Dr Symonds said that 'The victory was so outstanding that I looked at the clock as we rose to sing. It was on the stroke of 11 p.m.'[15]

However, they listened to the news broadcast at midnight, and it simply confirmed what Rees Howells had said: that unless some miracle happened, our troops would lose their beachhead before morning. But the next day on the front page of one of the daily newspapers was emblazoned 'The Miracle of Salerno'. The reporter who had been there described the impossible situation, and that the ceaseless bombardment of the enemy was so intense, that unless a miracle happened, the advancing army would rout our troops. Then he said the following: 'Suddenly, for no accountable reason the firing ceased and the Nazi artillery stopped its advance. A deathly stillness settled on the scene. We waited in breathless anticipation, but nothing happened. I looked at my watch – it was eleven o'clock at night. Still we waited, but still nothing happened; and nothing happened all that night, but those hours made all the difference to the invasion. By the morning the beachhead was established.'[16]

Such a testimony was the outcome of a God who intervened in answer to the passionate praying of Christians, not just in Wales, but in Scotland, and across Britain, throughout the war.

Winston Churchill and the Guiding Hand

When it was announced publicly by Winston Churchill in 1945 that the Second World War with Germany was over, we celebrated all over Britain. As we sought to rebuild our nation, plans were

---

15. Grubb, ibid., pp. 271-72.
16. Grubb, ibid.

made to bring about changes. One of those plans was enacted by the government: in gratitude for the recognition of God's deliverance in the war, a law was passed making the teaching of Christianity compulsory in the education system. Besides this, the National Health Service was set up by Parliament in 1948 through the work of Aneurin Bevan. As mentioned in a previous chapter, this had been a Christian vision for centuries with a significant Scottish influence, and William Temple, the Archbishop of Canterbury, had a key part in the establishment of the NHS, through his influential book, *Christianity and Social Order* (1942).

At one time, God's miraculous interventions during the war were recounted, but today very few are even aware of what happened. After victory had come, and Churchill had announced on the BBC radio that war with Germany was over, he went and read the same statement to the House of Commons, expressing his gratitude for their help and co-operation during the long struggle. He knew that there was something else of vital importance that needed to be done: asking for permission, he moved 'That this House do now attend at the Church of St Margaret, Westminster, to give humble and reverent thanks to Almighty God for our deliverance from the threat of German domination.'[17]

Churchill, even though he was not a religious man, had personally experienced this 'unseen hand' that had been guiding and protecting the nation. Once, while addressing three thousand mine owners and mineworkers' delegates, just over a week after the Battle of Alamein, he told them: 'I sometimes have a feeling of interference. I want to stress that. I have a feeling sometimes that some Guiding Hand has interfered. I have a feeling that we have a Guardian, because we have a great Cause, and we shall have that Guardian so long as we serve that Cause faithfully. And what a cause it is.'[18]

---

17. David E. Gardner, *The Trumpet Sounds for Britain*, Vol.2, p. 132, from the three volumes in one edition (Christian Foundation Publications, 2002).

18. Gardner, ibid., p. 130.

As we sought to restore Britain, discussions were going on about our purpose in the post-war world. William Temple, Archbishop of Canterbury, had already expressed this on Sunday, 26th September 1943, in his sermon at St Paul's Cathedral on the Battle of Britain: 'We may, and we must believe, that He who has preserved our land in a manner so marvellous, has a purpose for us to serve.'[19] What was that purpose?

When Field Marshall Rommel returned to Germany from North Africa in March 1943, he began to learn from other German officers about Hitler's ruthless regime: about the mass extermination of the Jewish people, about the gas chambers, persecution of the churches, slave labour and many other atrocities. He directly challenged Hitler about this, but the Führer was unmoved. Rommel began to see Hitler as 'the Devil incarnate' and that this evil rule would end in the destruction of Germany.

Meeting in secret with high-ranking officials who were equally dismayed at the Nazi monster, discussions centred on what sort of action must be pursued to stop it. A Draft Peace Treaty was put in Rommel's hands which outlined the plan for an armistice with Britain, America and their allies. The Treaty was 'founded on the idea of uniting Europe on the basis of Christianity' with 'the abolition of frontiers and bringing about the return of the masses to the Christian faith .... Only thus could the threat of Bolshevism [Communism] be defeated.'[20]

His intention was to meet up with Generals Eisenhower and Montgomery, knowing that they had a Christian understanding, and propose an armistice. He would probably have discussed the vision for a new Europe based on Christian values, but he was accused of being part of a conspiracy to assassinate Hitler on 20th July 1944, in *Operation Valkyrie*. Rommel was forced to commit suicide by cyanide by the Nazis, although the Nazi propaganda said he had died of a brain seizure on the way to a conference.

---

19. Gardner, ibid., p. 133.

20. Gardner, ibid., p. 135, citing from Desmond Young's *Rommel* (London: Collins, 1950), p. 225.

His son, Manfred Rommel, was an eyewitness of his father's last hour, who told what happened after Nazism had been destroyed. Rev. David Gardner wrote to Manfred Rommel when he was the Mayor of Stuttgart and asked him to confirm the vision of a Europe based on Christian values. Gardner received a letter from him in 1974, saying: 'I still have the vision of a united Europe based on Christianity.'[21]

Sceptics have questioned such a vision, but the fact of the matter is that straight after the end of World War Two there arose the Christian Democratic Union in Germany. This party, to which Manfred Rommel belonged, led the process of rebuilding Germany, and saw the preservation of West Germany from the Communist regime. It was a party made up originally of Catholic and Protestant politicians who were determined to steer a new path in Germany and Europe based on Christian-democratic principles. Even in this we can see the far-reaching effects of the Presbyterian influence, in that a Christian-based democracy was deemed to be the best form of government in a sinful world. However, the idea of a merger between Catholics and Protestants would clearly not have been popular with the reformers and Covenanters of Scotland, nor the liberal ideas that would be accepted later as biblical Christianity became diminished.

---

21. Letter of Manfred Rommel, Mayor of Stuttgart, to Rev. David Gardner, December 1974.

CHAPTER 14

SCOTLAND: WHERE ARE WE GOING?

Thousands of shouts and screams merged together in the night. Amidst the drumming and burning torches the colourful procession had woven its way to the top of Calton Hill overlooking Edinburgh. It was Beltane Fire Festival on the evening of 30th April, and a twenty-first century enactment of an ancient Pagan custom was being performed again, to the delight of an estimated twelve thousand excited and inquisitive viewers. As the performers focused their attention on the unfinished National Monument, also known as Edinburgh's Disgrace, because money ran out to complete the full construction in 1829, the May Queen and Green Man were being celebrated as a new summer was being ushered in. It was a fertility festival in which participants, daubed as spirits in white, green, blue, or red, played their part in the drama. The red spirits, being nearly naked, were especially mischievous. It is something the Edinburgh Council is proud of in its celebration of diversity, and as *The Scotsman* newspaper remarked, it is a 'world-famous attraction'.

'Beltane fires,' wrote Sir James Fraser the Scottish scholar, 'were formerly kindled with great ceremony on the first of May, and the traces of human sacrifices at them were particularly clear and unequivocal.'[1] With the coming of Christianity human sacrifice disappeared, but customs of offering cakes in the fire to the spirits for the blessing of crops and livestock remained. Today's

---

1. J. G. Fraser, *The Golden Bough: A Study in Magic and Religion* (World's Classics, Oxford University Press, 1994), p. 716.

Beltane in Edinburgh is a much more elaborate and theatrical performance, stripped of much of the rawness of its past.

The Lottery

Although it was a warm California night in the 1990s, the lecturer in an adult-education class was 'shivery, chilled to the bone.' The students had discussed a book written in the 1940s by Shirley Jackson called *The Lottery*. The scene is set in a small American town and the locals gather for a ritual to ensure the productivity of the crops. The silent participants each randomly draw a piece of paper from a box. Tessie Hutchinson, a wife and mother, screams, 'It isn't fair, it isn't right!' Her random selection of a piece of paper with a black mark means that she will be this year's human sacrifice, offered for the blessing of the crops on behalf of the others.

When *The Lottery* first came out in 1948 people were outraged, but now in the 1990s something had changed. When asked for a moral response to the book, the students did not even protest. 'They just do it; it's their ritual,' one student responded. A nurse in her fifties summed up what most felt. 'Well, I teach a course for our hospital personnel in multicultural understanding,' she declared, 'and if it's a part of a person's culture, we are taught not to judge, and if it has worked for them...'

The seasoned teacher, Kay Haugaard, who had taught for decades, was paralysed by a sense of hopelessness and despair. 'At this point I gave up,' she reported in *The Chronicle of Higher Education*. 'No-one in the whole class of more than twenty ostensibly intelligent individuals would go out on a limb and take a stand against human sacrifice.'[2]

Does such a scenario seem impossible for our so-called 'evolved culture' in Scotland? I asked the same sort of questions to young adults in Edinburgh and found that our capital city is so drenched with wokeness that most of them answered something

---

2. O. Guinness, *Time for Truth: Living Free in a World of Lies, Hype and Spin* (Intervarsity Press, 2000), pp. 21-24.

like, 'Well, I don't agree with human sacrifice personally, but we should not judge another culture that practises it. We all have different opinions. It might not be my truth, but it's theirs.' Meet the relativists of modern Scotland.

The irony, however, is that those same placid people can suddenly become enraged at the breaking of the modern secular code of ethics by others. For example, women, they say, have the right to abort their babies up to birth, for any reason, because only women matter; any contrary opinion saying that both lives matter is viewed as bigoted, unless the parents wish to selectively abort their babies based on their sex, in which case sexism trumps abortion. Questioning macro-evolution in the science classroom or research department can lead to expulsion. Woe betide anyone to question the right of children to 'change sex', or for anyone to state that it is scientifically impossible to do so.

In Scotland, we are witnessing the clash of two worldviews: relativism and absolutism. Relativism is the belief that truth is based on cultural preference, and absolutism is the belief that truth applies to everyone, irrespective of their beliefs and cultures. A group of people from different faiths, beliefs and cultures might have a different opinion about food, but at the same time there are absolute laws working on this planet, to which we are all subject, such as $1 + 1 = 2$, or the law of gravity, or death. The United Kingdom, and increasingly Scotland, finds the majority of the population sandwiched between what has been called woke, or ultra-liberalism on one side, and Islam's absolutism on the other. The frustration of many is bubbling over in protests, which some extreme groups make use of for their own agenda.

For the church, we find that four walls are closing in on it: atheism, woke ideology, New Age-Paganism,[3] and Islam. Under the pressure to conform, churches are either becoming chameleons and changing their colours to compromise and merge

---

3. The term 'New Age' was coined by Alice Bailey, an occultist and spiritualist, in the 1940s. She believed and wrote that a global movement would overcome the Age of Pisces, the period of Judaeo-Christian dominance, and be replaced by the Age of Aquarius, a period of multifaith Paganism.

with the spirit of the age, or they are increasingly becoming the targets of persecution, if they stand for traditional biblical values and beliefs.

Scotland was once called 'the Land of the Book,' meaning the Bible. Our ancestors understood that God had created the universe, and that His laws were shown in science and morality. From this foundation our culture emerged over centuries, as the previous chapters in this book have shown. Often, our Christian Heritage Tour guests are puzzled how Christianity, which had such a massive part in shaping our Scottish culture, has now shrunk to such a low ebb, that it has almost been extinguished as a voice in modern Scotland. It is as if the sea has gone out and just left rock pools on the shoreline of our land. However, the tide will turn; the sea will come in again.

The Enlightenment and its Daughters

Although the Reformation left a wonderful legacy in many ways, such as education, the beginnings of a Christian-inspired democracy, and a vision for the welfare of the whole nation, it also left a legacy of religious legalism. The freedom procured through the blood of the reformers and Covenanters paved the way for free speech and open debate, but many wished to be also free of what Jesus called 'the yeast of the Pharisees'. A growing number of intellectuals began to use the new platform of freethinking to challenge religion and devise alternative ideologies.

In this period, which we call the Enlightenment, we saw many good things being developed in Edinburgh and Scotland, but we also saw the rise of the ideas of David Hume, James Hutton and Charles Darwin. Hume challenged belief in God and the supernatural through his rationalism; Hutton hammered at Genesis through his fieldwork in geology; and Darwin assaulted the divine origin of life through his book on evolution, called *The Origin of Species* (1859). The late Daniel Dennett, a former Professor of Philosophy, and highly regarded as one of the New Atheists, along with Richard Dawkins, Sam Harris and Christopher Hitchens, outlined what happened to our Western culture:

Little did I realize that in a few years I would encounter an idea – Darwin's idea – bearing an unmistakable likeness to universal acid: it eats through just about every traditional concept, and leaves in its wake a revolutionized world-view, with most of the old landmarks still recognizable, but transformed in fundamental ways.[4]

The new *zeitgeist* entered the mainstream Bible colleges, with the rise of Higher Criticism, producing a compromised and liberal church. If the Enlightenment and Darwinism had produced secular liberalism, then secular liberalism gave birth to the sexual revolution of the 1960s, and to what was called political correctness; political correctness gave birth to wokeness, and now wokeness has given birth to extreme wokeness, a form of puritanical illiberal movement.

With the rise of extreme wokeness in the last ten years we find ourselves in a fog of confusion. It is as if some ultra-liberal élite wish to turn our culture upside down and remove all traditional boundary stones. Feminists, who fought hard and long for their human rights, are now faced with a transgender ideology which wants to dominate them and strip away their dignity. Those who dare to challenge the new creeping tyranny are labelled as Nazis, fascists and bigots, in what has been called the culture war. Do we really want to see a Scotland dominated by woke extremists? The strange thing about this is that the strong social consciousness movement associated with wokeness, actually had its origin in Christian values, but we have stripped away the biblical authority and boundary stones. Tom Holland, in his book, *Dominion: The Making of the Western Mind* (2019), perceptively wrote:

> Christian values ... like dust particles so fine as to be invisible to the naked eye, were breathed in equally by everyone: believers, atheists, and those who never paused so much as to think about religion. Had it been otherwise, then no one would ever have got woke.[5]

---

4. D. Dennett, *Darwin's Dangerous Idea: Evolution and the Meanings of Life* (Simon and Schuster, reprint, 1996), p. 63.

5. T. Holland, *Dominion: The Making of the Western Mind* (Little, Brown, 2019), p. 517.

Resurrection from the Dead?

For those who have eyes to see, something is also stirring again. There may appear to have been a burial of Christianity in Scotland and in Europe, but life is starting to rise up again. A thaw is in the air after a long, hard winter, but the church must go through purification first before regeneration explodes once again from the embers. There is hope, but it is time to regroup and rebuild. This hope is not lost on perceptive scholars who study world trends, especially in Europe. The late Professor René Girard, one of Europe's leading philosophers of ideologies during this century and last, underwent a conversion from atheism to Roman Catholicism. As one of the forty Immortals for the think-tank of the French Academy, he wrote in 2006: 'I believe we are on the eve of a revolution in our culture that will go beyond any expectation, and that the world is heading toward a change in respect of which the Renaissance will seem like nothing... we will live in a world that will seem and be as Christian as today it seems scientific.'[6]

Seeing the conflict between the domineering ideology of Islam and that of the prevailing extreme wokeness of our far-left culture, which is even expressed among the Conservatives, he understood that it will be a revived Christianity that will triumph. 'If it was really understood that Jesus is the universal victim who came precisely to surmount these conflicts,' he said, 'the problem would be solved.' According to this leading scholar, love and truth are needed at the crossroads of our culture, and 'in Christianity, truth and love coincide and are one and the same.'

Girard bemoans the fact that 'the Christian religion cannot even be mentioned in certain environments, or one can speak of

---

6. *2006: Anthropologist Foresees a Christian Renaissance*: ldsfocuschrist2. wordpress.com › 2009/04/10 › 2006-an, and also cited partially in *How Christianity Made the Modern World* (Paul Backholer, By Faith Media, 2009), p. 104. The initial sources are from *Truth or Weak Faith: Dialogue on Christianity and Relativism*, by René Girard and Gianni Vattimo, published by Pier Vittorio and Associates, and also from *Anthropologist Foresees a Christian Renaissance*, Zenit.org, 17th December 2007.

it only to keep it under control, to confine it, making one believe that it is the first and only factor responsible for the horror the present world is going through.' But he was not a romantic idealist: he realised that for this Christian renaissance to burst forth, it is inevitable that Christianity in Europe will go through persecution and burial for it to be refined and rise up again in a Christ-like form to shine with glory.

Restoring a Christian Worldview

There is a fresh onshore wind blowing for those with discernment. Among many thinkers, there is a growing sense that something is very wrong with our culture, which is heading into a storm caused by tyrannical ideologies. Among the outspoken liberal voices are the Scottish agnostic, Douglas Murray; Jordan Peterson, an agnostic turned theistic professor of psychology; the feminists Louise Perry, Joanna Williams and J. K. Rowling; the comedian-scholar, Andrew Doyle; the mysterious 'The Secret Barrister'; Toby Young of The Free Speech Union; Tom Holland, the historian who has moved from atheism to Christianity; Ayaan Hirsi Ali, a Somali intellectual who became an extreme Muslim, then converted to atheism, and recently became a Christian, and many others. Even the notorious atheist, Richard Dawkins, has declared himself to be a 'cultural Christian' (whatever that means). By using rational arguments, they are seeking to counter extreme wokeness and Islamic absolutism, but have been called fascists and Nazis because of their stand for common sense.

As we delve into their books and talks, we begin to discern that there is generally a common pull towards Christianity, even though most of the contenders are not believers. For example, Douglas Murray has a cure for those desiring revenge against so-called white supremacists, who apparently have the unforgivable original sin of racism: it is called forgiveness. 'Is there any route to forgiveness?' He asks. 'The consensus for centuries was that only God could forgive the ultimate sins,' he answers, 'but on a day-to-day level the Christian tradition, among others, also stressed the desirability – if not the necessity – of forgiveness.'[7] In despair he looks at the modern witch-hunting of those who go on moral archaeological digs to unearth any so-called incriminating evidence of heresy or sin against wokeness. In frustration he cries out that 'guilt and shame are more at hand than ever, and … we have no means whatsoever of redemption. We do not know who could offer it, who could accept it, and whether it is a desirable quality compared to an endless cycle of fiery certainty and denunciation.'[8]

Louise Perry, despite being driven by an evolutionary atheist and feminist philosophy, reacts against the sexual revolution and calls us back to something akin to Christian morality, lacing her arguments with quotations and reflections from Christians, such as C. S. Lewis, the social reformer Josephine Butler, G. K. Chesterton, and even the hated and ridiculed Mary Whitehouse, who campaigned tirelessly as a lonely public figure against pornography and child sex-abuse.

In seeking to fend off the mob, The Secret Barrister points us to law and order, and includes a section from Tom Bingham's book *The Rule of Law* in his own section entitled 'Equal treatment under the law'.[9] Bingham, as I have outlined before, was both the former Lord Justice of England and Wales, and a practising Anglican Christian who understood the Christian influence behind our laws and constitution. If our constitution and rule of law are removed, we will drift on the current of wokeness to the rocks of our own self-destruction.

Homecoming Scotland

Will Scotland hear the voice of Christ to come and follow Him? In this book I have sought to present the remarkable transformation that came to our nation through Christian

---

7. Douglas Murray, *The Madness of Crowds: Gender, Race and Identity* (Bloomsbury Continuum, 2020), pp. 181-82.

8. Murray, ibid., p. 182.

9. The Secret Barrister, *Fake Law: The Truth About Justice in an Age of Lies* (Picador, 2020), pp. 243-44.

movements of the past. Individuals were radically transformed by their experience and love of Christ, which led to communities undergoing transformation themselves. Out of this came the rise of fairer and more just laws; modern democracy and human rights; national education; ethical and compassionate healthcare and medical advances; scientific breakthroughs; social reforms for women, slaves and the working class, and so much more. If we lose biblical Christianity in Scotland, we will lose much of this and will find ourselves engaging in culture wars which will tear our nation apart. It is true that it is impossible for Scotland ever to be wholly Christian, but it is possible that we could swing back to a Christian worldview, although to do so would be an amazing miracle.

Tim Farron, former leader of the Liberal Democrats, was hounded out of office because he could not accept same-sex marriage. Commenting on what is going on in our culture now he said, 'Liberalism has eaten itself, because it has eaten the very world-view that gave birth to it, that made it possible. In discarding Christianity, we kick away the foundations of liberalism and democracy, and so we cannot then be surprised when what we call liberalism stops being liberal.'[10] It was for this same reason that Kate Forbes, one of the contenders for the post of First Minister of the Scottish Parliament, was torn to pieces by her own party for her 'sin' of holding a different opinion, that of traditional marriage.

Margaret Thatcher, a former UK Prime Minister, once said to the Church of Scotland General Assembly:

I think back to many discussions in my early life when we all agreed that if you try to take the fruits of Christianity without its roots, the fruits will wither. And they will not come again unless you nurture the roots. But we must not profess the Christian faith and go to church simply because we want social reforms and benefits or a better standard of behaviour; but because we accept the sanctity

10. Tim Wyatt, *Gordon Brown: I should have been more forthright about my faith* (Church Times, 1st December 2017).

of life, the responsibility that comes with freedom and the supreme sacrifice of Christ expressed so well in the hymn:

> When I survey the wondrous Cross,
> On which the Prince of glory died,
> My richest gain I count but loss,
> And pour contempt on all my pride.[11]

Jeremiah, writing so long ago in about 627 B.C., gives us the challenge: 'Stand in the ways and see. And ask for the old paths, where the good way is, and walk in it; then you will find rest for your souls' (Jer. 6:16).

May prodigal Scotland heed these words, avoid self-destruction, and return home.

---

11. Margaret Thatcher, *Christianity and Wealth,* Speech to the Church of Scotland General Assembly, 21st May 1988.

TIMELINE

c. 200: The first Christians were at *Alt Clud* (Dumbarton) amongst the Britons, a Welsh-speaking people, and the original inhabitants of today's Scotland.

303–313: Emperor Diocletian's massacre of Christians in the Roman Empire, which included the Britons.

314: Three bishops from the Britons were represented at the Council of Arles in France.

345: According to legend, Regulus brought some of the apostle Andrew's relics (bones) to Scotland.

397: Ninian the Briton re-evangelised southern Scotland.

410: Germanic tribes sacked Rome, so the Romans left Scotland, leaving the Britons exposed to the onslaughts of the Pagan Picts and Scots. Many Christians were massacred and churches burned between 410 and the 600s.

432: Patrick the Briton from *Alt Clud* (Dumbarton) became an apostle to the Irish (Scots).

540s: Kentigern the Briton began his mission in Scotland.

563: Columba came from Ireland and set up his mission base on Iona.

635: Aidan was sent from Iona to pioneer the mission community at Lindisfarne, to reach the Anglo-Saxons with the gospel.

664: The church in Scotland came under the authority of the church at Rome.

c.680s: Cuthbert preached in southern Scotland and a church in Edinburgh was dedicated by him below the castle (now called St Cuthbert's).

697: Adomnan of Iona initiated the Law of Innocents, to protect women, children and the clergy during war.

795: The Vikings began their destruction along the Scottish coasts.

806: Sixty-eight monks were slaughtered on Iona by the shore at Martyrs' Bay.

843: Traditional foundation of Scotland as a nation.

854: A church was built on the site of today's St Giles in Edinburgh.

1093: Queen Margaret died in Edinburgh Castle.

1095–1270: The Crusades were started to try and protect Christian pilgrims and liberate the Holy Land from Muslims. A small number of Scots became Crusaders.

1125–1197: The period of founding the great abbeys: Jedburgh (c.1118); Holyrood in Edinburgh (1128); Kelso (1128); Dunfermline (1128); Melrose (1136); Dryburgh (1150); and the cathedrals in Edinburgh (1125), St Andrews (1160s) and Glasgow (1197).

1230: King Alexander II founded the Dominican friary.

1305: William Wallace was executed by the English.

1314: Robert the Bruce defeated the English at Bannockburn.

1320: Declaration of Arbroath, in which the leaders of Scotland petitioned Pope John XXII for his intervention to stop the English from invading Scotland.

1328: The Treaty of Edinburgh-Northampton, by which Scotland became fully independent from England with its own ruling kings.

1380s: Preachers from John Wycliffe at Oxford University preached in Scotland, calling for reformation of the church.

1388–1414: Reformers were martyred and persecuted in Scotland.

1455–1458: Greyfriars' (Franciscan) friary was founded.

1460s: Trinity College Hospital was moved from Soutra Aisle (founded by the Church in 1164) to Edinburgh.

1505: The Royal College of Surgeons was founded.

1507: The first printing press in Scotland was pioneered by Myllar and Chepman, inspired by Bishop Elphinstone.

1517: Martin Luther nailed his 95 *Theses* on the door of All Saints Church in Wittenberg, which triggered off the Protestant Reformation. Scottish seekers travelled to Germany to hear Luther.

1526: William Tyndale's English New Testament was distributed from Leith Port near Edinburgh. Soldiers burnt copies and imprisoned people who owned them.

1528: Patrick Hamilton, the Scottish Lutheran reformer, was burnt at the stake at St Andrews.

1534: The reformers Gourlay and Stratton were burnt at the stake on Calton Hill, Edinburgh.

1538: Five reformer Christians were burnt at the stake next to Edinburgh Castle.

1560: The Scottish Reformation was led by John Knox, and the Protestant Church of Scotland was established.

1568: Robert Carver, the Scottish church composer, died.

1572: John Knox died and was buried behind St Giles.

1579: The first printed complete Bible was distributed in Scotland (the Geneva Bible).

1583: Gilbert Primrose, a reformer, raised surgery to its prime position amongst the guilds in Edinburgh. The University of Edinburgh was officially established (its roots were in Magdalen Chapel).

1592: The Great Charter was established, granting legal right of the Presbyterian, democratic system in the Church of Scotland.

1599: The Christian, Peter Lowe, left Edinburgh to found the Faculty of Physicians and Surgeons in Glasgow.

1611: The King James Bible was published (named after King James VI and I, who was born in Edinburgh Castle).

1614: The Christian, John Napier, invented the logarithm.

1628: The Petition of Right was written by the Puritan, Sir Edward Coke.

1638: Signing of the National Covenant.

1643: The Solemn League and Covenant.

1661: 'The Drunken Parliament' in Edinburgh, in which the nobles of Scotland signed the nation over to absolute control by King Charles II.

1661–1688: 'The Killing Time' in which over 18,000 Covenanter Christians suffered through death, starvation, torture, exile and slavery.

1679: Habeas Corpus.

1688: The Glorious Revolution of William of Orange.

1689: The English Bill of Rights and Scottish Claim of Right were established by law, beginning a movement towards religious and democratic freedom.

1690: The Act of Settlement, restoring the Presbyterian Church in Scotland.

1697: The atheist, Thomas Aikenhead, was executed for committing blasphemy outside the Tron Kirk in Edinburgh.

1707: Act of Union, by which Scotland came under Westminster's government.

1712: The Patronage Act, which was imposed on the Presbyterian Church, effectively squashing its democratic and legal right for the third time.

1726: Edinburgh Medical School was founded, based on the Christian doctor, Herman Boerhaave's Leiden model.

1741: George Whitefield's first preaching tour in Scotland (his final tour was in 1756).

1751: John Wesley's first preaching tour in Scotland (his final tour was in 1791).

1776: David Hume, the sceptical atheist, died.

1790: Adam Smith, father of capitalism, died.

1796: Rev. John Erskine challenged the Church of Scotland about world mission.

1797: James Hutton, father of modern geology, died.

1799: Lord Monboddo, Scottish pioneer of evolution, died.

1809: The Scottish Bible Society was founded in the Edinburgh City Chambers.

1820: James Wilson, John Baird and Andrew Hardie were hanged in Scotland for their stand as leaders for democracy for the common person. Both Baird and Hardie were Christians.

1824–1930s: Scotland's world missionary movement.

1826: David Nasmith founded the City Mission movement in Glasgow.

1829: The Christian, Thomas Young, inventor of the double-slit experiment, died.

1832: David Nasmith founded Edinburgh City Mission.

1839: Christian revival in Edinburgh and parts of Scotland.

1841: Grassmarket revival amongst the prostitutes.

1843: The Disruption in the Church of Scotland; the Free Church of Scotland was founded. The Christian, David Octavius Hill, with Robert Adamson, produced the first ever portrait photographs.

1847: Rev. Thomas Chalmers, a key founder of our free education system, died.

1859: A large, almost national, Christian revival began. Charles Darwin published his *Origin of Species*. He had been educated at Edinburgh University.

1868: The Christian, Sir David Brewster, discoverer of Brewster's Law (foundational for laser science), died.

1873: D. L. Moody, the American evangelist's first revival visit. Rev. Thomas Guthrie, founder of the Edinburgh Ragged School, died.

1879: James Clerk Maxwell, the Christian physicist from Edinburgh, died.

1880s: Moody's second revival visit.

1906: James Keir Hardie, a Christian, became the first leader of the Labour Party, thus properly representing the common person for the first time.

1910: The World Missionary Conference took place in Edinburgh.

1912: Lord Joseph Lister, Christian pioneer of antiseptics, died.

1914–1918: The First World War.

1939–1945: The Second World War.

1945: Eric Liddell, the famous Christian missionary athlete from Edinburgh, died; all of Scotland mourned.

1949–1952: The Hebrides' revival.

1955: The American evangelist, Billy Graham, had a huge impact in Edinburgh.

1966: Billy Graham preached to large crowds in Scotland, with many being converted to Christ.

APPENDIX

GOD, EVOLUTION AND THE CHRISTIAN FAITH

A movement of highly qualified biologists, biochemists and geneticists is beginning to rise up that is questioning Darwinism. For example, among those who have taken their stand as dissenters are over 1,000 scientists with PhDs, among them being hundreds of experts in the fields related to biology. They stand behind the following statement:

'We are skeptical of claims for the ability of random mutation and natural selection to account for the complexity of life. Careful examination of the evidence for Darwinian theory should be encouraged' (dissentfromdarwin.org).

Among the dissidents are theists, atheists and agnostics. Many come from the world's leading universities, such as Oxford, Cambridge, MIT, Harvard, Princeton, Yale and Berkeley; some are members of national science academies; others are Nobel Prize winners and leading research scientists. For every one person who has submitted his/her name to the list, there are reckoned to be at least ten other dissenters of this calibre who have not, due to fear of losing their jobs for questioning Darwinism, ignorance of such a list, or for other reasons.

Please find below a list of useful books on this important subject.

Denton, M., *Evolution: A Theory in Crisis: New Developments in Science are Challenging Orthodox Darwinism*, Adler and Adler, 1985. Michael Denton has a PhD in biochemistry from King's College, London. He wrote his book as an agnostic.

Lennox, John C., *God's Undertaker: Has Science Buried God?* Lion Hudson plc, 2007. Lennox is Professor of Mathematics at the University of Oxford.

Gish, Duane T., *Evolution: the fossils still say NO!* Institute for Creation Research, 1995. Gish's PhD was in biochemistry from the University of California, Berkeley.

Sanford, J. C., *Genetic Entropy and the Mystery of the Genome*, Elim Publishing: New York, 2005. Sanford was Professor of Genetics at Cornell University when his scientific work drove him to the conclusion that macro-evolution is untrue. He co-invented the gene-gun.

Bergman, J., and Howe, G., *Vestigial Organs are Fully Functional*, Creation Research Society, Monograph Series, No.4, 1990. Bergman's PhD was in human biology at Columbia Pacific University, and Howe's PhD was in plant biology (botany) at Ohio State University. The foreword is by David Menton, Professor of Anatomy at Washington University School of Medicine, and by Verna Wright, Professor of Rheumatology, University of Leeds.

Harrub, B., and Thompson, B., *The Truth about Human Origins: An Investigation of the Creation/Evolution Controversy as it Relates to the Origin of Mankind*, Apologetics Press, USA, 2003. Harrub's PhD was in anatomy and neurobiology from the University of Tennessee, and Thompson's PhD was in microbiology from Texas University.

Evolution's Achilles' Heels: 9 Ph.D. scientists explain evolution's fatal flaws – in areas claimed to be its greatest strengths, edited by Robert Carter whose PhD was in marine biology at the University of Miami, Creation Book Publishers, 2014.

Jeanson, Nathaniel T., *Replacing Darwin: The New Origin of Species*, Master Books, 2017. Jeanson's PhD was in cell and developmental biology at Harvard University.

Spetner, L., *Not By Chance! Shattering the Modern Theory of Evolution*, The Judaica Press, Inc, New York, 1997, 1998. Spetner received his PhD in physics from MIT, after which he was on a fellowship with the Department of Biophysics at John Hopkins University.

Wilder-Smith, A. E., *A Basis for a New Biology*, Telos, 1976. Wilder-Smith had the unusual combination of three earned PhDs in the natural sciences: organic chemistry (University of Reading); biology (University of Geneva); and biochemistry (E.T.M., Zurich).

Wilder-Smith, A.E., *The Natural Sciences Know Nothing of Evolution*, Master Books, 1981. In this book, Wilder-Smith shows the scientific impossibility of macro-evolution.

Gitt, W., *In the Beginning was Information*, Christliche Literatur-Verbreiting e. V., Germany, 1997, 2000. Werner Gitt received his PhD from the Technical University of Aachen in Germany, and was Director and Professor of the German Federal Institute of Physics and Technology.

Flew, A., *There is a God: How the world's most notorious atheist changed his mind*, HarperOne, 2007. Flew was Professor of Philosophy at the University of Keele, but he also held positions at the Universities of Oxford, Aberdeen and Reading. Although he did not become a Christian before he died, this leading atheist became a theist through his investigation of the scientific evidence, which challenged materialistic evolution.

Sarfati, J., *The Greatest Hoax on Earth? Refuting Dawkins on Evolution: A response to The Greatest Show on Earth: the evidence for evolution*, Creation Book Publishers, 2010. Sarfati's PhD was in physical chemistry from Victoria University, New Zealand.

Strobel, L., *The Case for a Creator: A Journalist Investigates Scientific Evidence That Points Toward God*, Zondervan, 2004. Strobel was formerly an atheist.

Mere Creation: Science, Faith & Intelligent Design, with contributions by Michael Behe, David Berlinski, Philip Johnson, Hugh Ross and others, edited by William A. Dembski, InterVarsity Press, 1998. This is a book containing articles by PhD contributors.

Behe, M., *The Edge of Evolution: The Search for the Limits of Darwinism*, Free Press, 2007. Michael Behe is Professor of Biochemistry at Lehigh University.

Behe, M., *Darwin's Black Box: The Biochemical Challenge to Evolution*, Free Press, 1996.

Wells, J., *Icons of Evolution: Science or Myth? Why much of what we teach about evolution is wrong*, Regnery Publishing Inc., 2000. Jonathan Wells was awarded two PhDs in molecular and cell biology at the University of California, Berkeley.

Wieland, C., *One Human Family: The Bible, Science, Race & Culture*, Creation Book Publishers, 2011. Carl Wieland was a medical doctor who graduated from Adelaide University.

Milton, R., *The Facts of Life: Shattering the Myths of Darwinism*, Corgi Books, 1992. Richard Milton is a science journalist.

Werner, C., *Evolution: The Grand Experiment*, Vol.1, New Leaf Press, 2007. Carl Werner is a medical doctor.

Werner, C., *Living Fossils: Evolution: The Grand Experiment*, Vol.2, New Leaf Press, 2008.

Kenyon, D., and Davis, P., *Of Pandas and People: The Central Question of Biological Origins*, Foundation for Thought and Ethics, 1989, 1993. Dean Kenyon was Emeritus Professor of Biology at San Francisco State University, and Percival Davis received a PhD in biology from the University of South Florida.

BIBLIOGRAPHY

Chapter 1: The Coming of the Cross

Adomnan of Iona. *Life of St Columba*. Second Preface, translated by Richard Sharpe. Penguin Classics, 1995.

Adomnan of Iona. *Life of St Columba*. Translated by Richard Sharpe. Penguin Classics, 1995.

Annals of Ulster: A Chronicle of Irish Affairs from A.D. 431 to A.D. 1056. Printed for her Majesty's Stationery Office by Alexander Thom and Co., 1887.

Bede. *A History of the English Church and People*. Translated by Leo Sherley-Price and revised by R. E. Latham, revised edition 1968. Penguin Classics, 1983.

Bede. *Chronica maiora*, 4131, and in his *A History of the English Church and People*. Penguin Classics, 1955, 1968.

Bede. *The Age of Bede: Life of Cuthbert*. Translated by J. F. Webb. Penguin Classics, 1965.

Bryce, D. *Symbolism of the Celtic Cross*. Llanerch Press Ltd., 1989, 2006.

Cooper, W. R. 'Special Appendix: The Early Writing of the Gospel,' *The Authenticity of the Book of Genesis*. Creation Science Movement, 2011.

Ehrman, B. *The Triumph of Christianity: How a Forbidden Religion Swept the World*. One World Publications, 2018.

Eusebius. *Life of Constantine*. New Advent (online resource).

Eusebius. *The History of the Church*. Penguin Classics, 1989.

Eusebius of Caesarea. *Demonstratio Evangelica*. Translated by W. J. Ferrar (1920).

First Letter of Clement (5). *Early Christian Writings: The Apostolic Fathers.* Trans. by Maxwell Staniforth. Penguin Classics, 1968.

'Fragment of the Life of St Kentigern,' contained with the *Life of Ninian* and *Life of S. Kentigern, The Historians of Scotland.* Vol. V. Edited by Alexander Penrose Forbes. Edinburgh: Edmonton and Douglas, 1874.

'Glastonbury Abbey uncovered.' University of Reading research. reading.ac.uk, 2018.

Gildas. *De Excidio Brittanniae, Or The Ruin of Britain.* Preface, edited for the Hon. Society of Cymmrodorion by Hugh Williams, a facsimile reprint by Llanerch Press, 2006.

Gildas. *On the Ruin of Britain.* Translated by J. A. Giles (1842) and T. Habington. http://www.heroofcamelot.co

Harnack, A. *Der Brief des britischen Konigs Lucius and den Papst Eleutherus.* Sitzungsberichte der koniglich preussischen Akademie der Wissenschaften, 1904.

Healy, J. *The Life and Writings of St. Patrick, With Appendices, etc* M. H. Gill and Son, Ltd, and Sealy, Bryers and Walker, Dublin, 1905.

Hippolytus. 'Hippolytus on the Twelve Apostles: The Same Hippolytus on the Seventy Apostles,' *The Ante-Nicene Fathers.* Vol. V, Eds. Roberts, A., and Donaldson J. Edinburgh: T&T Clark; Grand Rapids, Michigan: WM. B. Eerdmans Publishing Company, Grand Rapids, 1995.

Hurtado, W. *The Earliest Christian Artifacts, Manuscripts and Christian Origins.* Wm. B. Eerdmans Publishing Co., 2006.

Ignatius. 'The Epistle to the Ephesians,' from *Early Christian Writings.* Penguin Classics, reprinted 1982.

Jocelinus (Jocelyn). 'Life of S. Kentigern,' from *Two Celtic Saints: The Lives of Ninian and Kentigern.* Llanerch Press, 1989, 2000.

John of Fordun. *Chronicle of the Scottish Nation.* Edited by William F. Skene, first published in 1872 (Edinburgh), as Vol. IV of the *Historians of Scotland.* Republished by Llanerch Publishers, 1993.

Knight, D. J. *King Lucius of Britain*. Tempus Publishing, 2008.

Lactantius. 'Of the Manner in Which the Persecutors Died: Addressed to Donatus,' Vol. VII. *Ante-Nicene Fathers*. Reprinted 1994. Edinburgh: T&T Clark. Grand Rapids, Michigan: WM. B. Eerdmans Publishing Company.

'Life of Charlemagne by the Monk of St Gall,' from *Early Lives of Eginhard and the Monk of St Gall*. Edited by A. J. Grant, Alexander Moring Ltd, the De La More Press, 32 Hanover Sq., London, produced by Andrew Dunning and created from scans by Robarts Library, University of Toronto, available through the Internet Archive, a Gutenberg Project.

Nennius. *History of the Britons (Historia Brittonum)*. Translation by J. A. Giles. Cambridge, Ontario: Parentheses Publications, Medieval Latin Series, 2000.

Origen. 'Commentary on Ezekiel.' *From Origen of Alexandria: Exegetical Works on Ezekiel*. Edited by Roger Pearse. Trans. Mischa Hooker. Ipswich: Chieftain Publishing, 2014.

Pliny. *The Letters of the Younger Pliny*. Editor Betty Radice. Penguin Classics, 1963, 1969.

Scott, A. B. *From the Pictish Nation, Its People and Its Church*. Edinburgh and London: T. N. Foulis Publisher, 1918. Forgotten Books, 2016.

Simeon of Durham. *A History of the Kings of England*. Translated by Joseph Stevenson (1858) in the *Church Historians of England*. Facsimile reprint by Llanerch Enterprises, 1987.

Simeon of Durham. *Simeon's History of the Church of Durham*. Translated by Joseph Stevenson. First published by Seeleys of London in the series, *The Church Historians of England*. Facsimile reprint by Llanerch Publishers, 1993.

Spottiswoode, John. *The History of the Church of Scotland: Beginning the year of our Lord 203, and continued to the end of the Reign of King James the VI of Ever Blessed Memory*. Book 2, third edition. London: (original edition, 1639).

Stark, R. *The Rise of Christianity: How the Obscure, Marginal Jesus Movement Became the Dominant Religious Force in the Western World in a Few Centuries*. Harper Collins, 1996.

Tacitus. *The Annals of Imperial Rome.* Translated by Michael Grant. Penguin Classics, reprinted 1979.

Tertullian. 'An Answer to the Jews 7,' *The Ante-Nicene Fathers.* Editors Roberts A. and Donaldson J. Vol III. Edinburgh: T&T Clark. Grand Rapids, Michigan: Wm. B. Eerdmans Publishing Co., 1997.

Tertullian. 'Apology,' *The Ante-Nicene Fathers.* Editors Roberts A. and Donaldson, J. Vol. III. Edinburgh: T&T Clark. Grand Rapids, Michigan: Wm. B. Eerdmans Publishing Company, 1997.

The Anglo-Saxon Chronicle. Translated by G. N. Garmonsway. London: J. M. Dent and Sons Ltd. New York: E. P. Dutton and Co. Inc., The Aldine Press, 1953.

Thomas, Charles. *Christianity in Roman Britain to A.D. 500.* London: B. T. Batsford Ltd., 1981.

William of Malmesbury. *The Kings Before the Norman Conquest.* Facsimile version, Llanerch, 1989. Reproduced from Seeleys of London, *The Church Historians of England,* Vol. III, Part I, 1854.

Chapter 2: Transformations

Bebbington, David. *Evangelicalism in Modern Britain: A History From the 1730s to the 1980s.* London: 1989.

Burger, Delores. *Practical Religion: David Nasmith and the City Mission Movement, 1799–2000.*

Burns, Islay. *Memoir of the Rev. Wm. C. Burns, M.A.: Missionary to China From the English Presbyterian Church.* Forgotten Books, Amazon, 2019.

Bussey, Oscar. Whose PhD thesis at Edinburgh University was in 1947: *The Religious Awakening of 1858–60 in Great Britain and Ireland.*

Carwardine, J. *Transatlantic Revivalism: Popular Evangelicalism in Britain and America, 1790–1865.* Westport: Conn.: 1978.

Edinburgh City Annual Reports from 1832 to 1900, from their private archives.

Edinburgh Society for the Monthly Distribution of Tracts, Report in 1861.

Guthrie, David K. and Guthrie Charles J. *Autobiography of Thomas Guthrie and Memoir by his Sons.* Vol. I, quoting from his own manuscript. New York: Robert Carter and Brothers, 1873.

Holmes, Janice. *Religious Revivals in Britain and Ireland 1859–1905,* whose PhD thesis was published in 2000.

Jeffrey, Kenneth. *When the Lord Walked the Land,* whose PhD was published under the supervision of Professor David Bebbington at Stirling University in 2002.

Lennie, Tom. *Glory in the Glen: A History of Evangelical Revivals in Scotland, 1880–1940.* Christian Focus, 2009.

Lennie, Tom. *Land of Many Revivals: Scotland's Extraordinary Legacy of Christian Revivals over Four Centuries, 1527–1857.* Christian Focus, 2015.

Lennie, Tom. *Scotland Ablaze: The Twenty-Year Fire of Revival That Swept Scotland, 1858–79.* Christian Focus, 2018.

Marrs, Clifford. In his unpublished PhD thesis, *The 1859 Religious Revival in Scotland,* at Glasgow University in 1995.

Meldrum, P. *Conscience and Compromise: Forgotten Evangelicals of Nineteenth Century Scotland.* Foreword by Professor David Bebbington. Studies in Evangelical History and Thought. Wipf and Stock, 2007.

Memoirs of Charles G. Finney. Chapter XXXV: Labors in Scotland and in England. The Gospel Truth www.gospeltruth. net/1868Memoirs/mem35.htm

Nicholls, John. *Evangelising Our Cities – The Abiding Challenge of Thomas Chalmers.* London City Mission archive.

Orr, J. Edwin. *The Second Evangelical Awakening in Britain.* London and Edinburgh: Morgan and Scott, 1949.

Patrick. *Confession* 38 and 14. Royal Irish Academy, 2011.

'The Awakening in Scotland.' *Monthly Visitor,* No. CCCXLIII. January 1861.

The Monthly Visitor Reports, 1858 to 1900. Produced by the Scottish Monthly Visitor Tract Society. Archives at Edinburgh City Mission.

These Fifty Years: The Story of Carrubbers' Close Mission, Edinburgh, 1859–1909. The Tract and Colportage Society of Scotland, 1909.

William Robertson of the Carrubbers' Close Mission: Reminiscences of a Life of Blessing. Edited by his son Rev. R. M. Robertson, with a foreword by Principal Alexander Whyte. Edinburgh and London: Oliphant, Anderson and Ferrier, 1914.

Chapter 3: Education

BBC Magazine online. 2nd July 2008. http://news.bbc.co.uk/1/hi/magazine/ 7484282.stm as at 15th December 2015, referred to from *The Little Book of Non-Violent Extremists*, 2016, The Christian Institute.

Bready, J. Wesley, *England: Before and After Wesley: The Evangelical Revival and Social Reform.* Hodder and Stoughton, 1938, whose references are taken from Raikes in the *Dictionary of National Biographies*, and also from *Sunday Schools* in the *Encyclopaedia of Religion and Ethics*, and also from the *Encyclopaedia of Education*.

Brown, Callum. 'The Sunday-school Movement in Scotland 1780–1914.' *Scottish Church History Society*, 1981.

Brown, John. 'The Origin of Sabbath Schools in England and the Existence of these Schools in Scotland Fifty Years Before those of Mr Raikes.' From the *Scottish Christian Herald: Origin of Sabbath Schools*, Vol I.

Caesar, Julius. *The Conquest of Gaul.* Translated by S. A. Handford. Penguin Classics, 1951, 1976.

Durkan, John. 'The Royal Lectureships under Mary of Lorraine,' from *The Scottish Historical* Review (April, 1983). Edinburgh University Press: stable URL: http://www.jstor.org/stable/25529507 Accessed: 1906–2017 13:02 UTC.

Einhard. *The Life of Charlemagne*, 25. Translated by Samuel Epes Turner. New York: Harper and Brothers, 1880.

Eusebius. *The History of the Church*. Translated by G. A. Williamson. Penguin Classics, 1965, 1989.

Guthrie, David K., and Guthrie, Charles J. *Autobiography of Thomas Guthrie D.D. and Memoir*. Vol. 1. New York: Robert Carter and Brothers, 1873.

Guthrie, Thomas. *Out of Harness*. New York: Alexander Strahan, 1867.

Hunter, Henry. *A Brief History of the Society in Scotland for Propagating Christian Knowledge*. London: SSPCK, 1795.

Laquer, Thomas Walter. *Religion and Respectability: Sunday Schools and Working Class Culture*. New Haven, CT: Yale University Press, 1976.

Metcalfe, George. *The Life and Writings of St. Columban 542? –615*. Preface, first published in Philadelphia in 1914, a facsimile reprint. J.M.F. Books, Felinfach, 1993.

Ramsay, W. M. *Church History 101: An introduction for Presbyterians*. Geneva Press, 2005, quoted from *The Little Book of Non-Violent Extremists*, 2016. The Christian Institute.

Renwick, A. M. *The Story of the Scottish Reformation*. London: Intervarsity Fellowship, 1960.

Sabbath School Union for Scotland: Third Annual Report, 1819.

Schmidt, Alvin J. From *How Christianity Changed the World*. Zondervan, 2001.

The First Book of Discipline (1560): 'The Fifth Head: Concerning the Provision for the Ministers, and for the Distribution of the Rents and Possessions Justly Appertaining to the Kirk: For the Schools and The Necessity of Schools,' based upon the published edition in the *Works of John Knox* (edited by David Laing; Edinburgh: James Thin, 1895), Vol. 2. Produced in an edited version to comply with contemporary English, by Presbyterian Heritage Publications, 1993.

Walvin, J. *A Child's World: A Social History of English Childhood 1800–1914*. Pelican, 1982.

Chapter 4: Healthcare

A Scientist's Testimony: Sir James Simpson, Bart., M.D. Sovereign Grace Union.

Baron, John (1838). *The Life of Edward Jenner M.D. LL.D. F.R.S.* Vol. 2. London: Henry Colburn. :2027/nc01.ark:/13960/ t2t523s95, Hathi Trust.

Boerhaave, Herman. From *The Works of Samuel Johnson*. Vol. 14. Troy, New York: Pafraets Company, 1903.

Brown, Thomas. *Alexander Wood: A Sketch of His Life and Work.* Edinburgh: MacNiven and Wallace, 1886.

Buchan, James. *The Capital of the Mind: How Edinburgh Changed the World*. John Murray Publishers, 2003.

Canon Law LXX, Council of Nicaea, A.D. 325, *The Seven Ecumenical Councils, the Nicene and Post-Nicene Fathers.* Vol. XIV. Second series, Wm B. Eerdmans Publishing Co, 1899.

Fielding, H. Garrison. *An Introduction to the History of Medicine.* Philadelphia: W. B. Saunders, 1914.

Florence Nightingale: Extending Nursing: Collected Works of Florence Nightingale. Edited by Lynn McDonald. Wilfrid Laurier University Press, 2009.

Graves, Dan. *Doctors Who Followed Christ: Thirty-Two Biographies of Eminent Physicians and Their Christian Faith.* Kregel Publications, 1999.

Guthrie, Douglas. 'Centenary of Chloroform Anaesthesia,' *British Medical Journal.* 1st November 1947.

James-Griffiths, Paul, *The History of Edinburgh City Mission: David Nasmith, A Dynamic Founder of Missions (1799–1839),* which can be found online at https://www. christianheritageedinburgh.org.uk/category/ecm/

Lamont, Ann. *21 Scientists who believed in the Bible.* Creation Science Foundation Ltd., Brisbane, Australia, 1995.

Risse, Guenter B. *Mending Bodies: Saving Souls: A History of Hospitals.* Oxford and New York: Oxford University Press, 1999.

Schmidt, Alvin J. *How Christianity Changed the World*. Zondervan, 2004.

Simpson, E. B. *Sir James Young Simpson*. Oliphant, Anderson and Ferrier, 1896.

Simpson, Robert Russell. *A Diary of the Last Days of Sir James Young Simpson*. Transcribed by R. R. Simpson. Pansmanse Publications, December 2008.

The First Book of Discipline, 1560: 'The Fifth Head: Concerning the Provision for the Ministers, and for the Distribution of the Rents and Possessions Justly Appertaining to the Kirk.'

The text of the medical historian, Douglas Guthrie, in the Museum at Surgeon's Hall in Edinburgh.

Wilkinson, John. *The Coogate Doctors: A History of The Edinburgh Medical Missionary Society, 1841–1991*. The Edinburgh Medical Missionary Society, 1991.

Chapter 5: Law and Justice

Anderson, J. N. D. *Morality, Law and Grace*, Tyndale Press, 1972.

Atherstone, Andrew. *The Houses of Parliament: Cradle of Democracy*. Day One, 2011.

Augustine. *City of God*. Penguin Classics, 1984.

Bingham, Tom. *The Rule of Law*. Penguin Books, 2010.

Catherwood, Frederick. *A Better Way: The Case for a Christian Social Order*. Inter-varsity Press, 1976.

Eusebius. *The History of the Church*. Penguin Classics, 1989.

Gratian. *Decretum*, Caus. XV, qu.6, can.1

Hate Crime and Public Order (Scotland) Bill. The Christian Institute, Scotland, October 2020.

Hutton, G. M. *Stair's Public Career* in D. M. Walker (ed), *Stair Tercentenary Studies* (Stair Society Volume 33) 1 at 1, cited by Stephen Allison in 'Stair, Natural Law and Scotland,' *L&W Journal* 1112-2: *L&W Journal* 1009 14/12/2012 09:19, p. 189.

Montgomery, James Warwick. *The Law Above the Law*, Chapter 2. 'Witch Trial: Theory and Practice.' NRP Books, 1975.

Reid, D. 'Thomas Aquinas and Viscount Stair: the Influence of Scholastic Moral Theology on Stair's Account of Restitution and Recompense' (2008), 29. *Journal of Legal History*, p.189.

Siedentop, Larry. *Inventing the Individual: The Origins of Western Liberalism*. Penguin, 2015.

'Survey of Scottish Witchcraft.' History Department, University of Edinburgh. *The National*, Hamish MacPherson, 16th February 2021.

Tertullian. 'Scapula.' 2, Vol. III, *The Ante-Nicene Fathers*. Edinburgh: T&T Clark; Wm. B. Eerdmans Publishing Company, reprinted 1997.

The Bible in Scots Law, Scots Law News, 22nd August 2010. hmacqueen, uncategorized, University of Edinburgh, Edinburgh Law School, https://www.sln.law.ed.ac.uk/2010/08/22/the-bible-in-scots-law/

The Secret Barrister. *Fake Law: The Truth About Justice in an Age of Lies*. Picador, 2020.

Tierney, Brian. *The Crisis of Church and State, 1050–1300*. Toronto, 1988.

Chapter 6: Democracy

Aristotle. *The Athenian Constitution*. Translated by P. J. Rhodes. Penguin Classics, 1984.

Armstrong, M. *The Fight for Scottish Democracy: Rebellion and Reform in 1820*. Pluto Press, 2020.

Buchan, James. *The Capital of the Mind: How Edinburgh Changed the World*. John Murray, 2003.

Donaldson, Gordon. *Scotland: Church and Nation through Sixteen Centuries*. Bloomsbury St., London: SCM Press Ltd, 1960.

First Book of Discipline, 1560. 'The Eighth Head: Touching the Election of Elders and Deacons, etc.'

Forrest, W. G. *The Emergence of Greek Democracy: The Character of Greek Politics, 800–400 B.C.* London: Weidenfeld and Nicholson, sixth reprint in 1979.

Fry, Michael. *Edinburgh: A History of the City*. Pan Books, 2009.

Graham, Roderick. *John Knox: Democrat*. London: Robert Hale, 2001.

Herman, Arthur. *The Scottish Enlightenment: The Scots' Invention of the Modern World*. Harper Perennial, 2001.

Jones, A. H. M. *Athenian Democracy*., Basil Blackwell and Mott Ltd, reprinted in 1978.

Lewis, Donald M. *Lighten Their Darkness: The Evangelical Mission to Working-Class London, 1828–1860*. Greenwood Press, 1986.

Plato. *The Republic*. Translated by A. D. Lindsay. J. M. Dent and Sons Ltd, reprinted 1980.

Robison, John. *Proofs of a Conspiracy Against All The Religions And Governments Of Europe, Carried On In The Secret Meetings Of Freemasons, Illuminati, And Reading Rooms*, 1798. Reprinted by Amazon in Great Britain.

Rousseau, Jean-Jacques. *The Social Contract*. Translated by Maurice Cranston. Penguin Classics, 1968.

Siedentop, L. *Inventing the Individual: The Origins of Western Liberalism*. Penguin Books, 2014.

Watt, H. *Recalling the Scottish Covenants*. Thomas Nelson and Sons Ltd, 1946. The entire Solemn League and Covenant document is reproduced in the appendix (pp. 106-9).

Woodberry, Robert. 'The Missionary Roots of Liberal Democracy.' *American Political Science Review*. Vol. 106, No. 2. May, 2012.

Chapter 7: Human Rights

Bowen, C. D. *The Lion and the Throne, the Life and Times of Sir Edward Coke 1552–1634*. Hamish Hamilton Publishers, 1957.

Bryant, Chris. *Parliament – The Biography: Reform*. Vol. 2, Transworld Publishers, part of the Penguin Random House group, 2014.

Collins, G. N. M. *The Heritage of our Fathers*. Edinburgh: The Knox Press, 1974.

Cunningham, John. *Church History of Scotland*. Vol. II, second edition. Edinburgh: James Thinn, 1882.

Diary of Alexander Jaffray Provost of Aberdeen, one of the Scottish Commissioners to King Charles II, and a Member of Cromwell's Parliament. John Barclay, second edition. London: published by Darton and Harvey, Grace Church St, 1834.

Diary of Sir Archibald Johnston of Wariston (1632–1639), edited from the original Manuscript with notes and Introduction. George Morison Paul Ltd, Edinburgh, printed at the University Press by T. and A. Constable for the Scottish History Society, 1911.

Documents of the English Reformation. Edited by Gerald Bray. Series: Library of Ecclesiastical History, edition 3, The Lutterworth Press, James Clarke & Co Ltd, 1994.

Foxe, John. *Foxe's Book of Martyrs*. J. Milner and I. Cobbin. London: Morgan Scott.

Graham, Roderick. *John Knox: Democrat*. London: Robert Hale, 2001.

Howie, John. *The Scots Worthies*. Glasgow: Macgregor, Polson & Company, 1845.

Mackenzie, Sir George. *A Vindication of the Government in Scotland during the Reign of King Charles II against Mis-Representations made in several Scandalous Pamphlets to which is added the method of proceeding against criminals, as also some of the Phanatical Covenants as they were printed and published by themselves in that reign*. First printed in London, 1691 and reprinted in Edinburgh by James Watson, 1712.

Marshall, Rosalind. *St Giles': The Dramatic Story of a Great Church and its People*. Saint Andrew Press, 2009.

Peterkin, Alexander. 1780–1846; White, Andrew Dickson, 1832–1918. *Records of the Kirk of Scotland: containing the acts and proceedings of the General Assemblies, from the year 1638 downwards, as authenticated by the clerks of assembly: with notes and historical illustrations*. The Church of Scotland, General Assembly, Edinburgh: John Sutherland, 1838.

Scots Confession, 1560 and *Negative Confession, 1581*. With an introduction by Professor G. D. Henderson of Aberdeen University, Church of Scotland Committee on Publications, Edinburgh, 1937.

Second Book of Discipline (1578). 'Of the Kirk and Policy Thereof in General, and Wherein it is Different from the Civil Policy.'

The Letters and Journals of Robert Baillie. Principal of the University of Glasgow. Vol. I. Bannatyne Club, 1841, David Laing.

'The National Covenant of 1638.' Reproduced by Hugh Watt, Professor of Church History, New College, Edinburgh University, from his *Recalling the Scottish Covenants*. Appendix, Thomas Nelson and Sons Ltd, 1946.

Tyndale, William. *The Obedience of a Christen man, and how Christen rulers ought to govern, wherein also (if thou mark diligently) thou shalt find eyes to perceive the crafty convience of all iugglers*, section 38 forward. Published in 1528.

Vos, Johannes G. *The Scottish Covenanters*. Blue Banner Productions, 1998.

Wodrow, Robert. *The History of the Suffering of the Church of Scotland from the Restoration to the Revolution*. Vol. I. Glasgow: Blackie, Fullerton and Co., 1828.

Chapter 8: Plight of the Poor

Burger, Delores. *Practical Religion: David Nasmith and the City Mission Movement*, 1799–2000.

Eusebius. *The History of the Church*. Penguin Classics, 1989.

Ferrier, Hugh M. *Echoes from Scotland's Heritage of Grace*. Tentmaker Publications, 2006.

First Book of Discipline, 1560. The Conclusion: *Works of John Knox*. Vol. 2. Edited by David Laing. Edinburgh: James Thin, 1895.

Guthrie, David K., and Guthrie Charles J. *Autobiography of Thomas Guthrie and Memoir by his Sons*. Vol. I. New York: Robert Carter and Brothers, 1873.

Hanna, William. *Memoirs of the Life and Writings of Thomas Chalmers*. Vols. I-III. Edinburgh: Thomas Constable, 1849–1852.

James-Griffiths, Paul. *The History of Edinburgh City Mission: David Nasmith: A Dynamic Founder of Missions (1799–1839)*. Edinburgh City Mission, 2006.

Lecky, W. E. H. *History of European Morals: From Augustus to Charlemagne*. Vols. I and II. Longmans, Green, and Co., 1886.

Martyr, Justin. 'The First Apology,' *The Ante-Nicene Fathers*. Vol. 1. Edinburgh: T&T Clark; WM. B. Eerdmans Publishing Company, reprinted 1996.

Munn, Charles W. *Minister of Money: Henry Duncan, Founder of the Savings Bank Movement*. John Donald, an imprint of Birlinn Ltd., 2017.

Nicholls, John. *Evangelising Our Cities – the Abiding Challenge of Thomas Chalmers*. An article available through London City Mission.

Roxborogh, John. *Thomas Chalmers: Enthusiast for Mission: The Christian Good of Scotland and the Rise of the Missionary Movement*. Rutherford House, 1999.

Second Book of Discipline, 1578: David Calderwood's *History of the Kirk of Scotland*. Vol. 3. Edited by Thomas Thomson. Edinburgh: Wodrow Society, 1843.

Stark, R. *The Rise of Christianity*. Princeton University Press, 1996.

The Annual Reports of Edinburgh City Mission, held at Edinburgh City Mission.

The Monthly Visitor Reports, in the Edinburgh City Mission archives.

Turgot. 'The Life of S. Margaret, Queen of Scotland.' Prologue, contained within *Lives of the Scottish Saints*. Translated by W. M. Metcalfe. Llanerch Enterprises, 1990.

Chapter 9: Abolition of Slavery

Adomnan. *Life of St Columba*. Translated by Richard Sharpe. Penguin Classics, 1995.

Backholer, Paul. *How Christianity made the Modern World*. ByFaith Media, 2009.

Clement, bishop of Rome. 'Letter to the Church at Corinth,' from *Early Christian Writings*. Penguin Classics, 1982.

John Knox. *The Reformation in Scotland*. Banner of Truth, 2000, also quoting from Knox's letter to Anna Locke, 31st December 1559.

Lecky, W. E. H. *History of European Morals: From Augustus to Charlemagne*. Vols. I and II. Longmans, Green, and Co., 1886.

'Life of St Margaret,' by her confessor Turgot. Translated, by W. M. Metcalfe. *Lives of the Scottish Saints*. Llanerch Enterprises, 1990.

Macleod, Alexander. *Negro Slavery Unjustifiable: A Discourse*. New York, 1802.

Moore, Joseph S. 'Founding Sins: How a Group of Antislavery Radicals Fought to Put Christ into the Constitution,' 2015. Published online by *Oxford Scholarship*, September 2015, Oxford University Press, 2020.

Patrick. *Letter to the Soldiers of Coroticus*: https://www.iampatrick.com/wp-content/uploads/2020/01/IAmPatrick-St.-Patricks-Epistle-to-Coroticus.pdf

Schmidt, Alvin, J. *How Christianity Changed the World*. Zondervan, 2004.

The exhibition in the National Library of Scotland, Edinburgh, 4th October 2018–16th February 2019. *Strike for Freedom: Slavery, Civil War and the Frederick Douglass Family in the Walter O. and Linda Evans Collection, 200th Anniversary*.

Whyte, Iain. *Scotland and the Abolition of Black Slavery, 1756–1838*. Edinburgh: Edinburgh U.P., 2006.

Chapter 10: Emancipation of Women

Choi, Eun Soo. Whose PhD at Glasgow University was entitled, *The religious dimension of the women's suffrage movement: the role of the Scottish Presbyterian churches, 1867–1918*. Available online at https://theses.gla.ac.uk/3943/

'Former pupil in Nazi-occupied Hungary reveals act of defiance.' *The National*, 27th January 2020.

Hardage, Jeanette. *Mary Slessor: Everybody's Mother: The Era and Impact of a Victorian Missionary.* The Lutterworth Press, 2008.

Leneman, L. *A Guide Cause: The Women's Suffrage Movement in Scotland.* Revised edition. Aberdeen, 1995.

Miller, Basil. *Mary Slessor: Heroine of Calabar.* Bethany House Publishers, 1974.

Pankhurst, Christabel. *Unshackled: The Story of how We Won the Vote.* WeBuyBooks, Rossendale, Lancashire, UK.

Stark, R. *The Rise of Christianity: How the Obscure, Marginal Jesus Movement Became the Dominant Religious Force in the Western World in a Few Centuries.* Princeton University Press, Harper One, 1996.

Chapter 11: Science

Bain, M., Bentley, A., Squires, T. 'Sir Henry Duncan Littlejohn – A Dynamic Figure in Forensic Medicine and Public Health in the Nineteenth Century.' *Proc R Coll Physicians Edinb* 1999; 29:248-252.

British Medical Journal. Vol. 2, No.2806. 10th October 1914.

Campbell, Lewis, and Garnett, William. *The Life of James Clerk Maxwell, With A Selection from His Correspondence and Occasional Writings, And A Sketch of His Contribution to Science.* MacMillan and Co., 1882.

'Einstein Inspired by James Clerk Maxwell.' *The Guardian,* Tuesday, 8th December 2015.

Graves, Dan. *Scientists of Faith: Forty-Eight Biographies of Historic Scientists and Their Christian Faith.* Kregel Resources, 1996.

Hannam, James. *God's Philosophers: How the Medieval World Laid the Foundations of Modern Science.* Icon Books Ltd, 2009.

Harrison, Peter. *The Bible, Protestantism, and the Rise of Natural Science.* Cambridge University Press, 1998.

Kaiser, Christopher B. *Creation and the History of Science.* Vol. 3. Marshall Pickering, 1991.

Lamont, Ann. *21 Great Scientists who Believed the Bible.* Creation Science Foundation Ltd, 1995.

The University of Edinburgh website for the Bayes Centre: https:// www.ed.ac.uk/bayes/about/history

Chapter 12: The Arts

George MacDonald: An Anthology. Edited, with a preface, by C. S. Lewis. Harper Collins, 2015.

Stevenson, R. L. and Osbourne, L. *The Ebb-Tide: A Trio and a Quartette.* Heinemann (UK), Smith & Kimball (USA), 1894.

Stevenson, Robert Louis. *Prayers Written at Vailima,* with an introduction by Mrs Stevenson. Illuminated drawings by Alberto Sangorski, reproduced by the Graphic Engraving Co., for Messrs Chatto and Windus, who published the volume at 111, St Martin's Lane, London, 1910.

The Gospel in George MacDonald: Selections from His Novels, Fairy Tales, and Spiritual Writings. Edited by Marianne Wright, with appreciations by C. S. Lewis and G. K. Chesterton. Plough Publishing House, 2016.

Chapter 13: The War Years

Annual Reports of Edinburgh City Mission, 1914–1918, and 1939–1945, from their archives.

Gardner, David, E. *The Trumpet Sounds for Britain.* Vol. 2. From the three volumes in one edition. Christian Foundation Publications, 2002.

Grubb, Norman. *Rees Howells Intercessor.* Guildford and London: Lutterworth Press, first edition 1973, eighth edition 1983.

Metaxas, Eric. *Bonhoeffer: Pastor, Martyr, Prophet, Spy.* Thomas Nelson, 2011.

Pearce, Victor E. K. *Miracles and Angels: Evidence for Faith.* Vol. 4. Eagle Publishers, 1999.

'Remembering the acts of defiance which made Jane Haining a Second World War heroine.' *The Press and Journal,* Neil Drysdale, 27th January 2020.

'The Scottish missionary who died saving Jewish children in WWII.' 16th September 2016. *News,* Christians United for Israel.

Chapter 14: Scotland: Where are we Going?

Aitken, Robin. *The Noble Liar: How And Why The BBC Distorts The News To Promote A Liberal Agenda: What Needs To Be Done Now?* London: Biteback Publishing Ltd., 2020.

Anderson, Allan. *To the Ends of the Earth: Pentecostalism and the Transformation of World Christianity.* Oxford University Press, 2013.

Bergman, Jerry. *Hitler and the Nazi Darwinian Worldview.* Joshua Press Inc., 2012.

Communist Goals (1963), Congressional Record, Appendix, pp. A34-A35, January 10, 1963. Current Communist Goals, EXTENSION OF REMARKS OF HON. A. S. HERLONG, JR. OF FLORIDA IN THE HOUSE OF REPRESENTATIVES. Thursday, January 10, 1963 (capital letters copied as seen).

Darwin, Charles. *Descent of Man*, from *Charles Darwin: Evolutionary Writings.* Edited by James A. Secord. Oxford University Press, 2008.

Darwin, Charles. *The Descent of Man, and Selection in Relation to Sex* (1st ed.). London: John Murray, 1871.

Dawkins, Richard. *River out of Eden: A Darwinian View of Life.* Basic Books, 1996.

Dennett, D. *Darwin's Dangerous Idea: Evolution and the Meanings of Life.* Simon and Schuster, reprint, 1996.

Doyle, Andrew. *The New Puritans: How the Religion of Social Justice Captured the Western World.* Constable, 2022.

Fraser, J. G. *The Golden Bough: A Study in Magic and Religion.* World's Classics, Oxford University Press, 1994.

Gabriel, Mark. *Islam and Terrorism: What the Quran really teaches about Christianity, violence and the goals of Islamic jihad.* Charisma House, 2002. Page 136. This book was written by a former Professor of Islamic History at Al-Azhar University.

Guinness, O. *Time for Truth: Living Free in a World of Lies, Hype and Spin.* Intervarsity Press, 2000.

Hayward, John. 'Estimated Dates of Declining Denominations.' 15th May 2022, from *Growth, Decline and Extinction of UK Churches.*

Holland, T. *Dominion: The Making of the Western Mind.* Little, Brown, 2019.

Huxley, Thomas H. *Lay Sermons, Addresses and Reviews*, Appleton, New York, USA, 1871.

Mangalwadi, Vishal. *The Book that Made your World: How the Bible Created the Soul of Western Civilization.* Thomas Nelson, 2011.

Manifesto of the Communist Party. Chapter 2, 'Proletarians and Communists': Marxists: Marx and Engels, 1848.

McLaughlin, Rebecca. *The Secular Creed: Engaging Five Contemporary Claims.* The Gospel Coalition, 2021.

Murray, Douglas. *The Madness of Crowds: Gender, Race and Identity.* Bloomsbury Continuum, 2019.

Murray, Douglas. *The Strange Death of Europe: Immigration, Identity, Islam.* Bloomsbury, 2017.

Murray, Douglas. *The War on the West: How to Prevail in an Age of Unreason.* Harper Collins Publishers, 2020.

Pearcey, Nancy. *Total Truth: Liberating Christianity from its Cultural Captivity.* Crossway Books, 2004.

Perry, Louise. *The Case Against the Sexual Revolution: A New Guide to Sex in the 21st Century.* Polity Press, 2022.

Plato. *The Republic.* Penguin Classics, translated by Desmond Lee, second ed., 1974.

Reisman, Judith A., Eichel, Edward W. *Kinsey, Sex and Fraud: The Indoctrination of a People.* Huntington House Publishers, 1990.

Relationships and Sex Education: The Way Forward. A Report from the Lords and Commons Family and Child Protection Group. Introduction, September 2018.

Robison, John. *Proofs of a Conspiracy Against All The Religions And Governments Of Europe, Carried on In The Secret Meetings Of Freemasons, Illuminati, And Reading Rooms.* Originally published in 1798, reprinted by Amazon, UK.

The Secret Barrister. *Fake Law: The Truth About Justice in an Age of Lies.* Picador, 2020.

'Tom Holland interview: "We swim in Christian waters."' *Church Times,* by Andrew Brown, 27th September 2019.

Weikart, Richard. *From Darwin to Hitler: Evolutionary Ethics, Eugenics, and Racism in Germany.* Palgrave MacMillan, 2004. Weikart is an Associate Professor of Modern European History at California State University.

Williams, Joanna. *How Woke Won: The Elitist Movement that Threatens Democracy, Tolerance and Reason.* Spiked, 2022.

Yousef, Mosab Hassan. *Son of Hamas.* Tyndale, USA. Authentic Media Ltd., UK, 2010.

INDEX